TO TRAVIS
A FRIEND OF
MINE & MY SON
SFC *[signature]*

EVERY SOLDIER HAS A STORY

DONALD R. DUNN II

PublishAmerica
Baltimore

© 2012 by Donald R. Dunn II.
All rights reserved. No part of this book may be reproduced, stored in a retrieval system or transmitted in any form or by any means without the prior written permission of the publishers, except by a reviewer who may quote brief passages in a review to be printed in a newspaper, magazine or journal.

First printing

PublishAmerica has allowed this work to remain exactly as the author intended, verbatim, without editorial input.

Hardcover 9781462652235
PUBLISHED BY PUBLISHAMERICA, LLLP
www.publishamerica.com
Baltimore

Printed in the United States of America

DEDICATION

This book is dedicated to my father Donald Ray Dunn Sr, who died after a ten year battle with Alzheimer's and Parkinson's disease on December 2, 2006. Also, to Frank Shimfessel my father in-law who passed away from heart failure in October 9, 2002, he was also an Air Force veteran who served in Korea.

My wife Telena and my son Donald III, is also a soldier. I can't say enough about them for their sacrifices while I served and the way they put up with me during my Army career. Also, my mother Peggy Dunn and my mother in-law Mable Shimfessel and to all the soldiers I served with.

ACKNOWLEDGEMENTS

Lt. Col. Bob Williams, Lt. Col Paul Stamps, Lt. Cmdr Joe Biller, Master Sgt. James McAvey, Maj. David Bennett, Sgt. Major Mark Schultz, Sgt. Maj. Mary Starmer, Master Sgt. Troy Ratliff, Maj. Gary Conrad, GS 15 Morris "Mickey" Goldman Spec. Robert Valentine, Sgt. 1st Class Lindsey Hershey, Staff Sgt. Ray Korb, Staff Sgt. John Fuery, Staff Sgt. Richard Muller, CW3 Tito Vasquez, Sgt. 1st Class Carl Legore, Sgt. 1st Class Arvis Sutton, Staff Sgt. Steve Hayes, Staff Sgt. Joe Tolley, Sgt. Haig, Master Sgt. Tom Hovie, Maj. Chuck Pritchard, Sgt. Tim Jones who helped me get this book published and Colonel Paul R. Walker. There are many others, but these soldiers served as my best mentors and friends throughout my career.

CONTENTS

FOREWORD..................9

CHAPTER 1 ENLISTING IN THE U.S. ARMY AND BASIC TRAINING, FORT KNOX, KENTUCKY..................11

CHAPTER 2 ARMOR SCHOOL ADVANCED INDIVIDUAL TRAINING (AIT), 19E/K10, FORT KNOX, KY..................37

CHAPTER 3 THE ARMY RESERVE, LOUISVILLE, KY, 100TH DIVISION, 1982-1988..................50

CHAPTER 4 77TH ARMY RESERVE COMMAND, 361ST PUBLIC AFFAIRS DETACHMENT, FORT TOTTEN, QUEENS, NEW YORK, 1988-1992..................62

CHAPTER 5 81ST ARMY RESERVE COMMAND AND 300TH PUBLIC AFFAIRS DETACHMENT, FORT MCPHERSON, EAST POINT, ATLANTA, GEORGIA, 1992-1994..................111

CHAPTER 6 90TH REGIONAL SUPPORT COMMAND, 343RD MOBILE PUBLIC AFFAIRS DETACHMENT, CAMP ROBINSON, NORTH LITTLE ROCK, ARKANSAS, 1994-1997..................139

CHAPTER 7 THE 81ST REGIONAL SUPPORT COMMAND, 319TH MOBILE PUBLIC AFFAIRS DETACHMENT, FORT JACKSON, COLUMBIA, SOUTH CAROLINA, 1997-2003..................166

CHAPTER 8 THE 88TH REGIONAL SUPPORT COMMAND, 367TH MOBILE PUBLIC AFFAIRS DETACHMENT, COLUMBUS/WHITEHALL, OHIO, PART I 2003-2004..................258

CHAPTER 9 U.S. ARMY ACCESSIONS COMMAND, FORT KNOX, KENTUCKY, 2004-2007..................311

FOREWORD

If you would have asked me 26 years ago if I would join the U.S. Army and make it a career, I would have laughed and told them "Hell No." When I joined the Army back in 1981, I never had any idea it would take me where I am today. My cousin Joe Biller talked me into joining with him and I stayed the course and then some. This book is my story, the good, bad, and everything else which happened to me in my service to this great nation as an Armor Crewman to also being a Public Affairs Non-Commissioned Officer. I will talk about what it is like to be an enlisted soldier and a sergeant in the U.S. Army, not an officer or. What it is like to really be in the front leaning position. I have read many military books by general officers and commanders, but I thought it was time to tell what it is like to come from the enlisted ranks, private to sergeant first class. This is the real back bone of the Army. In this book I will tell you my story, the soldiers, civilians, politics, and the way things happened to me and how I survived all this to retire with over 25 years 8 months and two days service total. I want people to read this book with an open mind. Being a career soldier is a hard life. I will tell you exactly how I saw things and how they happened to me. I want to just be remembered as a soldier who took care of soldier's period. I will try to take you into my Army as I seen it through the eyes of a young man from Louisville, Kentucky on a long journey. As a young child to an adult, my teachers, friends, and some family members said I would never amount to anything. Well, let's just say, those people have a job, but I was a career soldier and no one can take that away from me. I was not the ordinary person, a soldier never is. I will tell you more than just one story, because there are many. I will take you from beginning to the end of my career, no holds barred from peacetime to death and destruction. I had many adventures here in the states and in foreign lands. I also dealt with and sincerely took care of my soldiers, through dealing with Army personnel, civilians and some son of bitches along the way. This is how it really was. I look back now and I am glad I served with a pride no other profession could have given me. It was the best decision I ever had, besides being married to my wife and having a great son. Every soldier has a story to tell and this one is mine. Once a soldier, Always a soldier this is the way it is and a whole lot of team work.

CHAPTER 1

ENLISTING IN THE U.S. ARMY
AND BASIC TRAINING
FORT KNOX, KENTUCKY

After high school, I had no idea what I wanted to do, except waste time with my friends and party. I had many teachers in school who called me a loser. I had a gym teacher who just called me dumb Donald Dunn. There was also an old man named Charlie who lived next door to me and he use to call me damn dumb Donnie Dunn every time he saw me. I have had my hair pulled and slapped in the face by teachers. A teacher in 6th grade called me a juvenile and turned her class ring around and hit me a lot of times on top of the head, leaving knots. I also was once literally picked up and shaken out of my desk in 2nd grade by the school principal and taken into his office where he bent me over a file cabinet drawer and beat me till he was satisfied. After the beating I had to sign the back of his paddle. I fought quite a bit in high school and even got stitches in my face twice and black eyes on a few occasions. With all this, my parents were great supporters and my mother especially believed in me, but I was told by some of my so called friend's parents that I was no good and would never amount to nothing. I was called a hood and was even arrested four times for under aged drinking and raising hell. The police even beat me up a few times. I tried to change all that, I went to college at the University of Louisville for one year, it did not work out. Then I decided to go to work and get one of those good ole factory jobs, which I never got. I worked every dead end job you can imagine. Being from Kentucky there are not a lot of opportunities for good work. I got friends who are still working dead end jobs with no way out.

My dad worked for Amour Meat Company on Story Avenue in Butcher Town, Louisville for 38 years and when he died of Alzheimer's his pension was only $600 dollars a month. My mother worked for over 30 years at General Electric Appliance Park and her pension is only about $900 a month when she retired. I was 48 years old when I retired from the Army and my pension as a sergeant first class is $3000 a month and I also have full health care too. I wanted the dream they could not give me. Then I made the decision of my life. Now, I do what I like and like what I do. I am financially stable and all I do now is travel and spend my time with my family. Every one of my friends and family who thought I was crazy for joining the Army after Vietnam are still working and slaving in their dead end jobs going nowhere in a bad economy. I am not better than them but I made better decisions and did what they wouldn't do. My real friends are some of the soldiers I served with, it is called common ground.

It all started with my cousin Joe Biller, when he said, "Donnie why don't we both join the Army. I needed to do something with my life and I took a chance. I got my shit together and decided I was going to be a soldier. I did not want to live the best years of my life in Louisville, working for someone else.

We both had this nutty idea about driving tanks at Fort Knox in the Army Reserve. So we went to see an Army recruiter. We talked to a Staff Sgt. Perkins. We were actually his first recruits. He only had an 8th grade education and we had to help him fill out all the paper work. He had finished Armor School in his career. So we figured if this guy can do it, we will have no problem. So we joined the Army Reserve and contracted for six years.

On September 29, 1981, We were inducted by a Navy Lieutenant from the Philippines, at the Louisville Military Entrance Processing Services (MEPS). The first thing we did was tell our parents. They did not support our decision, but my dad thought it was a good idea for me to start doing something with my life. Our report date was October 19th, so we had to get into shape fast. I was determined to see this thing through; I had been a failure at all my civilian jobs and wanted to make this work. Stupid me the day before basic training we had a keg party in my back yard. The next day was the hangover from hell. I felt like shit, but that was the least of my worries.

We reported to the Grey Hound Bus Station in downtown Louisville at 7a.m. I met Joe and he said, "Donnie, you look like hell warmed over. I said, "I feel like shit." Our parents saw us off giving us advice on something they had no idea about, because hell we did not know what was going to happen either. I and Joe had these orders and the cloths on our back and we were on our way to fabulous Fort Knox, Kentucky. The bus ride was about an hour. I remember looking out the window and seeing the Main Gate at Fort Knox and thinking what the hell am I doing here.

All of the sudden the bus stopped at the Reception Station. Everything and every building were white and looked like a bunch of chicken houses. Then the Bus door opened and this big black soldier in solid green who looked like Smokey the Bear in a hat said, "Listen up you ignorant civilian fucking bastards. I am going to call out your name and you will get off my fucking bus and get in the back of that fucking truck over there. This is not rocket science so listen up shitheads." Then I heard Allen, Biller, Caldwell, Carter, Dunn, I just jumped up and ran like hell to the door. Before I got off the bus, I heard another soldier say, "who are you ass wipe, your mine if you don't get the fuck off my bus." Once I got completely off the bus, I saw Joe in a truck and he motioned me over. There were other soldiers yelling and screaming from every direction at us. Fuck was the word of the day. "We are not waiting all day sweet fucking heart get on that truck. I rolled in next to Joe. Then a metal gate was locked in on the back of the truck. We were like cattle headed to a slaughter. It was also cold as hell and the exhaust from the truck was blowing back in all our faces. We finally stopped in front of a set of barracks. This soldier came around and let us out. All I could hear from where I was sitting was get out your son of bitches and line up over by that sidewalk. I remember standing there looking for Joe he was behind me in the second column. Then I heard, turn your ass around. I looked forward and there was Smokey the Bear in my face. He was yelling fuck this, and fuck that, "you are all going to get a fucking haircut, because you fucking hippies look like shit. I am a Drill Sergeant and you will call me that do you hear me."

"Yes Drill Sergeant."

"You dick heads sound like a bunch of old pussies." Do you hear me?"

"Yes, Drill Sergeant!" I want you to know something right fucking now. I don't know who you are or where the fuck you come from. When I tell you to do something you will do it, because if I repeat myself you will pay."

The barbershop was in a trailer. "First three get in there and the rest of you shit heels shut the fuck up. I remember the cold air hitting my head as I came outside. I looked at Joe and he looked at me and we had to hold ourselves back from laughing at each other. We all looked like a gang of skinheads. "I guess we will let you sorry fucks all get something to eat, also In this mess hall don't open your trash can shit hole of a mouth or I will nail it shut, do you hear me,"

"Yes, Drill Sergeant!" At the mess hall the food was terrible, but I was hungry. We did not get even ten minutes to eat. Drill Sergeant Lane then said, "get the fuck out of my mess hall we got a hell of a lot of shit to do today, this is not fucking Burger King." He then looked right at this fat soldier and said, "Did you eat shit this morning?" Then why the shit eating grin. We are going to help you get rid of some of that weight you fat son of a bitch."

It was now time to get our uniforms at the Clothing Issue Facility (CIF), All I could hear was take this shit and bag it. All my clothes were either too small or too big and my boots left me with nothing but blisters. Another thing you did not touch anything unless you were told to do so and you did not sign anything until you were told. Then we had to hump all our shit back to the barracks, at double time which is a real fast walk. I had two full duffle bags. I carried one on the front of me and one on my back. After two miles of this I was ready to quit. I got footlocker thrown at me while being called a mother fucker.

Then off to the PX (Postal Exchange), for our personal hygiene items tooth paste, shampoo, soap, etc. Then we went to evening chow at the mess hall. The food was the same with left over's from lunch mixed in like a mystery stew. When we all came back to the barracks, to clean the shitters and buff floors. The worst part was taking a shit, there were no stalls everything was open. It was not unusual to walk in a latrine and see two or three soldiers taking a shit right in front of you while you were going to the shower, brushing your teeth or shaving. Also the water was mostly cold, there was no such thing as real hot water in these old WWII barracks. Then the lights would be out at 2100 or 9:00 p.m. Drill Sergeant Lane said, "You little limp dicks get your rest and don't play with yourselves, because at O dark thirty, meaning 0430 we will be doing physical training, then you're sorry asses will be getting shots at the hospital and giving blood."

We were next awakened by a 30 gallon metal trash can thrown from one end of the barracks to the other with the lid flying in some poor bastard's bed hitting him in the head. Then the words grab your cocks and drop your socks. The barracks now had Drill Sergeants on both ends. Then came all the yelling and screaming again. All I heard was every swinging dick get out on the street in five minutes. It was cold in October and you seemed to notice it, especially at 4:30 a.m. outside with a shaven head, in the cold rain. We even had to stand in our underwear outside. There I was almost naked with this Drill Sergeant up in my face with bad shit eating breath calling me a motherfucker, it was enough to make you just lose it, but I just stood there and took it.

We went to morning chow in the mess hall for a runny egg with shell pieces in it and some SOS, no not help, but shit on a shingle, a mixture of gray beef chip gravy over stale toast. You also learn that chow is the only thing to look forward to besides church. Yes you prayed for God to help you through each day. It was now pushups, sit-ups and running till you throw up. One drill sergeant said, "You pukes make me sick, you all are slower than old people fuck." Then we were duck walking all the way to the hospital for those shots and giving blood. With white tee shirts on rolled up to our shoulders. No needles these were medicine bottle air guns. Shots were given in both arms at the same time it was a cocktail of shots. A soldier passing out was common. The drill sergeants just laughed. They said, "Do not move dumb fuck." Some soldiers who moved got stitches; because the air pressure out of these medicine guns would rip you wide open. One soldier had an allergic reaction and had to be taken away shaking profusely. All I could hear was a drill sergeant say, get that pussy out of here!

Marching back to the barracks we all looked sick. Then the Drill Sergeants gathered us around and explained to us what they expected for us to accomplish before we were sent to our basic training companies. The reception station was only the beginning. Every day, there was something crazy going on. Soldiers were going AWOL and some tried to commit suicide. At night it was lonely and every morning came like a new day in Hades. I have seen soldiers thrown out of their beds for being slow. Yes all the screaming, fuck this, fuck that, and fuck you and this place smells like feet and ass.

One night I was on fireguard and heard this big thump in the middle of the night. Every one woke up thinking; it must be one of the drill sergeants having some fun with us. I turned the lights on and there in the middle of the floor was Private Alexander unconscious, with blood running out of his head. He was on the top bunk and fell about six feet to the floor head first. I went for help. Drill Sergeant Lane came in and laughed at him, before he called the ambulance to take him away. Then he said, "I hope the rest of you dumb fucking shit asses can keep from getting hurt in your sleep, now get the fuck back to bed, 0430 will come soon enough for you dog shits. The next day we heard rumors of a private with brain damage who was injured in training. Training my ass, he fell out of bed.

We started out with about 35 soldiers in my platoon and they were slowly falling out. I made my mind up early that I was going to make it. One soldier was an American Indian; I don't remember his name, he had more tattoos than anyone I had ever seen. He also had crazy eyes. I just avoided him, because he was not all there. In other words he was one feather short of a head band. Drill Sergeant Lane called him Billy Jack. He was later found AWOL in the hills of Montana and court martial.

I remember none of us could do anything right and someone was always screwing up. Yes, we all paid for it. After a while, you get tired of the screw up and he usually got beat up for a cure. They tried to teach us how to march. The Drill Sergeants kicked this one soldier in his leg every time he missed a step. He had bruises all the way up and down his legs. It is amazing how many people don't know their left from their right, especially when it comes to legs and arms.

If you fucked upped you did pushups to the winds, which means 40 pushups to the east, west, north, and south. I even remember coming out of the barracks and hearing the word Drop from 100 yards away. My arms felt like lead weights at the end of every day. They continued to scream at you and yes back then they hit you. Pushups were not the worst exercise, it was the duck walking. I have also seen soldiers get kicked in the stomach while in the front leaning rest position doing pushups wrong.

Soldiers were getting beat down by drill sergeants. You did not disrespect the drill sergeant, because they would fuck you up. There was no trainee abuse back then, you took it and kept your mouth shut. We called them shark attacks being mugged by drill sergeants was your worst nightmare

Also don't ever question your Drill Sergeant. They were in charge period right or wrong. If a Corporal told you to shit bricks, your reply was how many and if that meant building a house you did it without question. After all, this was right after Vietnam and the way they were treated, they sure did not give a fuck about you and you're crying. My two basic training drill sergeants were from Puerto Rico and had both done double tours in Vietnam. Their last names were Cruz and Ramirez. At this point I and my cousin Joe were split up. Later after a call home I found out he had high blood pressure and was back home on a medical discharge, I was on my own. I knew then it was up to me to make it through this shit.

The Drill Sergeants told us, you joined us, we did not join you. They could instill the fear of God in you by just calling you to attention and screaming your name. You were never called private, you were a low life and your name was trainee, until the day you graduated. Training was long and painful. There was also no place for homosexuals/gays in the Army, back then it would have been a death wish.

Weather was no option; most civilians are used to going from point A to point B, in and out of their cars with their heaters and air conditioning on. When you are a soldier it does not matter, you stay in the weather till the mission is done, you learned to savor the elements and sleep is a luxury.

Classes are also hell, just to stay awake after being dogged all day long. If you fall asleep you could expect whatever happens to you. Example, we had a soldier fall asleep in class, he was dragged out of the classroom by his ear and made to do pushups till he cried. Another soldier fell asleep in class and while he was sleeping, the Drill instructor told everyone to move aside; when they did he took one of the old iron gray chairs near the podium and threw it at the soldier. It was truly a rude awakening, when the chair hit the soldier in the head and chest leaving him knocked out on the floor. There was this dumb who ass thought it would be cute to fart in class, needless to say he had to clean the latrine for a week. The sergeant giving the class told him, "How do you like that shit you filthy bastard?" There were no females in my basic training, because Armor School was next. They were not allowed in combat schools. No females, no easier rules, you were at their mercy.

A soldier forgot his protective mask in a class, wrong answer. This soldier was outside doing pushups to the winds. Then while in the front leaning rest position he was kicked in the ribs and told to say, "darling I will never leave you again" over and over. There was no candy of any kind. There were also no such things as sodas or even chocolate milk. Everything was white milk, juice, or water. There was this soldier who was overweight and the drill sergeants use to eat cake in front of him at his table and fuck with him. They even made him write home to his parents and tell them he had a good piece of cake today in the mess hall. This one day we were all really hungry from being in the field. While standing in line at Parade Rest with our hand behind our back interlocked. Drill Sergeant Ramirez told us he had a little surprise for us. He looked at the cook and said, "Do you want to see something funny." Then he waited till the last soldier in line got his food and said, "Dump it all, you bag of shits, now get your asses on the street, we are going for a fun run. He ran us on empty stomachs till some soldiers puked and others dry heaved.

I was finally starting to appreciate things we take for granite. I got hit only one time, I was waiting in the mess hall in line. Drill Sergeant Cruz came right up to me and pushed me into a window and grabbed me by my collar.

He said with an evil grin, "Dunn, I just wanted to make sure you were not forgotten." There was a soldier in my platoon who was a real screw up; you name it he fucked it up. Then one day he was shoved in a wall locker and locked in it by Drill Sergeant Ramirez. Then he ordered two soldiers to throw the wall locker down two flights of steps and out the door with him in it.

We had a dirty soldier who would not shower, his problem was solved by four soldiers holding him down with a blanket strapped around him, beating him and scrubbing him down with a wire brush. If you stood in the way of a Drill Sergeant, you first heard the words "make way or make a hole," then if you were not out of the way you would be physically thrown out of the way.

Fighting was always common among soldiers. The movie Fight Club had nothing on basic training fights in the good old days. In the eyes of a Drill Sergeant back then we were all equally worthless as a pile of shit on the side of the road. Drill Sergeant Ramirez said, "I see you all like to fight among yourselves. I will teach you to fight as a team. Ok, belts off all of you and get into a fucking circle. Now take your belt and put it in your hand and double it over, then I want you to hit the soldier next to you as hard as you can, give him your belt and now he has a chance to hit you while you run to your original spot in the circle, do it now you sons of a bitches. You people look like shit and you all hit each other like pussies. So I have a shit detail for you sons of pussies." He then made us all duck walk about a half mile and do pushups on a gravel road till our hand were bleeding. Then sit ups till our backs were bleeding.

Once we were on a twenty mile road march going up and down the two biggest hills at Fort Knox nicknamed Agony and Misery. Ambulances in the front of the road march and ambulances in the back and God help you if you fell out and ended up in one of those ambulances. We were carrying all of our Load Bearing Equipment (LBE). We had a few soldiers fall out. Drill sergeants played keep away about a mile with their gear throwing it back and forth while they tried to get it. I had a trainee named Private Hopkins in front of me on the march, he fell down and when I reached to help him out of a ditch, I was tackled by Drill Sergeant Ramirez, who told me, "Leave that sorry fat bastard if he can't make it, fuck him, now move on Dunn or you will be the next piece of shit going in that ditch." You had to take care of you, no one was going to carry your ass. At the end of the road march we did not even change socks or bust our blisters. All we could see was a building at the end of the road leading to the top of the hill called Misery. When we finally got there we saw a solid concrete center block building.

Then Drill Sergeant Cruz said, "Welcome to my Gas Chamber dickheads, let's have some fun seeing who can't breathe. First two trainees follow me now!" I was one of the first, this time I was glad to get this over with. We had classes and training on nuclear Biological Chemicals NBC, but nothing prepared us for the real thing. We walked in through the front door and the room was filled with Tear Gas. I was in there for about five minutes of what seemed like an eternity. The Drill Sergeants were in the front and back entrances to make sure you did not run out early. Then you were told to breathe and they asked you questions so you could not hold your breath. Then you were shoved out the backdoor. Your eyes and skin were burning like you just came out of a fire and it lasted till you thought you were going to pass out. The smell stayed in your uniform for days even after you washed them and each breath was a struggle.

It was the worst anxiety attack I had ever had. I coughed till I could not cough no more and I hugged a tree and just threw up on the other side where no one could see me. I could hear everyone around me with the same symptoms. There was no sympathy, I saw one soldier running around, freaking out and saying "I can't breathe, I can't breathe." Drill sergeant Ramirez grabbed him and back handed the shit out of him and said," you can breathe you stupid son of a bitch, you're talking to me." He then threw him down face first in the mud. After that he went to fuck with a soldier who ran out early. This soldier was screaming for his mother and Drill Sergeant Ramirez said, "I'm your motherfucker now, and back into the gas chamber your ass goes." He then opened up the door and threw him back in the gas chamber and told the other Drill Sergeants to make sure he got the full effect. This poor bastard staggered out of the gas chamber so full of smoke he looked like he was on fire and fell flat on his face. Drill Sergeant Ramirez walked up and said, "I hope you die you son of a bitch."

Now we were all counting how many days till this was over and our final wake up call. Basic Training was about eight weeks long. It felt like an eternity or prison sentence. You could always hear someone everyday saying how many days and a wake up we had to leave this hell hole. We learned real teamwork, and to walk, look, and be a soldier. There were no rides you marched everywhere you went. Going to and coming back from the mess hall we started carrying a wooden telephone pole with soldiers on both sides while marching with it. We also sang cadences. Like, "there ain't no use in looking back Jodie's got your Cadillac. Also Jodie had your girl and was gone with her too. It was always about Jodie, he had everything you left behind.

In basic training you were always saluting, coming to attention, or getting the hell out of someone's way with rank, because you had none. You did what you were told no questions asked, because this was not a democracy. When you enlisted you also raised your hand to protect America against Foreign and Domestic enemies, this means not just killing an enemy in a foreign land but also killing our own people if that's what it takes for America's freedom.

The Drill Sergeants even poised you against other even soldiers who you thought were your friends. We once were all gathered in a set of bleachers and were brought out one at a time in front of the whole company to talk about someone we hated. Drill Sergeant Ramirez loved this. He had soldiers spilling their guts on each other. When I got called, I said, "I was just trying to survive and do the best I can." You never want to be a rat. I like to talk and I was rebel on authority, but I bit my tongue on this one. All this did was given the Drill Sergeants more ammunition to use against you. They wanted to hear soldiers talk about each other, and then they knew how to break you down around your peers.

Speaking of bleachers, we were once learning minefield training. While the Sergeant was giving the class all at once the bleachers gave way where we were sitting. They folded like a pair of scissors and five soldiers were seriously injured. I pulled one soldier out myself, who obviously had a broken leg. They called for an ambulance, and picked up the wounded soldiers, and then we went back to having the class like nothing ever happened. It was then; I realized I am just an expendable part of the Army.

There were a lot of us and we all had different personalities and backgrounds. We had soldiers from New York City to Bear Creek, Tenn. Hell; we had one soldier from Vietnam. I was a local from Louisville, Kentucky and was only about 45 miles from my house. I thought it would be nice to be close to home, shit the woods are the woods no matter how close or far you were and this was not home. The Army is not like a civilian job, you just can't quit. It is also teamwork, something most civilians don't have. The Army is all about last names and rank. To be a soldier you have to have discipline and a will to reach down grab your nuts and say I am going to make it. Quitting is not an option. We continued to train everyday; we were beginning to be soldiers. Our uniforms were pressed and we were sharp. Our boots were spit shined and we were squared away. The weak had been weeded out. Perception and appearance was the key to success. You could tell a soldier by his boots, now it is by his beret.

There was no family days back then, you saw your family when you completed basic training and graduated, not before. Also you reported to the officer of the day when you received your pay at the end of the month and you saluted that officer until you were paid. There was no such thing as direct deposit on a computer. We were now just getting ready for our second road march, 25 miles to a bivouac site in the woods of south Fort Knox. We were all lined up outside the Company. When out of nowhere was this ambulance pulling right up in front of our formation. It seems that a trainee had decided to try and commit suicide by taken an overdose of aspirin and sleeping pills. This soldier's Drill Sergeant came out with the paramedics and was ranting and raving about the delay. I remember them putting him in the ambulance and hearing Drill Sergeant Andrews say, "I hope you die Butler you worthless piece of shit. I wish I would have known you were going to try and kill yourself, because I would have done it for you." The ambulance doors shut and Andrews said, "get this piece of shit off my sidewalk.' Then he turned to the first three soldiers in his formation and said, "I guess you boys will be next, I bet you will probably go AWOL. This one here looks like he might end up in jail. I can't forget about you scarecrow, you will probably end up in downtown Radcliff eating out of garbage cans. Yeah, you will want to come back to the Army, but we won't want you. Ok anybody else feels like committing suicide before we march you dickheads to death."

It was raining, sleeting and just damn cold. While marching down the road toward agony and misery again in a double time march it was evident this was not going to be a good day. I could see the drill sergeants starting to pick on certain soldiers, especially the ones who were lagging behind. They were doing everything from kicking soldier's legs to playing keep away with soldier's equipment again. One soldier fell out and they literally dragged him to the rear and threw him in an ambulance while he was crying. All I could hear was get this sorry cry baby dead ass off my fucking road. Now which one of you pussies is going to be next?" I still had bad blisters from the first road march. Then a jeep came down the road and got too close to our platoon and his outside mirror hit a soldier and knocked him off the road. A drill sergeant walked up and said," Parker you did that on purpose so you would not have to march." All I heard was anyone else wants to slow us up from reaching our fucking objective. Finally we were there, I felt like I was a dead man walking. I remember Drill Sergeant Cruz laughing the whole way up misery while walking backwards smoking a Marlboro Red cigarette. I thought he was superman, but he was use to being on the trail after all he had been an infantry soldier in Vietnam and he really enjoyed pain. Also the cycle for a Drill Sergeant is 2 years basic training on the trail.

We then checked our feet, popped blisters again and changed socks. We set up our shelter half's with two men per tent. We dug in for the night. I slept in my Ranger Bed, A hole to sleep in with sticks leaves and pines for a blanket. Digging a fox hole also brought sparks with an entrenching tool hitting solid rock. Me and Private Cousins, who I was teamed up with worked till night fall. He even fell asleep while digging. I said, "Cousins, you're the first person I ever seen fall asleep with a shovel in his hand dug in the dirt. I also feel like someone whipped my ass and got away with it." We finally finished, made the final formation and went to sleep without even eating chow. We just drank water out of our canteens and got some rest. We were awakened by Drill Sergeants playing games on us in the middle of the night. They tore down tents, dragged soldiers out in the mud. There is no real rest when you are in the field.

Still tired as hell, in the morning at 0430 there was training and work to be done. We first had to dig a latrine for pissing and shitting. We were broken down into teams and given map reading classes with a compass. Land navigation time; we learned grid coordinates, map features, and how to find reference points. We all teamed up with our shelter half buddies and then we were given reference points and had to locate them. You and your buddy read the map and pinpointed the locations and if you got lost, well let's say God have mercy on your ass, because the Drill Sergeant wouldn't when they had to go out and find you. We did have a few stragglers, but no one got lost for long. Here you are in the woods there are no roads, your protractor, compass and map are your directions and you better keep your map dry. Some soldier's maps got wet and tore, which was their main reason for them getting lost. They learned after finding their way back and a lot of pushups to remind them not to hold up the whole company. You see being late to a formation or movement is one of the worst things you can do in the Army. Not being accountable is a major fuck up.

After two more days of common skills training we were ready to head back. We filled in holes, policed, and cleaned up the whole area. Also equipment had to be turned in and cleaned. After getting back, there was nothing like that first hot meal in the mess hall. You see the little things most people don't think much about like taking a shower, or even getting something to eat, these things become a privilege.

Next, we came up on our turn for guard duty. This entailed 48 hours of 4 hours on and 4 hours off until the cycle was complete. We guarded everything from motor pools to Holder Complex a weapons and training station. In order to get ready for guard duty there was an inspection. Which meant black Kiwi Polish and a whole lot of spit shining till the boots looked as good as glass.

I remember one trainee had his pistol belt on with his ammo pouches dangling open. Drill Sergeant Cruz walked up to him and said, "Let see what else is fucked up trainee." He then reached into the ammo pouches and said, "What the fuck do you have here, the whole mess hall." He unloaded the soldier's ammo pouch and everything from cheese to a smashed donut fell out on the ground. "You stupid fuck you no its an article 15 for stealing food from the mess hall and you really fucked up letting me catch you. On your knees shit bag and get in the front leaning rest position. Ok, everyone we are going to march around this soldier till he eats all this shit he stole from the." It was pouring down rain we all were in it with no ponchos on. We went on to our guard duty stations and the trainee was given an Article 15 meaning he lost a whole month's pay.

Now basic training was only a few weeks from being complete; I was starting to feel my body change. I was actually getting into shape. At a Confidence Course we did everything from scale walls to pulling each other up seven story simulated buildings one soldier at a time. We were finally working as a team. The weak did not survive, if you couldn't pass a PT Test, you could not be in the Army. This meant pushups, sit ups, and running two miles. You were timed in each event. You had to also keep your weight down to meet the standard. PT and weight gets rid of a lot of soldiers, smarts don't get it, and you have to be in shape too.

There were 35 soldiers in my platoon and we now had 20. Some were put out of the Army and some were recycled. You definitely did not want to get recycled and do all of Basic Training over again. There were days I hurt real badly. I learned to deal with pain. Every day we would start out yelling our platoon motto "Razor sharp, tiger tough, what you get is not enough drive on Drill Sergeant Drive on."

Rifle training with the M16A1 and .45 pistols was next; you learned to worship your weapons, because it was like being married to it. When you train with weapons and go to ranges, there is no room for mistakes. I remember seeing soldiers get butt stroked for fucking up during weapons training. You also, never point a weapon at someone or it was your ass. You respect a weapon and you learn when to use it and when to clean it. You always keep your weapon on you at all times and it better be on safe at all times until you use it. I never fired a weapon in my life till I joined the Army, but I learned to take care of my weapon, because using a weapon in a life threatening situation is no joke. I qualified as an expert, only because I listened and learned what those Drill Sergeants were teaching me. I use to hate them now I was respecting them.

We were also trained with hand grenades and each soldier had to throw a live one before passing. We all stood behind a concrete wall and were brought out one at a time while watching through a periscope over the wall to learn how to pull the pin and throw it properly. You slip with a hand grenade and that's it not only for you, but others. Well, one soldier pulled the pin and dropped his hand grenade by accident. The only thing that saved him was a quick thinking sergeant. He grabbed the soldier leaped over the pit wall into the next pit right before the grenade went off. This soldier was on garbage cans and mess hall duty till the end of basic training. Also that day he marched around us all the way back to the barracks while running with his weapon over his head.

We learned about mines and how to recognize the different kinds, like anti-personnel and tank mines. We also trained how to disarm them. The Cold War was on back then and Russia was our primary enemy. We studied how to recognize Chemical threat signs, uniforms, weapons, and vehicles associated with the Soviet Army. While in one class on chemical weapons and chemical agents a soldier thought it would be cute to fart out loud in the class. It wasn't very funny when he was outside doing pushups until he fell over and one of the Drill Sergeants kicked him in the ribs and said, "Fart again for us laughing boy." We had one dummy push his ear plugs in too far on the pistol range and he could not get them out. Well, he never did that again. Drill Sergeant Cruz wasted no time in getting a pair of needle nose pliers and digging them out of his ear. He laughed as he made blood come out of the soldier's ears. "Get back in formation dumb dick, the next time I will rip you're fucking ear off and mail it home to your mother." He also said, the next time one of you shits eats C-Rations and can't go to the bathroom. I will help shove an ice pick up your ass and help your bowels move till you shit blood."

A final Physical Training PT Test was right around the corner. I was looking forward to getting this over and out of the way. First we woke at the usual, 0430. Then we went to the track. There were three lines of graders. One for pushups, one for sit ups, and others for the two mile run. The run was last and the hardest thing to do after getting done with pushups and sit ups. The minimum to pass the PT Test for me was 44 pushups in two minutes and they had to be right. Some soldiers did over 70 pushups only to have what they needed to pass. Then I had to do 50 sit ups in two minutes and they had to be right, with hands interlocked behind the head the count started when you came down for each repetition. If your hand slipped from behind your head or you did not come all the way up that repetition did not count. The same thing happened some soldiers did more and only got counted for less. The last part of the PT Test was a two mile run and that had to be done in 15 minutes. I passed and met the standards. Also in order to pass you have to pass all three exercises and score 180, which is 60 or more above in each category or you fail. If you fail one area and score over a 180 you still fail. I scored a mere 220. We had over 10 failures out of 20 and three of them were put out of the Army a week later.

We had inspections every week in our barracks and if your wall locker, boots, bed, and everything else including floors and latrine wasn't squared away. You worked until it was. We used Brasso Cleaner, wax and floor buffers every day. Well, let's just say it wasn't a good inspection when you see boots and beds flying out of windows two stories up. Drill Sergeants also took some beds to the shower and threw them out the window watered down at you while you were in formation. I also remember seeing one soldier pulled from formation by his nuts, Drill Sergeant Cruz. He said, "Your area looks like shit so maybe if I grab you by your nuts. This will also grab your attention. Now, I got a shit detail for all of you. We will clean these barracks to include this fucked up floor and then we will all get on our hands and knees and cut some fucking grass." We all got on our hands and knees for about an hour and pulled grass until the green on our hands matched our uniform. Last, but not least we all carried the long telephone pole in front of our barracks and duck walked to the mess hall.

Now, with a couple days left, we are finally preparing to graduate basic training. Everyone is on edge, because no one wants to screw up and get recycled at this point. We were all cleaning like crazy and turning in equipment. There was also plenty of drill and ceremony practices and marching.

The hold over's and the recycled soldiers had to watch us graduate back then. A few of the hold over's did get released early, but not without humiliation. It was raining hard the day before we graduated. I remember their Drill Sergeant making holdovers put on their Class A uniform, which is the Army Dress Uniform. The Drill Sergeants made them go outside in the rain until they were soaked. Then they made them roll around in a mud pit. After that they brought them back in the barracks and made them roll down the walls in their uniform. Them they made them clean the walls before they were released. It was bad enough not to make it through basic training, but to leave post in a muddy Class A Uniform was the end of the road. Kind of like Chuck Connors in the TV series Branded. The Drill Sergeants just laughed and said, "Take a good look at what it's like if you want to get out of the Army and be a civilian again."

Graduation, and the last wake up call, we all came out on the parade field at Brave Regiments Rifle Road and we all looked sharp in our Class A Uniforms. I also remember marching off the field after the ceremony feeling proud and thinking; I made it, thank God. I saw the look on my parents face when my name, rank, and platoon was announced. I will always remember hearing, "Alpha Company A1-A dismissed I also knew in a week after leave, I would be right back here for Armor School for another 14 weeks of combat training in the M60A3 tanks.

All the way home I just looked out the window and thought about all the things I had missed while in Basic. A home cooked meal was at the top of the list and then my bed. Right when I got home and saw our house, I thought basic was over. Then the phone rang and my mother answered it. I could hear Drill Sergeant Ramirez on the line. All he said was, "Let me speak to dickhead." what was really funny was my mother said, "I think it is for you Donnie, it sounds like someone from the Army." I took the phone and said, "Yes Drill Sergeant." He started ragging me about the barracks looking like shit before we left and that he was the one who had to turn the building in. Then, he realized he had the wrong soldier and it was another soldier he was looking for in another set of barracks. Instead of any apology which I knew was not forthcoming, I heard him say, "Get back to your fucking family dumb ass while I try to find out who the lame fuck was that left my barracks like shit." This was the last thing I remember hearing from Drill Sergeant Ramirez. With that said, basic training was finally over.

CHAPTER 2

ARMOR SCHOOL ADVANCED
INDIVIDUAL TRAINING (AIT)
19E/K10
FORT KNOX, KY

I had to report to the reception station at Fort Knox again before heading over to Armor school. After leaving the reception station, I was assigned to B-2-1 which was Bravo Company. The company logo was "Be a Hunter." I was assigned to Drill Sergeant Jacobs, who was a crusty middle aged sergeant first class and he hated all us and yes we were still called trainees. There were about 25 soldiers in my platoon and now we were ready to start becoming Armor Crewman on the M60A3 Tank.

The first day of training in our Military Occupational Skill (MOS) 19E, was hell all over again. Now was a combat school and even more was expected. Physical Training (PT) was every morning before chow at 0430. Weather did not factor into being a tanker either. Jacobs said "If you thought basic was hard you sorry bastards wait till you get a load of this 14 weeks. Some of you who made it through basic will not make it through this, I fucking guarantee you this."

I remember him coming in our barracks in the morning. You could hear his right foot hit the first step, then the door bolted open, and if the light came on and you were not up and out of your bunk, you were doing 40 pushups in the front leaning rest position. Wall to wall counseling was another one of his favorite pass times at night. If you fucked up not only did you hear it from your fellow soldiers, he would also pay you a visit and bounce you off a few walls.

The XM-1 Tank as it was called back then was still experimental and we rarely trained on it. Today it is the M1A1 Tank and the old M60's series tanks are gone. Everything on a tank is heavy. The back plates you had to open just to check the gas and oil weighed over 50 pounds apiece. I mashed my hands and had bruises on them from just checking the fluids.

A tank is made all around with 4 inches of steel and it will hurt and kill you just like it will kill the enemy. It weighs sometimes over 60 tons when fully loaded with ammo, 50 caliber machine gun, 240 caliber machine gun, and main gun rounds. A tank is all about cover and concealment. We learned first, anything that can be seen can be hit and anything that can be hit can be killed.

We had three gate tests to pass in order to make it through Armor School. We were familiarized with weapons to include as mentioned the .240 caliber machine gun, a .50 caliber machine gun, the 45 caliber pistol, and the main gun on a tank. Every weapon had to be function checked and you had to be able to take that weapon apart and put it back together in matter of minutes. Speed and accuracy were expected, nothing less. A 50 Caliber machine gun will literally eat your ass up it had over 25 components.

Tanks had mechanical, manual firing switches, and a master battery switch which operated the power in the whole tank. The main gun on a tank had a breach block and a firing pin and you better make sure the firing handle on the breach block is locked when a round is loaded. I once saw a loader on a tank lock in a round but did not lock in the breach block handle. Well the round went down range along with the handle flying up in position. Then the soldier's nuts went up after it too.

We were traveling down to the range once to fire table 8, a five tank on line firing exercise. The soldier was in the turret, which is the top part of the tank. He did not have the latch on the cover of the hatch he was standing in locked down. Well the tank came to a stop and the hatch came forward and caught his hand between the hatch and the tank. He had a broken hand in three places. Also in a tank you have four kinds of rounds for the main gun and they weigh around 50 pounds apiece depending on the rounds. There are SABO rounds, which are armor piercing used for destroying enemy tanks and other armor vehicles. Then there is HEAT rounds used to destroy vehicles like trucks and jeeps. There are HEP rounds used on troops and vehicles along with a Beehive round which are used on troops like a giant shotgun blast. There was a soldier in our squad who was the loader and did not lock one of the bustle racks behind him that holds these rounds. The tank stopped the round came forward out of the bustle rack and hit him in the head and he was recycled with a severe concussion. I also remember one soldier was not ready for the tank he was in to stop. Well he got launched onto the street head first from the top of the turret hatch where he was standing. He landed on the street in front of the tank unconscious on his way to the Ireland Army Hospital for some surgery on his face and neck.

You have to think safety at all times, I myself was too close to the turret ring which is exposed inside the M60 tank. When the turret turned it literally ripped my fatigue top right off of me. I was lucky not to get stitches in my side. One soldier had the same thing happen to him, he got thirty stitches in his side.

We had to learn communications and radio procedures, there are just four soldiers in a tank. There is a gunner, loader, tank commander, and driver. Everyone has to know each other's job. The loader loads the main gun on a tank when told to do so by the tank commander. The gunner identifies and zeroes in on the target to fire. The Tank commander gives the command to fire and the driver has to know when to move out after the target has been hit. An example of a fire command is "gunner SABO, enemy tank 100 meters identify, fire, on the way, target seize fire, driver move out. Vehicle Identification is very important; no one wants to kill a friendly tank. Also, a must is map reference points to tell where you are on the battlefield.

With a tank you check it from top to bottom, and then you drive it. The Army teaches maintenance. Also troubleshooting, we learned that if something goes wrong how to fix it. There are training manuals on every piece of equipment the Army has. If you sign for it, it is yours and if you mess it up it is out of your pay, especially if there is negligence involved on your part.

A tank can only be pulled by another tank. If a tank has to be towed it takes another tank or tanks. If the tank is stuck in thick mud or water it can take sometimes two tanks to get it out. Low and behold if a tank goes in the water and gets stuck up over its turret with mud, it can take three tanks to pull it out and you better have the towing cables crossed and hooked up and then some times that may not work.

Tank gunnery starts with how to properly engage the enemy and kill him. You have to know the machine guns and main gun on a tank. What rounds to use. How to clear weapons and also perform safety checks was next. Once on the range this is not the place to learn, because someone will get hurt. I remember being in a tank on the range and the 50 caliber machine gun jammed, the tank commander made the mistake of opening the feed tray before recharging it and clearing it. He also thought he could fix it on his own. Well, a .50 caliber round went off and the shell ejected. It kicked out of the weapon with the force of the bullet. I was the loader at the time and heard it ringing around inside the tank. I put my steel pot over my face for cover. Then I heard silence followed by a couple of screams. Well the shell from that round ended up going into the gunners side, coming out and was stuck in the tank commanders arm. I had to get on the radio and stop the exercise so the medics could take both of them to the hospital. I was lucky it was not me who got hurt.

The next day on the range things got even worse and another soldier got hurt. Pvt. Howard ended up being taken away and had to get over 20 stitches in his right arm. It seems after the main gun fired in his tank he did not get out of the way of the main gun as it recoiled 12 inches against his arm. One platoon on the range before us had a soldier get killed in a tank. The driver got killed at night while sleeping in his tank. He took the back off his seat. Well there is only a V shaped opening between the driver's seat and getting in and out of the tank from the inside. He was lying back with the back of the seat off halfway in the V shape part of the tank and the other half in the driver's compartment. A soldier got in the tank and yelled Turret Power! This warns anyone in a tank that he is turning on the power and to be ready. He never heard the soldier yell, because he was fast asleep. What he did not know was the turret was engaged in the neutral steer position. When the turret power was turned on the turret swung completely around cutting the driver in half. Also there have been numerous accidents with soldiers sleeping near or under vehicles. You have to think around dangerous equipment or fatigue will cause you to be a casualty. Also, if any vehicle rolls over, most people try to get out while it is rolling. Most of the time when you do this the vehicle will roll over you. Staying in a vehicle is the safest way in a roll over.

I myself got 15 stitches once, but never missed training; the medic stitched me up in the field. A soldier threw a radio off a tank and hit me in the leg during a field exercise. I was lucky he did not hit me in the head. One of the Drill Sergeants seen this and made him pay for the radio, along with extra duty.

Then we had to go to the gas chamber once again. I thought not again, this shit sucks, the burning skin, eyes and throwing up all over again. Then, yes another soldier got hurt. While we were road marching to the gas chamber up Agony hill at Fort Knox, a soldier got close to a ditch and fell in it breaking his arm. Well I faired a little better than the first time at the gas chamber, but my eyes and skin were on fire and I still could not breathe for a while.

We had just finished the Gate One Test and now we were on our way getting ready for Gate Two. We got back to the company area and had an inspection. You got soldiers who will pocket brass and ammo at ranges. The Drill Sergeants found one soldier with two 50 caliber bullets and some brass. He got an article 15 and lost pay for a month. While going through the barracks with a military police dog, the MP's found drugs. The funny thing was the drugs were not illegal, but the private as stupid as this may sound confessed to trying to buy real drugs. He was busted out of the Army on intent to buy drugs.

The Gate Two Test was harder than Gate One. Station one was the 240 Machine Gun. We had to clear, disassemble, reassemble, perform a function check, load, and perform immediate action in two minutes and if you screwed up any station, you were a NO GO! After being a no go you were given one more chance a week later and then you were reclassified into another MOS or you were out of the Army.

Station two, maintenance, we used manuals and filled out maintenance request on every weapon and radio to include the M60A3 Tank. Station three, starting and stopping a tank. You must know all the procedures to start and stop a tank. You have a master battery switch, you also have three other soldiers in a tank with you and they need to all be in constant communication with you through your tanker helmet to complete this. Stopping a tank is more than just putting on the brake. An example is, we had another dummy lock the brakes on the tank and the gunner who was looking out of his primary sights went head first hard into the sights. Well he had two of the biggest black eyes I had ever seen. He looked like Batman. A tank has fire extinguishers and they better be fixed in place and operational.

Station four, ground guiding a tank, when you are standing in front of a 50 ton armor tank you better know how to communicate to the driver and tank commander where to put it. You not only have to ground guide a tank during the day. You also have to know how to do it at night. There are many hand and arm signals and flashlight signals used to ground guide tanks. A tank is loud and your hand signals is all you have to show the driver when you are in front of him. He cannot see behind him. At night a flashlight is all you have to move and show the driver. Gunnery flags are very important if a green flag is up you know that tank is ready to fire. If you get behind or in front of a tank when it fires, you might as well order a hearing aid for life. A tank also has a back blast, Also tanks rock up in the air about two feet when they fire and you can feel it inside and out. A red flag means cease fire.

Station five, communications, you had to know how to talk on a military radio word for word. The tanker helmet has to be operational and you have to let one person talk at a time to properly communicate in a tank. You had to make sure everyone is on the same frequency and when to change frequencies. When you talk on a military radio you are precise and to the point.

Station six, first aid and Nuclear Biological Chemical Warfare (NBC). If you are poisoned with gas or stricken with a blistering blood agent you have to know what to do. You always carried a M17 Protective Mask and you have only nine seconds to dawn it, clear it, and make sure it is sealed. Stations seven, Map Reading, you need to know where your soldiers are, tanks, and where other equipment is on a battlefield. Reference points are essential and terrain features are a must. Learning how to properly use a compass is a big part of it too. Most people have heard of compasses, but they have no idea where north, south, east and west are from where they are standing.

The Gate Three Test; there were four stations in this the final gate. Station one, was the 50 caliber machinegun. We had to clear, disassemble, assemble and perform a function check all in 5 minutes. Station two was prepare to fire checking all weapons on the tank and making sure they have been maintenance and are all in operational order. The breach block in a tank has to be taken completely apart on the main gun and cleaned. This is done with a big cleaning rod that looks like a giant cotton swab going down the main gun into the front main gun. All road wheels and end connectors on the tracks have to be checked to include the outside rubber on the road wheels. I once saw a tank go over a bridge at Fort Knox and the end connector on a track break. The tank went into neutral steer, spun around and went into the water. Two of the four man crew sustained minor injuries, luckily no one was killed.

Station three, prepare to load, unload, and conduct misfire procedures on a tank. Just loading and unloading rounds on a tank can wear your ass out. We loaded tanks with over 70 rounds in five tanks and used an assembly line of soldiers to do it. Also when a command is given on a tank you load that round, you yell up to let everyone in the tank know that round has been loaded. If it does not fire, you wait till all three main gun triggers in a tank have been tried. If the round still does not fire then you take the round out of the breach block and you physically turn it and load it again. Then you yell up and the round should fire. If not you take that round out and get another round and try it. Also you have to be careful when loading and unloading main gun rounds on a tank. You are standing as a loader on batteries with covers on them below your feet. If one of those covers gets kicked lose and a round falls on an open battery stem, because it only takes a few volts to set off a main gun round on a tank inside it.

Station four, Conduct of Fire exercise is to be executed perfectly. You must perform this as the gunner on a tank. Battle sight gunnery, identifies a target, know it is the enemy, and coordinate where to hit that target at center mass. Usually the center of mass is between the road wheels and the center of the turret. You don't wound another tank you kill it in one shot. Because once you fire at another tank you have been seen and you don't want the enemy tank to have a chance to retaliate. You strike, and you move out and you use cover and concealment. It is all about timing and accuracy. We were tested with laser sights too, you either hit your target or you missed it.

You also have primary sights and secondary sights. The instructors were extra hard on us at this final station. Now it was time for a road march to fire and spend our last two weeks on the range for gun weeks. There was a line of three Mack trucks pull. Drill Sergeant Jacobs, said, "You boys are going to love these next two fucking weeks. You see those big trucks and trailers, well they got enough ammunition and tank rounds to win a war and your names are on them start unloading." The next morning at 0430 we started unloading rounds. "Well boys we need to have every tank out here loaded before chow and then we will have some fun firing and cleaning up this shit, said Drill Sergeant Jacobs." It was 0730 and we unloaded all of those Mack trucks before we had anything to drink or eat and we did it in three hours. Amazing what you can do when a few Drill Sergeants are up your ass. We all were then assigned four man teams to each of the five tanks on line. It was hot in July 1982 and man it was dusty too. Back then there was no such thing as bottled water. You had canteens and water buffalo's, which are vehicles with tanks of water attached to them on trailers. We also had duck bags that are like a big duffel bag filled with water hanging down off a tree branch. I was 23 years old at the time and I felt like an old man at the end of the first day. You wore your whole uniform, not like today where they break soldiers down to t-shirt and unloosed pants in the heat. When you're in a tank made of solid steel at 90 degrees the temperature in the tank is well over a 120 degrees by four inches of steel all around. All you can do is drink water and hope you don't pass out. You humped from sun up till sun down and then some.

We started with firing the M240 Machine Gun at targets after we set up our bore sight targets 1200 meters down range for zeroing. We had to make our own targets out of wood with hammer and nails. We also had to fill sand bags to set up around the tank positions. We started loading the 50 Caliber Machine guns. After carrying rounds double belted around your neck and chest, mounting 50 caliber machine guns, and locking in the barrels we were ready to fire. Then we prepared the main gun for firing and loaded every tank on the line, along with changing out the machine gun barrels that were hot.

Then it was night firing with the M240 Machine Gun, and 50 Caliber Machine Gun together. You could see every five rounds with the tracer bullets. The next few days we fired every round of ammo we had. We had one day to clean the range. Cleaning all the brass and shells off the range was a killer. It had to be all picked up by hand. We also had to put out some minor fires out and tear down all the targets taking them apart and loading them on trucks. We had to clean all the weapons. One stupid soldier almost got killed when he and another soldier cleared and dismounted the barrel off a 50 caliber machine gun. He stood right in front of the 50 caliber machinegun while his buddy charged the weapon while holding it steady against his chest. Drill Sergeant Jacobs saw this and had a shit fit dogging both soldiers.

We then walked back the same way we came in. Two weeks on a range, no shower and just enough water to live on makes you really appreciate the little things in life. Then there were haircuts, uniforms, boots, and brass to shine. Then we had one final weigh in to meet weight standards and one final Physical Training Test.

The day before graduation one ignorant soldier went into town and got a tattoo. This was not a big deal, except the tattoo was on his right hand. When he saluted an officer with his hand the words Fuck You were written across the outside of his small finger and hand. I guess he thought it would be funny till he got caught and had to have it removed. He also got an Article 15 and forfeiture of pay for a month. Last but not least 3 soldiers shaved their heads and being completely bald is considered destruction of government property, with them being the property. They also received Article 15's and yes loss of a month's pay.

14 weeks of Armor School was over and everyone stood in formation in their class A uniforms. We marched as one unit over to the gym near Wilson Road and graduated about 70 soldiers total in a company that had started out with about 110 soldiers. All our families were there and we all stood sharp and ready. Even the Drill Sergeants were proud of us. This was now our job in the Army. Today we were finally soldiers with a purpose. One of the happiest moments of my life was when I heard Drill Sergeant Jacobs give the command Bravo B-2-1 "Dismissed and fall out." I was now a 19E/K Armor Crewman.

CHAPTER 3

THE ARMY RESERVE
LOUISVILLE, KY
100TH DIVISION
1982-1988

I reported to my Army Reserve unit for my first drill and handed my orders to Sgt. 1st Class Katlet, the training NCO. I was now assigned to the 100th Division Training Group. My whole idea was to go to college and be a soldier on the weekends and go to annual training two weeks out of the year. Sergeant Katlet took me to meet the company first sergeant, Master Sgt. Hall. I sat down with 1st Sgt. Hall and he told me what he expected and emphasized being on time especially for Drill Weekends and formations. "Accountability is the key to being a soldier," he said. Then he took me to meet my platoon leader Sgt. 1st Class Sutton. He also told me what he expected of me and showed me where supply was to get new unit crest and uniforms if I needed them. Then I went to meet Sgt. Carter who was the unit administrator. He went over my personnel records, medical records, and made sure everything was up to date for pay.

I then met my fellow soldiers in my squad. They showed me around the Reserve Center. Then we went to some classes on common task training (CTT). We also did some maintenance on some weapons My first weekend in the Army Reserve was a good experience and non stressful, not like Basic and AIT.

My first year, I went to college and studied Public Relations at Eastern Kentucky University. It was college mixed with one weekend a month drill and then in the summer we would spend two weeks at Fort Knox keeping up my Armor skills in tanks and learning how to become an instructor in case of a mobilization. I was treated good and got promoted to Private First Class (PFC) or E-3. I learned a lot from the Vietnam Veterans in my unit. Back then a lot of these NCO's had seen real combat and I listened and learned from them. The commander, Col. Sinclair had one eye with a black patch over his lost eye. He was a firm believer that a soldier learns best in the field. He could put the fear of God in you with one look and you never questioned his authority. Also, Sgt. 1st Class Sutton, my platoon leader had been a squad leader in Vietnam and had received a Purple Heart. He was fully aware of how to train soldiers. I remember going to the field and at night we would go out into Radcliff a town outside of Fort Knox and drink in some of the clubs and look for girls. At 0630 in the morning we would be right back on those tanks. I was young back then and could work all day and party all night. I did extra annual trainings when I was out of school and worked for extra money and retirement points also when possible.

The Army Reserve was my best part time job. I also worked while I went to school. I worked at Holiday Inn as a bell boy in Richmond, Ky. I was working on a degree in Public Relations, being a soldier one weekend a month, and doing 30 hours a week as a bell boy. Most kids at school had their mommy's and daddy's pay for their college. Anything free is never appreciated and I see this even today. Most of my friends still live in Louisville and they have never done anything with their lives, but work dead end jobs and stay close to mommy and daddy. I still had some fun with my friends, but I also had set goals I wanted to achieve. I did not want to wander job to job and blow my mind with partying all the time and working for someone else's dream. I did not want to be a burden on my parents either. They raised me and now it was up to me to become somebody and start taking care of myself.

I went to my first annual training in the summer of 1982. I worked on tanks and went to the field. I was also introduced to Sergeant Major Barren, he was also a Vietnam veteran and his favorite saying was, "we are not here to play games." He worked believe it or not with my mother at General Electric. He asked me if I knew her when he saw my name and I said, "yes she is my mother."He said you have a great mother. I just hope you are a good soldier. Sgt. Maj. Barren was a quirky soldier. Once I could not resist having a little fun. His radio name in the field was Top Dog. One time on patrol he called and said," this is Top Dog.' I said, "I got your Top Dog hanging." Sergeant Sutton burst out laughing and he replied, "who is this?" I just hung up the mike set. When he got where we were all he wanted to know was who was on the radio. Sergeant Sutton, said sergeant Dunn, "I won't give you up. I think this is one of the funniest things done to Barren in a long time. Keep quiet and it will blow over, but don't do that again."

Also, I had a little run in with Sgt. Carter, the administration NCO. One night while I was on Command Quarters CQ I was looking for a pen to write down a message I had received on the telephone. I went over to his desk to look for one, when I opened up the top drawer; low and behold there was my paper work for my college reimbursement. It had not been sent in and it was three weeks over due. I questioned him about it and he asked what I was doing in his desk. When I told him I was looking for a pen, there it was. He started yelling at me for getting in his desk. Sergeant Sutton was there and said, yes Sergeant Carter why have you not paid my soldier. Sgt. Carter knew he had been caught, he said, "oh I was busy planning annual training." Sergeant Sutton said, "I want to see you send that paperwork up now and if you ever hold up another one of my soldiers pay. We will talk this over with the Old Man," meaning the Company Commander. Sgt. Carter did it and by the end of annual training I got my school money.

My second Annual Training in 1983, I went to school in the Army Reserve. This was my first school since becoming Specialist or E-4. I went to a three week Instructor Training Course (ITC). I had been a student, now it was time for me to help with some of the teaching. In the Army you teach like this. I do, we do, and you do. Also you learn to make up lesson plans. There is a Task, Condition, Standard, Reason and Objective. With the mission being first, also, standing up in front of others was a challenge. In order to pass this course and I had to teach a class in front of enlisted soldiers and officers. Damn, I was scared even more than I was in basic training. I taught my first class on hand and arm signals on a tank. You were given three chances to show you could instruct and then you were cut. I was able to make it on my second try. I had a little coaching from Sergeant Sutton. The second time I was less scared and used better body language with my hands. I was also more efficient in my presentation of the class. Teaching is something you have to learn and gain experience at.

ADVANCED INDIVIDUAL TRAINING (AIT)
46Q20
FORT BENJAMIN HARRISON
INDIANAPOLIS, IN
JOURNALISM SCHOOL BJC-11
1984

Along with teaching classes, came my golden opportunity in the summer of 1984. There was an announcement in formation for the need of a Sergeant E-5, Public Affairs NCO to cover our missions and events. I went to Sergeant Sutton and he took me to the first sergeant and I got orders to the Defense Information School at Fort Benjamin Harrison in Indianapolis, IN. The course was 12 weeks from June to August and a great summer job. The real kicker was it was worth eleven semester hours toward my degree. The school was much different than Armor school. It was harder mentally not physically. You had to know how to write to be a journalist in the Army. I had to pass a typing test before being accepted. The typewriters back then were also manual. There were no electric typewriters and no computers and everything was edited with a pencil. Also there was a grammar test, which I barely passed. I made it in and once again I was determined to get through my second Military Occupational Skill (MOS).

I was in a small class of twenty service members. This was joint service course and was made up of Army, Navy, Marines, Air Force, and Coast Guard personnel. This was my first time being exposed to all the other branches of services. We had a class leader, not a platoon sergeant. He was a Marine, Staff Sgt. Baines and he had just come back from Beirut. He set the standards for the class and he helped me make it through this course. We all started the course with 25 students, but only 15 of us graduated. There was news writing, photography, feature writing, broadcast writing, and everything was edited and graded. Either you learned it and passed it or you went on probation for a week and then you were gone with no recycling. My instructor was Staff Sgt. Teel, he was hard, but he was fair. We learned how to use an Associated Press Style Book. This was not like English 101 or 102 in college, this was journalism and the rules were different. The style book was your guide and if you spelled a name wrong and it was a person, you were docked 25 points out of a 100 before you even got started on your story. I myself misspelled a name wrong right off the bat. I was told the name was Geoffrey and I spelled it Jeffrey.

My first news story I wrote I had failed with a 57 percent. Not only was a name misspelled, but there were other editing flaws, that included punctuation. Also if you are writing a news or feature story for the

Army or any other publication you better attribute who said it. Also who, what, where, when, why and how better be included. There are many rules to writing for a publication; you also better know the difference between Libel and Slander. Libel is when it is written, Slander is when it is said to a third party. Also many words mean more than one thing and you have to learn how to use them in a story.

My favorite part of the course was the photography. Back then there were no digital cameras. We all used manual Canon F1 35mm Cameras and shot plenty of film. Then you had to be trained in a darkroom to develop black and white pictures and contact sheets. This was the only way to get the photos printed for our story boards and cut lines. It would sometimes take more than two days using an enlarger and easel to get the photos you needed for publication. Today darkrooms are a thing of the past.

I was glad to use the darkroom, because digital cameras do not always work in harsh environments such as extreme cold and heat in the field. I know how to use both digital and film cameras and today's students only know digital.

I also spent many a night burning the midnight oil getting through this course. Sergeant Teel could have failed me two weeks before graduation. I had a 69.8 grade average and I needed a 70 percent to make it to the final project. I had one story left. Final Project consisted of two weeks for the class to create its own publication. The thing that saved me was he told me to write my last story on any subject and make it a good one. I wrote my last story on the 40th anniversary of the bombings in Hiroshima and Nagasaki in Japan. I found a veteran of WWII, who was getting ready to retire from the Defense Information School. He actually worked on the trigger mechanism for the atomic bomb that was dropped in Hiroshima. He was a Navy warrant officer in WWII, and worked in the back of a furniture store to cover up the fact that he and some other Navy officers were working on a part of the atomic bomb.

Sergeant Teel loved it, and told me "I knew you could do it." I got a 100 percent on the story. To get a 100 percent on a story is almost not heard of. Especially, when there is so much to edit in a story and pick at. I ended up graduating with a 74 percent overall grade. I made it to final project and we put out our publication called "The Final Cut." It was an eight page tabloid newspaper. We had to use a mimeograph machine back then. There were no copy machines, PageMaker or computers to produce it.

I graduated once again with my family coming from Louisville to Indianapolis to see me. It was an accomplishment that would set the tone for my career in the Army Reserve and later on in Active Army.

PRIMARY LEDERSHIP DEVELOPMENT COURSE
PLDC, FORT BRAGG, NC
1985

The next year I was teaching classes at Annual Training not just sitting in them or helping. By 1985, I was not only an Armor Crewman; I was also a certified Army Instructor with a Hotel Skill Identifier and also a Public Affairs Specialist who wrote stories about our training.

Now I was working my way to making Sergeant E-5, but first I had to go to another school to earn this. You see no one gets anything in the Army without training and earning it.

I had orders for my Primary Leadership Development Course (PLDC) at Fort Bragg in Fayetteville, NC. I was assigned for one month in the Second Army Non Commissioned Officers Academy in 1985. This NCO Academy was a killer. We had to learn everything from map reading to being in combat operations. We were also in the classroom for two weeks and in field for two weeks. I remember getting bit one night in the field by a poison spider, a Brown Recluse Spider to be exact. I had been to sick call that morning, but I talked the doctor into letting me finish my land navigation course. If you did not finish any portion of PLDC you failed. Also my platoon sergeants had already done a cycle before ours. He got pissed off one morning and went back to his unit after having words with the first sergeant who was a pain in the ass. I remember them almost coming to blows mid way through our cycle over bad water for the troops. The worst part was his replacement.

I walked all night and day to check points with a map and having my turn as platoon leader in a daze from the medication given to me for the spider bite. You see everyone had to be put in a leadership position to pass this course too. I packed everything from a radio to a M60 machine gun in 90 degree plus weather and even went through the swamps of Fort Bragg packing. Some soldiers fell out and we moved on in the heat and humidity and there was no bottled water back then either. You had two quart canteens. I went over a week without a shower and we all smelled like raw shit when it was over. Being dogged and tired with no rest was part of the test along with packing over 60 pounds to include a rucksack, sleeping bag, back pack with entrenching tool, and full LBE.

We graduated outside in the August heat and boarded a C130 plane the same day headed back to Fort Knox. I don't even remember the flight I was so tired after that month in hell. I was just glad I made it through PLDC.

Two months later I was a promoted to buck Sergeant E-5 and my mission changed. I was now responsible for soldiers and was a squad leader. My biggest thing was to take care of soldiers. I also knew their families. I continued teaching classes and even did some stories for The Century Newspaper an eight page tabloid. I especially liked to do stories about soldiers such as personality features, because every soldier does has a story to tell.

Still working and going to school. I decided to go into the Active Army Reserve and be a full time soldier. So I put in my paperwork and sent it to St. Louis, MO. This is where the Reserve Components Personnel Center was at the time (RC PAC). I applied in early 1986. I missed being a full time soldier, this was my way to get back to making this my career. It was over a two year wait. If it had not been for two warrant officers helping me, I would never have got all the paper work right, Chief Warrant Officer Holden and Chief Warrant Officer Johnson, both personnel warrant officers gave me the guidance I needed to finally get accepted into the Active Guard/Reserve Control Group known as the AGR Program.

I was excited, I had just finished college for now and I was living in Louisville at the time. I had been dating Telena Shimfessel, a girl who I met in Louisville. She had been working for Kroger and we were both living together in a trailer on Dixie Highway and going nowhere. After two years of living together, I asked her to marry me when I got my orders back to active duty and she said yes. I was now ordered to the 361st Public Affairs Detachment, Fort Totten, located in Queens, New York City as an editor and Public Affairs NCO. We were married on February 6, 1988 and my orders to report there was for February 22, 1988. I had also just got promoted to Staff Sergeant four months earlier in November of 1987. I was 29 years old and finally getting my life together with the support of a great mother Peggy Dunn, mother in-law Mable Shimfessel, father in-law Frank Shimfessel, who had once served in the Air Force during the Korean War, and my father Donald Dunn Sr. I was ready to make the second biggest decision of my life, the first was getting married.

Me and Telena sold the trailer and quit our dead end jobs. I first had to go to Fort McCoy, Wis. for one week of training before I was assigned to my new unit. I remember how cold it was at Fort McCoy that week in February. My old 1969 mustang barely made it up there and back. Also, there were only three people in my class, me, a Lieutenant, and a Captain. You see the AGR Program was very small back then and unlike today you where lucky to get back in and become a full time active duty soldier.

I was nervous, I did not know what to expect. There was no welcome packet and sponsor like there is today for a new soldier coming on active duty. I showed up to Fort McCoy and was on my own to find out where I had to report to. Then I began training for my new job before I was assigned to the 361st Public Affairs Detachment at Fort Totten, a post I had never heard of.

CHAPTER 4

77TH ARMY RESERVE COMMAND
361ST PUBLIC AFFAIRS DETACHMENT
FORT TOTTEN, QUEENS, NEW YORK
1988-1992

    I was now a full time active duty soldier in the 77th Army Reserve Command (ARCOM), which supported New York and New Jersey. I had just got off the airplane at LaGuardia Airport in Flushing, Queens. I could see Shea Stadium in the distance. Then I went to get my luggage in what seemed a United Nations microcosm of different people. Then I went to get a cab. I waited and waited, then I noticed you have to flag one down or jump in front of the cab or someone to get one. I finally got a cab to stop. I was in my Class A uniform and told him I needed to go to Fort Hamilton, in Brooklyn. It was a death ride with this guy. Finally, two hours later through massive traffic we made it to Fort Hamilton. The entrance looked like a war zone; there were stripped cars outside the gate. I had seen the movie I did somehow make it to the right building for billeting that night. The first thing I did was call Capt. Fallon; she was the Public Affairs Officer for the 77th ARCOM. She told me to sit tight for the night and they would send someone to pick me up at 0700 in the morning. I tried to get some sleep. I tossed and turned all night long wondering if I had made the right decision to come up here.

The next day I met Staff Sgt. Valez. He said, "How are you doing Staff Sgt. Dunn. Did you have any problems getting here?" I just looked at him like I had come out of a coma and said, "No."

We left Fort Hamilton, going under the Verrazano Bridge, it was daylight now and I thought well, I have not been to Fort Totten yet, let's hope it is better when we get to my real assignment in Queens. It took about two hours to get to Fort Totten, traffic was crazy. I saw the police chasing a man just outside the gate in a car. Then I saw the man jump out of the car and take off running with the car still going. The car hit two other cars and a telephone pole before it stopped. I looked at Sergeant Valez and he said, "Welcome to Fort Totten, things like this happen all the time around here." I thought to myself forget the new assignment just take me back to the airport. Then we reached the Ernie Pyle Center, named after the famous WWII Journalist. Sergeant Valez took me to see Capt. Fallon.

She called me in and said, "Great to see you made it Sergeant Dunn." I said, "Thanks." Then Sergeant Valez said he had to go to his section in personnel. Capt Fallon showed me around and introduced me to everyone. I had to in process too, this included making sure my pay was right. I had to be set up with housing. I also had to go through personnel and get a new ID card and security badge for Fort Totten. Then she said, "This is Mr. Morris "Mickey" Goldman's office and if he tells you what to do, make sure you do it before you do anything else, he is God around here." He was the senior civilian of the 77th Army Reserve Command. Finally, Capt. Fallon got me to my new unit. The 361st Public Affairs Detachment was located at the far end of the building on the second floor. The unit had 13 soldiers, four officers and nine enlisted soldiers including me. I was the only active duty soldier, responsible for this unit. Then she opened the door, what a mess. I said who was here before me. She said "Staff Sgt. Roho". "When did she leave? Capt. Fallon told me the story of sergeant Roho not wanting to be here, because her husband was stationed somewhere else. Later I found out that she had gone absent without leave AWOL to be with her husband. The unit had not had an active duty soldier in over two years.

What a shock, here I am staring at this room in an Army Reserve Center in Queens, New York and thinking, what the hell am I going to do. I noticed the unit had no word processors or any automated equipment. There were just two old gray manual typewriters and one old Royal Electric Typewriter. Also the darkroom had limited equipment. I had a whole lot of work to do here and I had not even met the first sergeant and commander. Later I went to lunch with Capt. Fallon and she told me, "This must be a big change for you coming up here from Kentucky." I said, "It sure is." Capt Fallon was nice enough, but I could tell she was a feminist by the way her office was set up. There was a sign on her desk that said a woman's place is in command.

That afternoon I met the commander, Capt. Gabriel, another female officer. This unit had a wide variety of ethnic groups in it too for just 12 soldiers. I had two soldiers from the West Indies and a variety of Italian and Jewish soldiers. I also had a soldier who was from Germany. She told me not to worry, because she had not been in the unit long and this was her first command. I thought well the blind leading the blind. I just hope we both don't fall in a ditch.

Later the first sergeant came in, he was a New City police detective named McClain, and he was the Master Sergeant in the unit. He also asked me questions about myself and my family. He said jokingly, "Sergeant Dunn, I know you must feel like an Irish hillbilly from Kentucky, but don't worry I will help you and don't take everything so serious here in New York." We work hard and we party hard and remember your one of us and we are a like family here in this unit." I thought I am not in the Army; I am in the Mafia now. I would meet all the other soldiers in the unit at my first drill weekend in about a week. I also met some of the soldiers in our sister unit the 340th Broadcast Public Affairs Detachment.

I had to do nearly everything. First I had to go through all this paperwork over two years. I found things missing in the unit that had never even been ordered or reported. The supply and maintenance for equipment was a wreck. The soldiers had no direction; they were just coming to drill and doing whatever.

I had to fix this and yes it took a lot of time and effort on my part. Even though I was in New York City, this was still the Army. I didn't make waves, I first made friends. You have to show New Yorkers you are one of them then they trust you. I started out by making sure everyone had the supplies they needed.

I had to recreate the whole unit supply property book first and get the soldiers and the unit what it needed. Capt. Gabriel, had also made the mistake of signing for the units property prior to my arrival without ever looking to make sure everything was there. Luckily nothing was missing. I told her, you should never sign for equipment without seeing it and always check the serial numbers to make sure it is the right equipment you are signing for." Supply is serious and you pay for what you sign for if you lose it.

Also, a commander is responsible for everything in a unit and then it is delegated down to the user's level. Next, I got new video equipment and cameras so the soldiers could train on weekends. This unit had a Public Affairs mission in less than six months to do three weeks in Heidelberg, Germany and I wanted to make sure we were ready. I helped Staff Sgt. Miller with the darkroom. He needed supplies to do pictures for the command. I fought with the logistics people in the command and made sure our Mandatory Table of Equipment (MTOE) was up to date and everything was there.

Fort Totten had been a post since the Civil War. It was a Union Hospital and was also used during WWI and WWII as part of the 77th Division. It is now used only for the Army Reserve, Coast Guard, and the New York City Fire Department. It was the smallest installation I had ever been stationed at.

I was authorized 10 days of permissive TDY, time off to go get my wife and settle in to our housing quarters at Mitchell Field, Navy Base 15 miles from Fort Totten, located on Long Island, in East Meadow. The movers brought our household goods and there were things damaged and missing. Luckily, the things could be replaced. Telena was also able to get a job as a cashier at the commissary on base.

Being in New York was a big adjustment for me and Telena, after all we had been married less than a month and here we were over 600 miles away in a strange place with no family. We made due and saw some of the sights to include the World Trade Center, which is gone now. People here were always talking fast and in a hurry. I used to laugh at their accent as I am sure they laughed at mine. People here were also very leery of each other. Nothing was safe and you had to get street smart.

Recruiters had cars stolen. One of them was trying to recruit a teenager in Brooklyn. He was in the house and his friends were stripping his car. I once saw a New York cop chase a guy with a car door in one hand and a car battery in the other and he never caught him in Far Rockaway, Brooklyn.

I and another soldier were running one day out by the Cross Island Parkway getting ready for a PT Test. When we looked and there was an elderly couple having sex in the bushes, We were laughing so hard we had to stop running. On another occasion we were running in the same place about two weeks later and the police was pulling a dead man out of the water. What was so ironic about this was there was his wife cursing him and telling him she was glad he was dead.

Once I was at the recruiting station in Time Square, in Manhattan and opened the door to leave this lady ran into the door and dropped all her drugs on the sidewalk. She screamed at me and told me I had to pay her for knocking her drugs out of her hand. The police saw this and locked her up. The gays and lesbians were like their own recruiters. I use to pass them on the other side of the street. There were also a lot of these little groups of trouble makers on a lot of the corners.

You never parked your car in the back streets of New York City either. If you did you better take your stereo out of your car. I remember seeing cars with signs posted in the window, "no radio." If your car breaks down in New York City forget a wrecker, you just call your insurance company and tell them it has been stolen.

I always walked close to high rise buildings in New York City, because if something falls out of a window, your chances of getting hit are less likely. Who wants to be in the middle of the side walk and have an air conditioner land on their head? I once saw a bottle hit a man and drop him to the ground. I called the police and he was rushed to the hospital with a severe concussion and cuts.

Never ask for directions in NYC, because there are many phone booths. This was way before cell phones. A person will call down the street and tell his buddies a tourist is on the way and they will be waiting to rob you. It's like carjacking in the Bronx. A car will stop in front of you and in back of you they will get out on both sides throw you out and take your car.

Subways always get in a train car with a lot of people and look for the ones with the conductors. Always keep away from the train till it stops. People are always in a hurry to get on and off the trains. I have seen people almost pushed in front of a train and I have seen them rolled down by the side of the train coming to a stop. Kids jump from one train to another after pick pocketing passengers. There are who like to get close to passengers and feel them up, especially the women passengers.

Some of the buildings also serve as markers or turf as gangs call them. I once seen an empty building with hangs men nooses in the center of the windows and stuffed animals hanging out of ever empty window, welcome to The Bronx. A cop once told me this is the sign of a crack house.

One time I went to flag down a cab and the cabby pulled over and asked me where I wanted to go. This was while his cab was on fire. I said, "I will wait and get another ride." You had to watch for gypsy cabs too in common cars.

Another great story is the day I was with a Colonel. We were crossing the street in downtown Brooklyn, near Bensonhurst. When out of the blue he yelled to two guys across the street. There were these two Italian men dressed in real nice suits and one was holding the umbrella for the other. The Colonel said," How is it going John," and he said, "Fine, what brings you down here to the old neighborhood." The colonel said, "am doing a little Army business." Then John said who is you friend."

"Oh, this is Sergeant Dunn." How are you doing Sergeant Dunn," I am John Gotti and this here is Sammy Gravano." I shook hands with them and then the colonel said, "see yooz later John and Sammy, we got to get back to Fort Totten. I told the colonel, their names sounded familiar and he said, "Yeah, they are always trying to put John and Sammy in jail, but they run this neighborhood. I grew up with them as kids on this street before I joined the Army." A few months later I saw

John Gotti and Sammy "The Bull" Gravano on television, before a grand jury for gangster related activity and tax evasion. I thought to myself, I met Teflon Don, but I am sure somewhere there is a FBI surveillance tape with my picture on it shaking his and Sammy's hand.

Me and Spec. Mike Golub a broadcast journalist in my unit went to the tenth anniversary of John Lennon's death in early December 1990 near the Dakota Apartments, located on 72nd street and Central Park West. What a wild day that was, people were everywhere around the building drinking, smoking dope, and doing whatever came natural. There was this girl who took off her clothes and said she was John Lennon's girl friend. These other people were gathered around the Imagine Circle throwing everything they could into the circle. We had to leave because the Cops were moving in on the crowd.

My first sergeant also helped me get a New York City Police Press credential. It helped get me where I needed to get in and out of the crowds in the city, especially when you had to cover parades on the Fourth of July and Veterans Day for the Army. Once at a Knicks game, where our color guard did the National Anthem. Michael Jordan fell on me going for a basketball out of bounds. I had the ball and threw it back to him after he got up. A few friends saw me on television, my claim to fame.

There was this old lady who got knocked down and had her purse stolen. I tried to chase the guy down until he wheeled a long knife on me and I just let it go. I did go back and try to help the lady. She said all she had was ten dollars in her purse.

Traffic is another story in the Apple; I was on the Brooklyn Bridge and the guy in front of me got out of his car and grabbed a phone out of the guy's car in front of him and threw it in the Hudson River. Then the police came and broke up the fight. A few weeks later a handicap person in a wheel chair bungee jumped off the Brooklyn Bridge. After that this guy jumped off the World Trade Center with a back pack parachute and landed in Central Park. That night the whole thing was on television, it seems his buddies taped him on the building and in Central Park where he landed. I also remember being in a traffic jams that lasted so long, everyone tailgated with lawn chairs and grills.

Paying tolls was expensive, at every bridge too. I use to have to go get tolls for the command. Once I picked up over $75,000 dollars worth of tolls at Randall's Island and had to make sure I made it back to Fort Totten in Queens. I was nervous; because, this is a lot of money and tolls are money. Even the Army had to pay tolls, our vehicles were not exempt, you always made sure you had tolls before leaving the command or you paid the tolls out of your pocket. Getting gas with a government credit card was another nightmare. Only two places took our cards between Fort Totten and Fort Hamilton. Also if you had to go to Fort Dix in New Jersey it would take all day just to go 95 miles there back.

There are also five Burroughs in New York City besides Long Island, which is not a Burroughs. I thought New York City was New York City. Let me tell you there are Manhattan, Queens, Brooklyn, The Bronx, and Staten Island. Every one of them has their own cultures and ethnic groups and you better know the streets and where you are going. You see when you ask for directions you can't always trust the person giving you them. I hated having to drive in New York in military vehicles; you stood out like a target. I had to fend off bums who would and wind shield washers trying to get money from me.

There were gangs to deal with too. I remember eating in a restaurant in China Town once and this group of Chinese youths came in and ate then they left without paying and no one seemed to care. I heard the guy next to me say. "There goes the Ghost Shadows, they never pay here." The owners of businesses were feared and they ruled the streets in China Town. There were many other gangs. If you are intimidated you are a target. I always walked into crowds and traveled with other soldiers in the city.

Back to my job, our unit and command had a quarterly newspaper called the Liberty Torch, a tabloid which circulated over 15,000 copies to every soldier, unit and command associated with the 77TH Army Reserve Command. I had to make sure it had 12 pages of news in it every quarter and I was responsible with my editor Lt. Cedell to meet deadlines. I had to go into Manhattan to a contracted printer and make sure it was printed right each quarter. I can't say enough good things about Lt. Cedell. She made sure it was edited and took it to Maj. Gen. Donahue, the 77th ARCOM Commander for approval before it went to print. Usually a General Officer does not approve the paper, but Donohue was different he was a district attorney in his civilian job and always pre edited our paper. It was all politics with him. I always tried to stay out of his way. I never concerned myself with most field grade or general officers; to me they were just there. I was an NCO and I was a soldier, not a politician. I made sure there were stories about enlisted soldiers, because who wanted to hear an officer toot his horn! I would pick up the slack and do more stories and pictures myself if need be. You have to be especially careful when you are dealing with public affairs in and out of the Army every day. Everything you do has a perception.

One of my proudest moments was when after less than three months in this unit we had a General's Inspection (IG) and the unit passed with just a couple of minor discrepancies. This was the first time in over two years the unit had been inspected and things were improving. It's all about taking care of soldier and then they take care of you. The key is readiness. We might have been a small detachment, but we were all qualified and were quality soldiers. In our unit there were no hideouts, either you got Military Occupational Skill (MOS) qualified in one year or you were out looking for another reserve unit. If we were ever get mobilized and deployed, this was not the time to learn.

It was September1988 and we were off to Heidelberg Germany for an overseas annual training. We had three weeks to support an operation called REFORGER, helping with the Cold War mission. East Germany still had the Wall up and we had to cover stories while we were in Heidelberg and other parts of Germany too. We worked with the 7th Medical Command (MEDCOM). We supported mostly medical units we also did stories for a tabloid called 'The Yank." Once in Germany we were bused down to Heidelberg from Frankfurt. There we met up with our point of contact. A Mr. Stevens, He was the chief public affairs officer in the 7th MEDCOM. Mr. Stevens got us our billeting and all our missions during this three week training period. This was my first time to Germany, but my commander and first sergeant had been here the year before. We all had to work in a small basement in the confines of the headquarters. It was tight and we all slept in the same room except for the females. I liked Germany; the Autobahn (highways) was great. I got my rental car up to almost 130 miles an hour and never had to worry about a speeding ticket. It was like driving on a road course in a NASCAR race. The food was great too; no one cooks pork like the Germans. I also can't forget the beer; especially the pilsner and the glasses/steins were huge. I did not get to drink that much, but the wine festival at Bad Durkheim one weekend was one to remember. Funny thing, I was there, but I don't remember how I got back. We also had a German in our unit. Staff Sgt. Korb, he was born and raised in Stuttgart before he came to America with his uncle.

He was also a New York Police officer. He could speak the language and new all the places to go when we were off duty. I am not a big fan of the police, but, the New York City Police officers in my unit were some of the best people I had ever worked with and met in the Army. We worked hard and we partied hard. Mr. Stewart, expected a lot of stories to be told about the Army's mission in Germany during REFORGER, but he also wanted us to get out and experience Germany.

I remember going and visiting Dachau near Munich. This was one of the worst concentration camps used by the Nazi's in WWII. You literally feel the pain this place held for those who were tortured and died there. I remember seeing the sign at the entrance which translated into "Work Will Free You." I remember visiting the ovens. You can only imagine the feeling the people had knowing they were going to be killed after being separated from their children and loved ones. The fences were doubled with barbwire and there were towers all over the perimeter. The people in the town did not even know what was going on behind these walls, until it was over. Even if they did they could not stop the wooden carts going in and out with dead bodies under the covers. This makes you realize how good we have it here in America. We don't have any problems once you see what went on here.

Staff Sgt. Korb, also took us to Stuttgart to meet his brother and some of his family on a weekend. It was nice to see how people lived in Germany. Me and Sergeant Korb are still good friends to this day and stay in touch.

The last day in Germany there was a real Hypnotic show put on by one of our officers Capt. Gary Conrad. He is to this day a well known hypnotist and works in comedy clubs all over the America. He is now retired as a Major. At first, Capt. Conrad seems strange, but he is very educated and versed in the mind. We were in Heidelberg Germany and he had some soldiers volunteer for a small show. He put them under and it was one of the funniest things I ever saw, till he had one of them almost go out a window thinking he was Superman. Even he was scared, because the last thing you would want to see is an investigation on how a soldier got hurt or killed, because he was hypnotized by his training officer and told he was superman flying out a window. We use to kid Capt. Conrad, calling him Captain Houdini or the Great Conradi. To this day whenever Gary Conrad is near or around Louisville, he sends me free tickets to his shows. I never miss a show and I enjoy seeing him.

You see in the Army it is all about being brothers. You never forget who you served with in the Army, it is all about comradery.

Being a full time soldier your job never ends and one weekend every month you are working for free while the reserve gets paid. Unlike a civilian job when you are a AGR soldier you don't get paid for overtime. The hours are long and no comp time either. Also Small unit no passes. When you go on leave no one covers for you either the work is there when you return and it is double. This is the way it is for an AGR Active Soldier. You are the only one and you have to make it happen or it's broken and you get the blame because you are the green card and active duty.

I was already planning for our next annual training which was ten months away and it was going to be in Germany again. Overseas deployment preparations never end. When one is over the next one begins. I also had to pull CQ and stay in the center all night once or twice a month as extra duty too. Then I was finally allowed to go home and see my wife, who sometimes was a little less than understanding about my job. I am lucky, I had a good wife, but being away is hard on the family and the soldier, especially when you have children. My marriage has lasted, but many soldiers get divorced in the military. I also never got comp time for working over like soldiers in other units who had more than one AGR soldier. I was by myself period in the unit and the weight of every section fell on me one way or another.

There were some interesting civilians and military personnel at Fort Totten. I will start with the senior civilian Mr. Morris "Mickey" Goldman. He was known as just

Mickey. He was 70 years old and had been in the 77th ARCOM since it was a Division right after WWII back in 1946. He was a GS-15, some soldiers even referred to him as the Godfather or The Boss. He had been in the Federal Government as a soldier and civilian for over 50 years. I did a story on him once and he could arguably have more sick time built up than anyone in the whole Federal Government with over 15, 000 hours accrued. He's even got a plaque on his wall by his desk when he reached the 10,000 hour mark. He had been in direct support for 16 different commanding generals. For a man with all the power, he was a good man and friend to me. He used to call me in on occasions to make pictures for the command and I reported to only him when I worked for him. He also knew more people in the government than anyone I ever met. He had a rolodex on his desk and if he needed something he just pulled a number out of it, made a call and it was done. He never even drove to work; he was always picked up by someone in the command and taken everywhere he needed to go. He had a secretary and usually three Staff Sergeants that worked directly for him.

Everyone liked working for Mickey; he had a charisma about him. His office was right in the middle of the command behind two glass wooden doors, with the commander's office on the left and the deputy commander's office on the right. Once Maj. Gen. Donahue tried to use his authority on Mickey telling him he had to move him, because he said he did not like going through his office to get to the deputy commanders office. I happen to be there at the time and I heard Mickey tell him and I quote, "I was here sir when you were a

2nd Lieutenant and I will be here when you are gone." Guess what, Mickey was there when he was gone. It was one of the rare occasions I ever saw him get mad. Once I was given an Army Commendation Medal for a lot work I did for him. The award never even went through the chain of command like most awards. He walked it directly into the general's office and told him to sign it and then he handed it to me with the order in less than 5 minutes. He had a way of making it happen, especially when it came to taking care of soldiers. He never called me Sergeant Dunn; he always called me Donnie by my first name. Names and ranks did not matter to him he always called a person by their first name and he never forgot a face or a name. He always got a Christmas card every year from Tom Seaver and Nolin Ryan, Major League Baseball pitchers on the 1969 Miracle Mets. He once showed me a Military Police Report where they were both in the 77th as Army Reserve Soldiers back in the late 1960's. The report said they showed up for pay and forgot their covers, another Army phrase for hats or berets. Mickey had to go to Fort Hamilton and get them paid after making sure the MP's released them before a baseball game at Shea Stadium that year.

    I once had to go into Manhattan and pick Mickey up at Tavern on the Green a restaurant near Central Park. There he was talking to Walter Matthau and Michael Douglas at a table, he knew everybody. You could be on the subway in New York City and if there was a soldier on board you would sometimes hear his name. Not only did he know all the Mets, he also knew all the New York Yankees too, especially the greats like Mickey Mantle and Joe Dimaggio. I liked going out with

Mickey, because you never knew who you were going to meet. He knew the politicians too, and once I took a picture of him with Senator Demato. At the New York City Parade for the returning soldiers of Desert Storm, Mickey had a VIP ticket and the general of the command could not get one. There I was also standing in the VIP section with a camera taking pictures of Mickey sitting between General Colin Powell and General Norman Schwarzkopf. I even got an autograph and pictures with them. I also met General Powell on the Intrepid, which is a WWII Aircraft Carrier in the Hudson River, where he was getting an award from his Persian Rifle buddies from Manhattan College. I was the only enlisted soldier there and my sole job was to get pictures of him with the command. Later I mailed some of the pictures to him. When he saw me months later, he approached me and said, "how are you doing Sergeant Dunn," I just stood there and looked up at the four stars on both of his shoulders and said, "Fine sir." He looked at me again and I thought, this is the Joint Chief of Staff and he is talking directly to me. There were other generals and field grade officers looking at me. Then General Powell said, "I want to personally thank you for the pictures you sent to me at my office and I appreciate your service." I said, "Thanks sir." Then he said, "If there is anything I can do for you just let me know." I was dumb founded and said, "thanks sir." A few colonels, I who I never met said; boy you left a good impression on him.

   Mickey, introduced me to people I never dreamed I would meet. I was asked by him to take photos and do a story of the reopening of Ellis Island in1990. For me it was like going to Hollywood for the Oscars. I met Paul Simon, Lou Pinella, Alexander Haig, Danny Thomas, Casey Kasem, Telly Savalas, Stan Musial, Phil Rizzuto, Anthony Quinn, Barbara Walters, Dan Quayle, Lee Iococca, just to name a few. I even got to sit down and have dinner at the same table with some of these celebrities. You had to donate $2,500, just be invited and here I was eating and mingling with celebrities. I was there because Mickey wanted photos and he loved his pictures for the Army.

Mickey's office was like a museum. He had pictures everywhere there was no space on the walls. He also has a coat rack with hats and coffee cups galore. Yes, Mickey was quite a man; He was never married and lived with his sister. This small Jewish man from New York City was a unique individual and I had the opportunity to serve with him for over four years. If he wanted something for the Army he got it and everyone liked Mickey. He was not selfish either. He once even helped a civilian named Mr. Hall, who worked in the training section. One day the Criminal Investigative Division (CID) came in and locked up Mr. Hall, they said he had misappropriated funds and was double dipping with his orders overlapping his civilian pay on military duty as a reservist. On the way out Mr. Goldman told him not to worry. The following day he was back and Mickey did not even ask him if he had done it or not. He helped him retire, without going to jail.

Mr. Goldman believed in his staff right or wrong he made sure Mr. Hall left with his dignity. He always had time for me or anyone else. If he wanted to know something he would talk to a private before he would a general. He told me, you will always hear what is really going on at the lowest level, while an officer will usually tell you what you want to hear. A few years ago I heard he died. I was in Columbus Ohio at the time and the news of his death came down even through their chain of command. Miles away from New York, soldiers and civilians admired Mickey Goldman. I know I did and I wish I could have been there at his funeral, but as a soldier you are never in one place for long. I was just honored to know him.

I left New York on TDY for a while and went to my Advanced Non Commissioned Officers Course (ANCOC) at Fort Benjamin Harrison in Indianapolis, Indiana. It was the summer of 1989 and I needed this school if I was ever going to make Sergeant First Class. The course was almost four months long and it was demanding. Just being married and being in the Army was also demanding. I was away from my wife, who worked at the commissary, but I was holding things together and my career was moving along. The first part of ANCOC was mostly soldiering, and team work. I was one of two AGR soldiers in the class, of 18 soldiers. I had one roommate and he was a staff sergeant too named Staff Sgt.Morten.

We worked as a team. We went to the field for a week and every one of us assumed leadership roles with field missions. Map reading, setting up a perimeter, field newspapers, Physical Training PT, and also setting up a Public Affairs Operations Center to do media operations on the battlefield.

The best part about the course was getting to know other soldiers in our field from other places. I was with soldiers in positions just like mine and now I was getting to know where slots were in the Army. It gave me a networking opportunity to find out where I might want to go once I complete my assignment in New York City. Back then there were few opportunities for advancement and we only had a few sergeant first class slots to choose from. We did not even have a master sergeant in the AGR program, little on a Sergeant Major. I and Sergeant Morton were the first two AGR soldiers in this class. I was trying to find out and plan for my future assignment and promotion opportunities. In the Army there are soldiers and there are a lot of politicians. I hated politics, but you had to know the right people to move up. I never was a ass kiss and I wasn't going to start now. I figured the Army had enough cut throats and assholes and I was about taking care of soldiers not just myself. I passed all my field operations and common task training CTT. Now it was time to spend the last three weeks of this three month course on public affairs. We started out learning how to do operation orders and running them through the chain of command for approval. Well, I like to improvise when I can, because to me all an Operation Order does is give approval. I always walked on the edge, because I took care of soldiers no matter what. Paperwork does not mean a thing to me when you are actually doing the real thing. It's about being a leader and my soldiers first. This thing about the mission first in the Army is shit. I knew if I took care of my soldiers the mission would take care of itself. I was learning and I figured if you did not make mistakes you weren't learning. I was always kind of a rebel, but I knew how far to push the envelope and I would not ever ask a soldier to do something I was not willing to do with them.

We learned how to do annual evaluations on other soldiers. This is another gray area for me and the Army has a problem with it too. This is the Non Commissioned Officers Evaluation Report or NCOER. It is done once a year with quarterly counseling, I think the NCOER literally sucks in today's Army and they have not figured it out yet either. All it's any good for is killing careers on paper if a few individuals don't like you. I have had good NCOERS and I have had a few that I personally questioned and rebutted with success marks. The ones I rebutted were a long and drawn out process and everyone in the chain hated to do it. First let's get one thing straight civilians, Department of Defense Civilians should not evaluate or rate a soldier. Just like I as a soldier I should not rate civilians. The reasons are that very few DOD civilians know how to properly fill out the form, little on rate a soldier. If someone in this world of politics does not like you and you are a good soldier, they will use this against you. I have never kissed ass to get a good evaluation from any of my raters in the Army either. This is probably why I only made E-7 of Sergeant First Class in my career. The Army is full of ass kisses getting good NCOER's and Officer Evaluation Reports OER's. Some of the worst leadership is the ass kisses with rank, because they only care about number one soldier no matter who they hurt on their way.

Well after all the operation orders and everyone in the course learning how to evaluate soldiers. We started learning about our jobs as senior public affairs NCO's. We learned how to operate a Press Camp Headquarters, which included everything from doing Army press releases to media escorting. We also had to hold our own press conferences and know the Army Regulations that doctrine public affairs the AR 360's series.

Writing and communicating are also probably the two most effective methods, by this I mean applying the KISS method, which means keep it simple stupid. Believe it or not it takes a certain amount of skill to write on the 8th grade level. Just because you paid for words in college does not mean everyone knows what you are talking about when you are writing a story. The course was coming to an end and I was satisfactory and met the Army course standards. In other words I got my ticket punched.

I went back to New York City, it was now October 1989. We were slotted to go to Germany in January 1990 and we were going to be doing REFORGER again, for the last time.

On November, 11, 1989, the wall had finally run its course. I had to schedule the unit for a SAEDA Briefing, which is basically a safety and terrorism briefing before we went overseas to Germany. This time things were different, the wall was gone and the east was meeting the west. The cold war was coming to an end. This time we flew out of McGwire Air Force Base in New Jersey. We stopped over in New Foundland to fuel up and then we were off to Rein Mein, Germany. This time the airport in Frankfort was heavily guarded, there was security guards everywhere carrying automatic weapons. I and the Master Sgt. McBain got the unit through customs. Capt. Mazzaroti was our new commander. Everyone was a little nervous, but we made it through and met up again with Mr. Stevens who we worked with last year. Right off the bat I could see friction between our new commander and him. We went back to Heidelberg and supported the 7th Medical Command again. We got set up and started covering stories and providing media escort for REFORGER. We were off duty the first weekend and Capt. Mazzaroti wanted to go to Berlin. Some of us were excited about going too. I went to DCSOPS another acronym for the Army security section, to find out what we could and could not do to go. First, we all had to have passports, second we had to have flag orders approved, and third we had to go on a military train. Last we had to be briefed again on East Germany, because in order to go to Berlin you had to go through East Germany to get there. One Major in public affairs got killed when the wall was up just tasking picture!

Capt. Mazzaroti, told us he would take care of it. I had my doubts, but he told Master Sgt. McBain, Staff Sgt. Miller, me and Spec. Golub to bring our passports. I and Staff Sgt.Miller had to get the tickets. We bought the tickets on Friday morning and left out at about 2200 hours or 10 o'clock that night from the train station in Heidelberg. We figured we would ride all night and be there early in the morning and visit the wall, where it was in the process of still being dismantled and taken down.

We were on the train for about four hours when all of the sudden it stopped, I looked out the window and noticed they were putting some people off the train. It was still dark and all I could see was German Shepherds and barbed wire fences. They grabbed this one guy and threw him off the train. Things just did not seem right. I remember Sergeant McBain and Sergeant Miller who are both New York City Police officer looking at each other. I said jokingly, "either the train is broke, headed for the yard, or we are finally at Dacchau," they both busted out laughing. Then the curtain was thrown back in our cabin and there was this East German soldier looking right at me. He turned and said, "Passports!" I pulled mine out and so did everyone else. He grabbed all of our passports and looked at them real quick. He had a box around his waist and neck; he pulled out a DDR stamp and stamped our passports. Then as fast as he appeared, he was gone with the curtains pulled back quickly. I looked at Spec. Golub who was still terrified and said, "Welcome to East Germany it was sure nice meeting the Fehurer." Capt Mazzaroti started laughing and we all joined in.

Finally, morning broke and we could see the wall outside our cabin window. We were excited, Staff Sgt. Miller said, "The first thing we are going to do is get to the Brandenburg Gate and get a piece of the wall." Everyone said let's do it. So once the train stopped we got off at the train station in Berlin. Spec. Golub knew this girl who met us and took us to a nice hotel for a fair price. He knew her from school in Brooklyn. I tell you this was all starting to feel like a James Bond movie. I mean, things were happening real fast, trains, this girl, hotel, and now I am standing with Staff Sgt. Miller and Master Sgt. McBain in front of the Brandenburg Gate, were the East meets the West in Germany. Then I pulled a hammer and concrete chisel out of my bag. Which, I borrowed from our Army carpenters tool kit. I gave them to Staff Sgt. Miller and he began knocking pieces off the wall. While he was knocking pieces off the wall, I decided to climb on top of the wall right in front of the Brandenburg Gate. The wall already was showing wear and tear from people taking pieces of it. There were holes in the concrete big enough to walk in. I first had

Spec Golub take my picture inside the wall with me in it. Then I scaled the wall and stood on top of it with some other Germans who joined me. I yelled down to Staff Sgt. Miller and said, "Look at me', he just laughed and said, "I hope your stupid ass falls." I then came down and started helping them gets some more pieces of the wall. We had a whole duffle bag full of rock.

We thought we had struck a gold mine. I also went across the wall and came back, just so I could say I did it. The East German border guards just looked at me and then some of them tried to sell me their uniforms. Staff Sgt. Miller and Master Sgt. McBain got out their cameras and all five of us had our picture taken in front of the wall by the Brandenburg Gate. We looked like a rock 'n' roll band doing a publicity shot for a new album. Then we headed back to the hotel for the night. Once we arrived at the hotel we divided up the rocks in Master Sgt. McBain's room. We were all sitting there at the table like we had just robbed a bank and sorting out rocks from the Wall like they were gold, laughing and drinking German beer.

The next day we headed back with rocks from the Brandenburg Gate in each of our own separate duffel bags. We got on the train in downtown Berlin right near a church which was one of the few things left standing after WWII as a reminder. We got back to Heidelberg that night late.

Only the commander Capt. Mazzaroti was not too smart about telling where we went and how we got there and back. He told the whole story about us going to Berlin. We vowed not to say a word and he tooted his horn. This brought attention all of us who had went on the trip. We also thought he had taken care of everything before we left to go to Berlin. Well guess what, he fucked up and it cost him his command. Once the word got out that a few soldiers from the 361st Mobile Public Affairs Detachment (MPAD) had made an unauthorized trip on a weekend to Berlin, all shit hit the fan. I was sitting at my desk in the 7th MEDCOM Public Affairs Office typing up one of my stories. I heard the door slam behind me and before I could turn around there was a BDU hat with two stars sailing and landing on my computer keyboard. Then I looked around and there was Maj. Gen. Richardson, the commander of Operation REFORGER looking right at me. He had come all the way down from Bonn in Northern Germany and he was pissed. I called the whole room to attention. All I could hear was, "Who do these two overweight soldiers belong to Sergeant Dunn." I could not say anything, because he had seen Sgt. 1st Class Mays and Sgt Bisby, who between them both were 50 pounds overweight. The funny thing was he had to press his way between them to get through the door. Inside I was laughing, but I did not dare show it. This was not a social visit. He then said, "where is your commander sergeant Dunn," and I said "he is in here sir." I opened the door to Capt Mazaroti's office and said; "sir general Richardson is here to see you." His eyes were as big as two eggs in a slop bucket. Maj. Gen. Richardson, said, "Thank you Sergeant Dunn and close the door on your way out." I said "yes sir," he then said, "Sergeant Dunn, get me Mr. Stevens right away." I ran down the steps. I saw Mr. Stevens and he was already on his way. I went back to my desk and just pretended to work and listened. All I could hear was General Richardson, yelling at Capt.

Mazarotti. His last words were as the door opened." I am going to slam dunk you for pulling me away from this operation and making me come down here captain." Mr. Stevens had his head hung down and Capt. Mazarotti was white as a ghost on Halloween. Then Maj. Gen. Richardson looked at me and said, "where is my hat sergeant Dunn." It was beside my computer keyboard, I picked it up and handed it to him and he looked at me and said, "Your commander is an idiot!" I thought about saying, I know that sir, but he did not look like he was in a laughing mood. So I just stood there at attention till he left the room romping down the steps and yelling at his driver to get him the hell out of Heidelberg. Right after Maj. Gen. Richardson left, the commander called me, Master Sgt. McBain, Staff Sgt.Miller, and Spec. Golub into his office. He wanted to know if we had talked to anyone about our trip to Berlin.

We all said no. Shortly after our meeting with the commander, Mr. Stevens took Master Sgt. McBain into the Deputy Chief Security Operations Section (DCSOPS) where he was questioned about our weekend in Berlin. Being the highest ranking enlisted soldier, Master Sgt. McBain told the truth. We then found out Capt. Mazarotti had wrote a story in third person about our trip to Berlin and turned it in to be published in the 7th MEDCOM's Tabloid, "The Yank." This was real dumb. We all were asked questions about Capt. Mazarotti, not about ourselves. I knew who they were after, it was obvious, and they wanted Capt. Mazarotti bad. We also found out he had lied about even going to Berlin, which put his integrity as an officer on the line. We did not give him up, he did that to himself. One thing I learned about being in the Army, always tell the truth, no matter what. He lied to DCSOPS Chief and a stenographer who was there recording everything. Later, Master Sgt. McBain called me, Staff Sgt. Miller and Spec. Golub to his room. We discussed what we had all been questioned about.

The trip to Berlin, to me was a minor thing, but to the 7th MEDCOM it was a big deal with implications. I am loyal to my chain of command and to my soldiers, but this was way out of my hands. All they wanted to do was get Capt. Mazarotti relieved of his command and they accomplished their mission. It was just a matter of getting back and watching the shit happen.

Now we were on our way back from Germany. We landed at JFK Airport in Brooklyn, New York. It was raining outside and I and Sergeant Miller had to get all the unit equipment from the belly of the plane through customs and out to the vans. Once all of this was done we went back to Fort Totten in Queens to unload everything and see our families. We had no sooner got to the unit and in walked the Commander of the 77th Army Reserve Command, Maj Gen. Donahue and he was with Col. Larado, the 77th Public Affairs Officer. I remember thinking, oh here comes shit on the griddle.

Capt. Mazarotti had the same look he had in Germany when Maj. Gen. Richardson had walked in. Maj. Gen. Donahue said, "Come with me Captain Mazarotti, we need to talk and bring your 201personnel file with you." The worst part is Maj. Gen. Donahue was a prick to say the least, I never did like him he was also the district attorney for Westchester County. I had to go up to the unit and unlock the file cabinet to get Capt. Mazarotti's 201 file, and then I had to bring it back to him personally.

We all looked at each other while Col. Larado, said, "I am upset with all of you in this unit, because the commander is on his way out and you all caused it. I am also ashamed, because I was the one who brought you all Capt. Mazarotti, but be advised, I will not make the same mistake twice." I also feel bad for you Staff Sgt. Dunn, because you are the only active duty soldier in this unit and will have to deal with this for a while when everyone is gone back to their civilian jobs." After, Col. Larado left; I looked at Sergeant McBain and Sergeant Miller and said, "Do you think I should have offered him a piece of the Wall." They looked at me and laughed and said, "I don't think so," Sergeant Dunn.

Well to make a fucked up story short, Maj. Gen. Donagan did relieve Capt. Mazarotti from his command and gave him a reprimand which is a bad letter of leadership, put in his 201 file. He came in and said goodbye and I out processed him. He was a good officer, but he was not a smart commander. I told Capt. Mazarotti goodbye and shook his hand and thanked him for his time in our unit.

Now let's talk a little bit about Maj. Gen. Donahue, the 77th ARCOM Commander, first he replaced Maj. Gen. Border who had been the 77th ARCOM commander for my first year being stationed at Fort Totten. I never knew much about Gen. Border, except he was divorced and liked the ladies. Every time I seen him at an Army function he always had a new girl friend. Other than that he was a politician like most general officers. Well, Maj. Gen. Donahue was a different kind of general officer. He was very arrogant and pompous to say the least. He wanted everything his way no questions asked. The first thing he did when he took over was to get rid of all the section chiefs in the command. I remember walking by his office on the day he assumed command and seeing a row of about eight to ten full bird colonels with their 201 Files in their hands.

Maj. Gen. Donahue also loved to be noticed and always wanted to be the center of attention. He made sure when he walked in a room there was someone there to announce his presence at the top of their voice. He loved authority and he was like Lyndon Johnson, a bully. Also, when he came down the hall with his cronies everyone made a hole and moved out of the way or sometimes you were literally knocked out of the way by his military police bunch, which he always had in front of him. He always had the band play "New York New York" by Frank Sinatra and made sure everyone stood at attention until it was over at functions.

Time for leave, my parents came up to visit me and I took them into Manhattan, my dad was petrified. When we got off the train at Penn Station and started walking down the street, he looked at me holding tight to my mother's hand and said, "Boy I don't know where you got us, but you better get us out of here now." I laughed, although he did not think it was funny. I told him,' just stay close to me and Telena. I took them to the Empire State Building and then we went on to the World Trade Center. At the top my mother said, "All the buildings and the people and cars look like ants." I finally went back to the World Trade Center in 2009 and I went to ground zero. It was then I realized what I fought for in Iraq. It was nothing like I remembered, and now it was gone. After leave it was always lonely after our parents would visit us and then go home. It was also the same when I drove back to New York City from Louisville, Kentucky after the holidays.

Another crazy story was when I had to cover Master Sgt. Benders's 40th birthday party. She was the Public Affairs NCO for the headquarters in the 77th ARCOM. First, they put two of my soldiers on orders to cover it, under my unsuccessful protest. We were ordered to videotape it, which I still have a copy. It was a bunch of women, civilians, and Army personnel, there to include a female Inspector General from the 77th ARCOM. All females in attendance made a disgrace that day of the memorial room in the Army Reserve Center. This room was a museum dedicated to the soldiers past and present who served in the 77th Division in WWII.

This particular day it was used for a paid Chip and Dales Stripper who they were able to sneak on post in a Battle Dress Uniform BDU for her birthday party. This guy came in and I knew something was not right when I saw him in an Army BDU uniform with long hair and no name tags or rank. To me it was a disgrace to the uniform and those that put him in it. He then jumped up on the table and took off the uniform and began doing a strip tease act for all the women. The worst thing is no one thought this was wrong, except me and my soldiers who were on orders to cover this. I told my two soldiers to make sure they filmed this, because I wanted to mail this to the Department of Defense and let them take a look at it. This guy did everything you could imagine sexually; it was disgusting and disrespectful to say the least. I went to the post Inspector General's Office at Fort Hamilton with the tape and they did nothing. I mailed the tape to the Department of Defense and they did nothing. I was also ordered by Capt. Fallon and Master Sgt. Bender to turn over the tape over to them. I did, but I kept a copy and I have it to this day.

It was bad enough that the tax payer's money was wasted on my soldiers to cover such an event on orders. Also, the commands females' were fraternizing with a stripper during duty hours. Also the female IG, a Major putting dollar bills down the strippers G-String. Then there was the fact of passing off a civilian male stripper for a soldier to get him on the post. It does not matter male or female if behavior is unbecoming of a soldier and in this case female soldiers, it is wrong. They could have had this party anywhere else, but they chose to do it in the 77th ARCOM museum. I was told to drop it or suffer the consequences. This was the first time in my career I was threatened and it would not be the last.

I went on leave again with Telena she was pregnant; we wanted to go on vacation before the baby was born. I was able to get off for two weeks, it was early spring 1990. The weather was nice for May and we started out from New York to Connecticut. It was great we visited Mystic, Bridgeport and worked our way up to Cape Cod in Massachusetts. From there we went to Boston and then on up to New Hampshire, Rhode Island, Vermont, and Maine. We really did a lot in a short period of time. But, like most leaves it ended all too soon and I was back in New York. The work load was always massive after I returned from any of my leaves. This was the way it was my whole career. It always took a few weeks after leave just to see daylight and catch up. In the Army you never get totally caught up, it is not like a civilian job. There is no overtime, sometimes 12-16 hour days depending on the mission. If I had the money the Army owed me for overtime, hell I would be a millionaire!

Now we had a new commander and another new beginning. I had seen Capt. Gabriel go and I had seen Captain Mazarotti get relieved. It was now the Capt. Jacobs era. June 1990. My wife is now expected to have our baby sometime in July. I am excited and nervous, because I know a child is a big responsibility for me and Telena, especially living and being in the Army in New York City without our families. My mother and her mother were also excited and making plans to visit us once the baby was born. I know it will be tough raising a child in the Army, but my family always comes first, then the Army.

A new annual training mission to Panama was set for April of 1991. While trying to plan for an Annual Training mission over a year away it was busy. We had the usual Physical Training (PT) Test and weapons qualifications. There were also a few public affairs conferences and functions. One I remember in particular, it was held in San Diego, California. I was brought there to meet other public affairs NCO's, officers, and civilians in our field. I went along with Capt. Jacobs, Sgt. 1st Class John Diablo and Staff Sgt. Quick for three days. The first day of the conference was a meet and greet deal or as I call it a dog and pony show. I was never one for just hanging out with a bunch of soldiers and civilians trying to make political connections and hear all their problems. I and Sergeant Quick had a better idea. We were close to Tijuana Mexico and we went. They told us earlier not to go to Mexico. This was more the reason to go. I got in my rental car and we drove to the border. Then we hopped in a cab and went to Revolutionary Blvd., in the center of TJ. We did not have to be back until 0800 the next morning. I and Sergeant Quick drank a few beers, had a few shots of tequila.

We had a cab driver take us to my car at the border parking lot and I drove me and Sergeant Quick back across the border back to San Diego. We got back at about 0430 in the morning and we had to be in the conference for day two at 0730. Man, I remember looking at Sergeant Quick, he looked at me and said, "Hell I know we are both hung over and look like shit, but damn it was worth the trip." I looked at him and said, "Sergeant Quick you almost landed us in the TJ Jail." He laughed and said, "Wait till tonight." Well day two began with aspirin and water. I also bailed out once to throw up in the bathroom. Then Capt. Jacobs and Sergeant Diablo said, "You two look like shit."Sergeant Dunn I see you let Quick talk you into going to Mexico. I said, "No it was my idea." Sergeant Diablo said to me, "Once this conference gets started, Sergeant. Dunn, "I want you and Sergeant Quick to go get some rest.

I will cover for you." So we ducked out of the conference and headed to our room. About two hours later Capt. Jacobs and Sergeant Diablo knocked on my door. They were with Sergeant Quick. They said, "come on Sergeant Dunn we are going to visit Gilligan's Island." I said what the hell," they said, you will see. So we all walked out of the hotel and went down to the dock near Coronado and there was a boat with a man saying come on lets go. So we all got on board and headed out. While we were pulling away from the dock you could see people in the conference room windows looking at us. Sergeant Diablo said, "Aw fuck them and that shit,"

"This is our three hour tour." I said, "I know I'm going to get in trouble for this one." Capt. Jacobs smiled and said, "Lighten up I'm the commander, and I said, "alright sir.' It was a great trip; another hang over, with all the boat drinks, but it was better than a boring conference.

I remember getting up on day three and saying to myself. I don't remember anything about what we came here for. This was just one big party, I was just happy to not get in trouble, New Yorkers know how to have a good time and we did. Sometimes in the Army you just have to say what the hell.

I also worked with the 340th BPAD and I sometimes worked with Sergeant Tito Vasquez we were not just soldiers we were good friends and he helped me greatly when I first came up here to New York City. He was from Puerto Rico and he also played Semi Professional Baseball at one time with Major League slugger Ruben Sierra, who at the time was playing for the Texas Rangers. One day after we got off work we went to a game at Yankee Stadium over in The Bronx. We got there early and while we were there outside in the players parking lot. Tito saw Ruben and yelled to him the words Indio, which is a Spanish phrase for Indian. Ruben came right over and talked to Tito and me. Then Tito yelled to Jose Cruz who was long time player for the Houston Astros and was now coaching. He was also from Puerto Rico. He came over and talked with us too.

Sergeant Vasquez loved baseball and he still played in different leagues in New York. Ruben also talked to us and took pictures with us. It was a day to remember. He is now a CW3 Warrant Officer in Supply in Gainesville, Fla. The last time I talked to him was last year he is trying to pull 30 years and then retire. I still stay in touch with him and have visited him a few times since I've retired.

Now it is back to getting ready for the mission in Panama. Operation Just Cause was gone along with Noriega, who is now in jail in Miami. Things were heating up for a real world mission in Panama and they needed Army Public Affairs Units to cover the restructuring and rebuilding of the country. Our mission was to do stories on the building of schools and roads. I was right in the middle of planning our new overseas mission, when on July 25, 1990 my son, was born in Long Island at Winthrop Hospital in Garden City. I was on staff duty that night and my wife called me and said she was having back pains. I called the staff duty officer and he told me he would cover for me. I drove home as fast as I could and called Doctor Nadel our pediatrician and took her directly to the hospital. She was in pain and they had to induce labor. She also had the baby naturally. At 0500 that night Donald Ray Dunn III was born.

He is the best thing to ever happen to me and Telena and our life would never be the same. Thank God, he had no complications and was a healthy baby boy. I told my wife to quit her job at the commissary and stay home to be with him until he was old enough to start school. I always wanted a son.

I was now a real family man and I decided at that point to make a career as a soldier and father.

One week to the day Donald III was born. August 2, 1990, Sadaam Hussein, a dictator in Iraq took over a little country called Kuwait. This was the beginning of Desert

Shield/Desert Storm. I had to make sure my whole unit was contacted for possible mobilization.

Things had to be done right away, our Unit Manning Report (UMR) was sent forward and the Army was looking for units and individual soldiers with certain MOS's to be deployed. Until this time a Unit Status Report (USR) was done every six months. Now they were done quarterly. This report was a snap shot of the unit and all its soldiers and where they were for readiness. This was a very busy time. I had to put some of my soldiers on orders to help me with the media and escorting.

I had to go cover and take pictures of one of the first units deployed a maintenance unit in Jamaica, Queens. The day before their deployment some vandals had gotten into their motor pool and destroyed a lot of equipment and vehicles. It was a mess, but the unit still deployed. The new equipment was ordered and would follow them once they were in Kuwait.

There were 26 other units that were identified by Forces Command to be deployed from the 77th ARCOM and we had to handle all their media needs. This included going to every unit in New York and New Jersey and making sure media events leading up to the unit's deployment were complete. We were briefed on what to say and what not to say and you never speculated on an Army issue unless you had firsthand knowledge and were given clearance to do so.

We also logged who we talked to and the questions the media asked. We had question and answer sheets and you did not deviate from those sheets. You also never gave interviews without command guidance and permission. I remember a specific instance where this was not followed and it cost a soldier in the 340th BPAD to be transferred and reprimanded.

Staff Sgt. Bergman was the soldier's name he was a broadcast journalist. He was put on orders to help with the very high volume of media calls we were receiving. He got a call from a newspaper reporter from the New York Post and he asks him a series of questions. He answered them without thinking of what was going to be printed in the next morning's paper. There it was on the front page of the paper. The headline read "Soldier is Reserved about Going." when the article was read by Maj. Gen. Donahue he was pissed. Sergeant Bergman said, "I do not want to go to another Vietnam." Also, saying that he did not have proper training in chemical warfare and only joined the Army Reserve, to make a car payment. Well, Maj. Gen. Donohue called down to the unit commander Maj. McGentry and told him he wanted that soldier out of his public affairs unit and to send him anywhere but here. By that afternoon Sergeant Berman was transferred to another unit.

I myself having a new born child, the media was over at my house talking to my wife. I did not even know this till I was watching TV that night at the Army Reserve Center and saw her. I was really glad she did not say anything controversial and it never was a problem. I also had to go to units being deployed with news media and make sure the commander and the first sergeant of those units were briefed on what to say and what not to say. This was crucial; I had to give interviews myself to the media on television when the commanders did not feel comfortable talking to the media. I was very careful what I said. One rule of thumb if you do not know the answer to a question, never say "no comment." This makes you look guilty of hiding something. If I was ever asked a question by the media and did not know the answer, the first thing I would say is, "I don't know, but I will get back with you and find someone who does." Think, before you speak and always leave yourself a way out if you can. I was also told where to take the media and where not to take them. We had refrigerated metal boxes in the motor pool. I was told they were for dead body parts and they also had body bags in them to ship to Kuwait for the war. Luckily, the media did not know what they were and they did not ask. So I never had to explain this to them. I also made sure we all had the proper credentials we needed. I always made sure the media made contact with us before they just showed up at a unit looking for a story. Never leave the media alone, because they will write a story, but I can assure you it will not be the one you want to read or hear.

Most of all you want to make sure they get maximum disclosure with minimum delay and that the story puts a positive light on the Army. Unlike the civilian media who writes whatever they want to just to sell the papers. In the Army you tell the positive story period.

Desert Shield turned into Desert Storm and more units were activated. We had specific things Maj. Gen. Donahue wanted at each deployment, like a band, color guard, and media coverage. What we did for one unit we did for them all no matter how big or small. Desert Storm ended in less than 100 hours in February 1991.The redeployments was more hectic than the deployments, but it was great to see the families and all Americans coming out to welcome the soldier's home.

We now had to prepare for The New York City Desert Storm Parade and it was massive. It came at a price of over $50,000 dollars per square block in Manhattan. It was going to take place right down the middle of what they called in WWII, the canyon of heroes. There had to be units contacted all over the country to participate in this including coalition forces. Also massive amounts of vehicles and equipment had to be brought in to New York City for the parade. I worked with many people doing my part. I had to be one of the photographers for the 77th ARCOM and I was lucky enough to get inside the VIP area for taking pictures. I met General Norman Schwarzkopf and General Colin Powell again. I also met Marine General Grey and a slew of other military coalition leaders from around the world. I also met Secretary of Defense Dick Cheney, who was later the Vice President. Then after the parade we all went to the Intrepid Aircraft Carrier and celebrated with soldiers from all over the world. I remember an incident between an Army Ranger and a French Foreign Legion Soldier. The Army Ranger let him wear his beret, but when the Army Ranger wanted to try his hat on, he flat out said no in French. There was almost a fight till one of their officers broke it up. I also remember this 82nd Airborne Soldier jumping off the aircraft carrier into the harbor, because his soldiers dared him too. He then swam into shore got out and came back to the party without incident. Another funny thing happened to me when one of the units came back from Desert Storm. I was on the bus with the unit taking pictures. I was standing at the front of the bus and all the sudden we stopped and the door opened.

I was the first one off the bus and all the media started taking pictures of me. I could not resist and gave them a few interviews as a joke. Capt. Fallon did not think this was funny; she came over and lectured me about not messing with the media.

Now the next Annual Training mission to Panama had to be done and it was moving upon me in a hurry. It was going to be two weeks in April 1991 and the Operation was called Fuertes Caminos meaning Strong Roads. We had to cover the news of the road building and school reconstruction operations in small villages in Panama and Honduras. Arriving in the Tomah Airport in Panama City was totally a new experience. Unlike the last two years in Germany, this was a third world country. We had to watch our luggage and equipment, everywhere we turned someone was bumming money or wanted to take what we had. We were finally able to secure our equipment in two vans with help from the soldiers who came to pick us up and take us to Fort Clayton, which was right next to the Flores Panama Canal Zone.

After being taken to Fort Clayton we set up for work. We were introduced to the U.S. Southern Command (USSOUTHCOM) PAO soldiers; then we started to unload our equipment. It was about 2300 hours or 11 p.m. before we were done. We were taken to our barracks and told that we were not allowed off post after 1200 hours at night. If you were off post after that, you would not be allowed back on post till 0600 hours the next morning, those 6 hours the base was closed. It was hot and you could see the heat on the street after a quick rain storm. I was too tired to sleep; I had a lot of work on my mind.

The next day came early we went to the mess hall and then at 0730 hours we had to meet the PAO staff to begin our mission. We spent most of the morning setting up all our video and broadcast equipment. Then we were given our assignments, by Col. Jenkins and his staff, which included Air Force and Army personnel jointly combined. I had to stay in Panama, but a few of my soldiers went to Honduras and El Salvador to cover road building operations and schools being built.

I did a few stories, but my job was to make sure everyone coming and going were logistically taken care of and had orders. I got to go to the city of Colon in Panama and do a story at Fort Sherman. The Panama Canal was different there. You actually drove your vehicle through the gates on the way to and from post. You could look up and see the gates holding back the water as you went across. The ships were pulled by two trains one on both sides of the canal which pulled them through. I even got to actually walk across the gates from one side to the other. I also got to visit the Pacific and Atlantic Oceans in the same day. Panama is only 50 miles wide from one ocean to the other and some of the beaches had black sand created by volcanic ash. When it rained it poured and when it stopped it looked like it had never even rained, because of the humidity and heat. I remember using a video camera while at Fort Sherman and it was so hot the tape melted to the head of the recorder. You always packed water with you, dehydration could come in less than an hour of being outside in the rainforest and jungle.

While at Fort Sherman I got a chance to go to their zoo. It was much different from zoo's I had been to in the U.S. I saw a 500 pound Anaconda Snake and they were feeding this thing rats, not mice. I also saw a Sloth, which looked like a small tree bear climbing a palm tree.

I also covered an earthquake in Panama. The earthquake killed over 100 people and we went there and helped the Panamanians find shelter, stop looters, and fed their children.

Fort Clayton and Howards Air Force Base was a different place at night, here in Panama. There were all these girls lined up outside the gate asking soldiers if they would take them on the base to party. When we went to the NCO Club, I would see all the same girls with soldiers bringing them in and out of the club and having sex in open cars in the parking lot. I also wondered why the base commander would allow this. These girls were looking for soldiers to marry and get them out of the country. I also saw Panamanian girls standing on the walls of the club inside and out. They propositioned you at will. If you had a military ID and you signed them in at the gate, you had your date for the night. They also came in with their friends and they would ask you to take them home with you.

I never drank the water, but I did have a few moments to try some of the local brew. They had a beer called Balboa and Atlas. Speaking of Balboa, the coins all had his picture on them. I think because he discovered Panama. The paper money used in the country was the American Dollar. It was kind of odd; the Balboa coins were the same size as our coins and were even minted in Denver. Another thing the roads were also dangerous in Panama; we ran off the road many times and had to watch for herded cattle and horses traveling through the villages.

The missions were over and now it was time to go back to the Big Apple, NYC. We first had to turn in all our stories and make sure they were edited. Then they were used by USSOUTHCOM. They broadcasted all our stories back home on Armed Forces Network (AFN).

While at the airport in Panama City, one of my soldiers a Spec. Delgado a journalist who was not the brightest light on the Christmas tree purchased a machete. Well, he put it on the security belt while they were looking at everyone's carryon luggage. I remember hearing one of the airport security guards yell "Machete." Then they grabbed him up and we had to go get him from the grasp of airport security.

The next week after being back from Panama, I had to do another dog and pony story. I had to take pictures in 77th ARCOM of a new memorial room being dedicated to Colonel Alt. I had the chance to meet Ron Gershner, a hockey player who played for the New York Rangers and his wife super model Carol Alt. The room was being dedicated to her father for his service to the 77th.

The next day, I came into the center and there was a fist fight going on at the copy machine. Sgt. Maj. Ramon was in charge of the copy room was fighting with CW3 Perkins. Well, the MP's showed up and they both were taken away. I came in another day and there was someone breaking into a car with a tent pole. Before he could finish there were two NCO's and MP's throwing him to the ground. The last thing I saw was this civilian handcuffed in the back of an MP pickup truck headed for jail. It never ends, later some new computers showed up on the dock near the back of the command. Before the driver could go in and get them signed for, they were gone. Now everyone who was supposed to get a computer including myself had to personally drive to Fort Hamilton and sign for theirs. I also remember this Captain screaming and talking to himself in the bathroom of the Center. He had to be restrained and evaluated; the stress level was high in certain command sections. Then this old warrant officer who was about 75 pounds overweight and could barely walk without stopping to get his breath died one day on the way out to his car in the parking lot of heart failure.

My job was to make sure this unit was ready. The key to any unit is readiness. This is the mission. I saw commanders get relieved during call up for Desert Storm. Especially when their equipment was broke and they reported it as being at 100% mission capable. Also not having enough personnel and fudging the numbers and qualifications for MOS's in the unit was a major no go. I made damn sure I could show our strength, weaknesses and also made sure they were being addressed. I put soldiers in school; they did not just hang out on their weekend drills. I also had four different commanders while in the unit.

I also took in all of New York City, I loved sports and there were the Mets, Jets, Knicks, Yankees, Islanders, Rangers, Giants, and a slew of other sports in the area. I went to the Triple Crown in horse racing and even stood in the winner's circle at the Belmont when Go Go Ire, the only Irish horse to win the Belmont won. Then there were the theatres, bars, movies, concerts, restaurants, uptown and downtown. You name it, The Statue of Liberty, where

I walked to the Crown, Ellis Island, Little Italy, China Town, South Side Sea Port, Jones Beach, Coney Island, Radio City Music Hall, Madison Square Garden, Carnegie Hall, Rockefeller Center and more, it was all here. I love Rock 'n' Roll. I went to every concert you could imagine in Madison Square Garden, Greenwich Village, CBGBs, The Apollo, The Beacon and the Ritz. I was at the tenth anniversary of John Lennon's Death at 72nd street and Central Park west. I remember the Imagine Circle and the main entrance leading into the Dakota apartments where he was shot and killed. Also the Broadway Shows were awesome, like Phantom of the Opera, Cats, Miss Saigon, A Street Car Named Desire just to name a few. I was even invited to parties with celebrities at places like the Waldorf Astoria Hotel. I spent time on weekends in Atlantic City and once I met Donald Trump and got his autograph in his Casino. I went to Governors Island and saw Ronald Reagan, George Bush Sr., and Mikhail Gorbachev speak. I ate at Tavern on the Green, Mama Leones, and Terrace Tower in Queens. The food was great in New York City; especially the pizza. It was another world beyond Kentucky.

This was the capitol of ethnic food. I spent over four years in New York City and I took it all in. I got to go to the U.S. Open, The Mets in the 1988 Playoffs, the National Invitational Tournaments in college basketball and Big East games.

I put Army assets in all kinds of places. Color Guards, Army Bands, soldiers, and all the things the 77th ARCOM had to offer for Community Relations. I remember the World Trade Center and standing on top of it and going into the two towers many times. Later in my career I would go to Iraq and fight the war on terrorism and I would remember all the people who lost their lives in those towers, I was a New Yorker back then. I still talk fast sometimes and use the slang. While my friends were at home in Louisville, mostly working dead end jobs and just hanging out. I got educated, and I experienced real life situations, and met many different people here. I stood on the top of the Empire State Building. I seen all five Burroughs, Brooklyn, Manhattan, Queens, The Bronx, and Staten Island were all part of my adventures. There was so much to do in New York City; I was working in the real world in the Army and I liked being in Public Affairs. I finally felt like I was going somewhere and becoming somebody.

My time was now coming to an end here and I was told by the Army Personnel Center (ARPERCEN) in St. Louis, Mo., that my next assignment would be in Atlanta, Georgia. I had to start getting ready to move me and my family. Moving in the Army was a pain in the ass. This time I made sure Telena and my son Donald were home with her parents in Louisville and I took care of the move. Next, I was off to Atlanta as a Public Affairs NCO and editor of the Wildcat Magazine in the 81st Army Reserve Command (ARCOM).

It was also time for me to reenlist again. The funny thing is I reenlisted 5 times in my career at 6 years a pop and only the first and last time did I ever swear in with an officer present. The other 3 times I did all the paperwork and signed the names and sent it forward. Once I even signed my own name for the commander. This tells you how much the personnel section noticed signatures on an enlistment.

Before I left Col. Lorado and my unit gave me a dinner and a going away party. It was great, except I was put in for a Meritorious Service Medal and it was downgraded to an Army Commendation Medal. It seems the reason was Maj. Gen. Donahue said, he does not give MSM's to soldiers under the rank of E-7 or Sergeant First Class. Yes, I was a Staff Sergeant then, but it was funny that he gave one of his female E-5 Sergeants an MSM, who by the way only worked for him just during Desert Storm and was a reservist on orders. Col. Lorado knew I worked hard and so did my unit. I was stationed here over four years and the unit never failed an IG Inspection, besides that we met mission at all our annual trainings being the only active duty soldier in the unit. You see being AGR and being in a unit is sometimes an ungrateful job. I also seen reservist gets better NCOER evaluations than me and they would only come in one weekend a month. The last thing I had to do now was start out processing New York was headed for the rear view mirror of my car.

I also had to go to Fort Devens to do more out processing in Massachusetts for three days TDY, go figure. I had to go to personnel there and carry my records to include my medical and dental records to make sure they were moved to my new command. I was now officially headed for 81st ARCOM

CHAPTER 5

81ST ARMY RESERVE COMMAND
AND 300TH PUBLIC AFFAIRS DETACHMENT
FORT MCPHERSON
EAST POINT, ATLANTA, GEORGIA
1992-1994

I arrived 1 June 1992, East Point in Atlanta, Ga. Here I could afford to buy a house. I bought a house in Riverdale, just near Hartford Airport, between Fort McPherson and Fort Gillem, which was located in Forest Park. I brought Telena, my wife and son Donald III, down with me. I could have never bought a house in New York City with the money I was making as a Staff Sergeant in the Army, especially a brick house on over an acre of land.

I was now in a new command the 81st Army Reserve Command (ARCOM), I went from wearing the Statue of Liberty patch to wearing the oldest patch in the Army, The Wildcat Patch. It was first designated by General Black Jack Pershing during WWI and was the first patch in the Army.

The first day I came to work, two different people approached me to bum money in the parking lot. The building I was in was over a 100 years old, it use to be used to build buggies and was even named The Buggy Works. On the outside you could see where a lot of windows had been replaced from being broken by vandals. It was also near the Social Security building and the MARTA (Atlanta's Subway System). The East Point Station had plenty of criminal activity. I remember having to help take the military vehicles to Fort McPherson for storage in one of their Motor Pools. The windows had been knocked out numerous times in the commands parking lot. One morning after coming into work, I was looking out of my window on the first floor near the street, when all the sudden a car slid sideways almost hitting our building near my office. I jumped up from my computer. Out came two men with 9mm pistols, I was that close. They began firing at a person running down the railroad tracks near the MARTA Station. They shot one man who was working on the tracks, but the person they were shooting at got away. I called the East Point Police and they responded and actually caught the two gunmen. Other soldiers in the building saw this too. They gave the police their story and I told what I had seen. Although, I gave them a full statement, it seems this was a drug deal gone badly and the gunmen were retaliating for not being paid. After it was all over, there was a severely injured MARTA worker and two cars in our parking lot had bullet holes in them. I thought to myself, I just left New York City and I surely don't need this shit.

We also had lots of break-ins at the center. I even had windows knocked out once in my office, but luckily they did not take my computer. We also had to put paper in back of the windows on the first floor of the building so no one could see in them to steal things. I even knew two officers who carried hand guns to work. One of them was a young Lieutenant. He showed me his 38 revolver and told me "Sergeant Dunn, my advice to you, especially where your desk is located near the street is for you to get a gun of your own and carry it with you here at work." I bought a gun, because crime had gone up and my car got broke into and the police were called twice and they never came. So I figure if someone attacks me or steals my property I will do what it takes to protect me and my family.

I met who I replaced, Staff Sgt. Elder. Most people just called her Elly, but I always call soldiers by their rank and last name. Well, let's say after coming into the office on the first day. I was a little nervous about meeting my first line supervisor, Maj. Simpkins, a reserve officer who was also a GS11 Civilian during the week. I could tell right away that she and Staff Sgt. Elder did not get along at all.

Staff Sgt. Elder showed me around and told me who would help me and who to stay away from. You got to always watch your back especially when you are the FNG (Fucking New Guy). I met most of the chain of command. I met one Colonel who at first I thought was crazy. His name was Col. Walker, he was a Vietnam Veteran, who had served many tours. I went to his office; he shook my hand it was like shaking hands with a bear. He was a powerful man and his voice was like thunder. Behind his desk was a snake skin on a board tacked to the wall? Also he had an entrenching tool hanging on the wall. I admired him and I got to know him and he liked me. He would come into my office and take me with him to his farm outside Atlanta. I helped him with his horses. He trained show horses and when he spoke they would listen. I once helped him pick up a horse that had fallen over. Once the horse was on its feet, Col. Walker would look it in the eyes and say. "Don't you ever fall on me again or I will kill your dead ass." The horse looked at him as though it knew exactly what he was talking about you could see fear in its eyes.

One time Col. Walker came in and told Maj. Simpkins he was taking me out with him. She asked where we were going and why he needed me. He turned and looked at her and said. "You are a major and I am a colonel and if I want to take Sergeant Dunn out to get drunk then I will do it." After that, she never questioned him again when he came to get me. Also, when I received my first year's evaluation NCOER (Non Commissioned Officers Evaluation Report), he said, "let me see it". Col. Walker looked at it and in less than a minute said, "Hell No!" He then went into Maj. Simpkins office and told her to get off the phone, he told her to rewrite my NCOER and make it look like she worked for me instead of me working for her. Col. Walker took care of soldiers. Once my wife needed to be looked at because the doctors thought she might have cervical cancer. Well to make a long story short, the hospital at Fort McPherson was dragging its feet on her appointments. Col. Walker came in where I worked and overheard me on the phone trying to make another appointment. Later on that day the hospital called me and told me they would see her right away. When I and my wife arrived at the hospital, there were two nurses and a doctor waiting for us. They rushed out and literally wheeled her in to be looked at. They also made sure all the tests were run that day. The next day the doctor called me and told me my wife just had a mild female infection. I was relieved because my wife had worried about this for over two weeks. The next day I went back to work, I saw Col. Walker and he walked up to me and said, "Sergeant Dunn, how is your wife doing?" I told him she is doing great and everything turned out all right with the tests." He said, "I am glad to hear this." Later that day a soldier told me he overheard Col. Walker giving Col. Osgood a hard time about taking better care of soldiers at his clinic and then he told him about your wife and he demanded it be taken care of immediately.

He was like this with all soldiers not just me; this is who Col. Walker was. He was not your typical Colonel; he wanted his enlisted soldiers to have the best and made sure it was done. Once, I got an Army Commendation Medal for my duty after Hurricane Andrew and he insisted on giving it to me. I really never liked getting awards in front of my peers, because I felt like others think you are a kiss ass. Colonel Walker gave me the award and the whole command was there along with others getting awards. Col. Walker, walked up and looked at me, then while he was pinning me with the medal. He shook my hand and said, "This is for you Sergeant Dunn, you are one hell of a Son of a Bitch!" I did not know what to say you could hear the laughter from all the soldiers in formation. He told me things about Vietnam that most vets would not even begin to talk about. He told me when he was there he wanted to come home and when he was home he wanted to go back. Once he took off his shirt after PT and I saw lots of marks all over his back. He looked at me and said, "Sergeant Dunn, I got shot so many times

I got tired of waking up and seeing purple hearts at the end of my bed. I once got shot once while being put on a helicopter and I will be damn if the little bastard didn't shoot me again. After that I always carried my rifle with me no matter where I was." I think he would have been a great general if he had not been so outspoken, but this is what I liked about him. He would tell it like it is and he did not give a shit if the command didn't want to hear it. He taught me how to really take care of soldiers.

Later, I was honored just to be at his retirement, I think it was in the fall of 1994, he had served over 36 years. I once asked him what he would do when he retired, he looked at me and said, "Sergeant Dunn do you see that plastic bucket over there by the MARTA subway." I said, yes sir, he laughed and said, "You will probably see me over there sitting on it and talking shit to everyone riding the subway on their way to work." Col. Walker told me, "Never take any shit from a civilian, because you already know what it is like to be one of them." I only saw him once in a Class A Uniform and that was the day he retired. He had so many rows of ribbons and medals, they barely fitted on his uniform and I think he even forgot to put a few on. He also had an impressive 12 service stripes on his sleeve for every three years he served. The overseas hash marks were too many to count. I remember laughing telling him damn Colonel you look better than any general officer I have ever seen. He told me, "hell you can go get all this shit at the Clothing and Sales Store if you want." To this day I will never forget him, because he was a true soldier, and a great friend and I was proud to have served with him.

I also worked directly for Lt. Col Phelps, but he was only at the 81st ARCOM on weekends, because he was a reserve public affairs officer. He was a good officer, but he was no Col. Walker. He was nice, but he would not go out on a limb for you. He liked things low key and did not get into conflict even if need be. I credit Col. Walker with teaching me; if it is wrong fix it! Don't just let it go, because it will never go away. Lt. Col Phelps would not help get my position upgraded from staff sergeant to sergeant first class. When I asked him about this his reply was "we did not do it for Elly (Staff Sgt. Elder), so we are not going to do it for you."

When I was in the 361st MPAD in New York, I always made sure my lower enlisted soldiers were advanced through going to my commander. Here in Atlanta in the 81st it was different, they wanted to hold you down and leave you in place. So I had to take care of myself.

Also working for Maj. Simpkins during the week was no bargain, she never said hello to me in the mornings and the office was a cold place to work. She was hard to get along with, but I tried to work with her. It was difficult and she liked to keep you in the office for long hours. It was funny about the hours in the Army. In the Army work long hours is just the mentality. If I had all the overtime I put in the Army in 26 years, I would be a millionaire. I always let my soldiers go if there was nothing left for them to do. I wanted them to be with their family and have personal time when I could give it to them. When I did need them to stay longer, they knew I really needed them or someone else with more rank was calling the shots.

Back to Maj. Simpkins, even the civilians and soldiers in the command did not like her. She would get someone mad or rub them the wrong way and I would have to go and smooth it out. I worked hard and long hours, especially when the Wildcat Magazine was on deadline. The 24 pages I had to do every quarter would be done way ahead of time, she would edit them and make me work long hours doing her editing. She was a procrastinator, always waiting till the last minute to get things done. Then she would try and jump through hoops. I did six full issues and two special issues of the Wildcat Magazine while I served at the 81st ARCOM. She also did Lt. Col Phelp's job, who she kissed up to. I always felt like I was on my own. She always held information from me that I needed to know too. I never had any guidance or training, no wonder Staff Sgt. Elder wanted to get out of here in a hurry. I never argued with Maj. Simpkins like Staff Sgt. Elder did. It was not worth it, especially when she told Lt. Col. Phelps what to do. He liked her doing his job. She was always on the phone from the beginning of the day till the end of the day. Things were not that great in Atlanta and in the 81st, there were a lot of prejudices and I did not to be here. Most of those who said they would take care of you never did.

My best time was with the 81st Wildcats Softball Team and we won the 1993 championship at Fort McPherson. I played right field and second base. I did not always start, but I did what I could to contribute as a team player. Our team was as diverse as any major league team. I made new friends and we won the league, because we all stuck together. We all got trophies and I did the team photos. It was the best part of being in the 81st Army

Reserve Command and a great way to relieve tension and stress.

I also got to cover the 1992 World Series in Major League Baseball. I did stories and helped with the Fort McPherson, Forces Command (FORSCOM) Color Guard. I went with them to Fulton County Stadium. The Atlanta Braves were hosting the Toronto Blue Jays. Yes, I got to meet some of the players too and also got a few autographs from Tom Glavine, Fred McGriff, and John Smoltz. We would take a van from Fort McPherson and drive right into the stadium. We would be parked in with the player's cars. Collecting autographs is one of my hobbies and this was a dream come true. I also got to walk out on the field and take pictures of the FORSCOM Color Guard. When you are on a baseball field during the World Series and you look around and see literally thousands of people full circle, the players, and cameras. How many people ever get to be a part of sports history and get to document it too? I wrote a story and did photos and I even shook hands with former President Jimmy Carter as he walked through the tunnel. He came right over to me and the color guard and personally thanked us for our service. I also got to walk out and talk with country music singer Billy Ray Cyrus who was singing the National Anthem. After the color guard presented the colors we got to go up to the skyboxes and watch the game.

The next home game for the Atlanta Braves, the Marines did the colors. I was watching it on television with a few of the soldiers in the Forces Command Color Guard and it was a nightmare. They came on the field late and presented the colors with the Canadian Flag upside down. There it was the next day on the front page of the Atlanta Journal and it caused havoc and was considered a national embarrassment. The Canadians were furious, this was the first time The Toronto Blue Jays were in the World Series and their fans were livid. I remember Sgt. Vaughan and Staff Sgt. Whitehead of the FORSCOM Color Guard saying I am glad we never made that mistake. Too this day the FORSCOM Color Guard for the U.S. Army has this front page picture on the wall in their office with a sign below it saying, "This is what not to do when you present nations colors." We were scheduled to do Game Six. Even though they did not make any mistakes with the flags and presenting the color, there was a full bird colonel with us that night. Col. Butler, from the FORSCOM Public Affairs Office was there personally to make sure we did not mess anything up. He personally checked each flag and soldiers uniform before they went out on that field. I took pictures and I could hear a few hecklers in the crowd saying, "Make sure you get the flag right tonight and I hope you all can march better than you can hold flags."

I just ignored them. I knew we had our shit together and we really did not need the Colonel there either. We made the Army proud that night and we were well received after the national anthem.

It wasn't long after this we had a problem of our own in the 81st ARCOM. I was sitting in the office with the television on CNN. They showed one of our Army Reserve Centers in Chamblee, Ga. There was this soldier, holding his own press conference and telling everyone he was gay. I did not vote for Billary Clinton and I still do not like what he did by trying to put gays in the U.S. Army and our military. At that time I could not talk about it, but I can now. I had to run and get Lt. Col Phelps and we had to go out and meet the media there. It was Lt. Col. Phelps who had to speak and go along with the current administration. After it was all over I told him, "I sure am glad I did not have to talk to them sir, because I know I could not have went along with it."

Next, Hurricane Andrew hit south Florida in late August 1992 and the Army helped out. I was told I was going to be on orders for 30 days. I flew to Miami and I set up a public affairs office in Florida City at the Perrine Army Reserve Center to cover the family support mission for the Army. I first had to go to the old Eastern Airline building at the airport, to set up a Joint Information Center (JIC). We did media escort, Broadcast, and Print Journalism stories. I also had a four man team from the 300th Mobile Public Affairs Detachment MPAD I was in charge of to cover stories in the aftermath of Hurricane Andrew. We also delivered food, water and helped displaced families to the tent city near Homestead Air Force Base.

I saw looting and shootings in some neighborhoods. The Army had to call in the 82nd Airborne from Fort Bragg, to help with creating order in the streets. I remember a gang in south Florida trying to take over one of our family support centers. They were told to leave, but refused. They changed their minds when this Captain I was with called in some 82nd Airborne soldiers on the radio, who removed them physically from the center. I and my team also took a helicopter each day to survey the damage and provide media escort to everyone from CNN to ABC. I did a special issue of the Wildcat Magazine on the 81st ARCOM and its efforts in helping the 500 Army Reserve families displaced by Hurricane Andrew. I went in the houses and helped soldier and their families get out. I remember removing people trying to take advantage of some people by selling them water at $5.00 a bottle and overcharging them for RV's and generators near their homes. Some people would even come from other places in Florida not affected by Hurricane Andrew and get groceries in our Family Support Centers. We had to start asking for driver's licenses to make sure these people were really from those areas. We even had some of them arrested. People would stand in front of what was left of their homes, to guard against looters. I saw a former Marine in a bathtub in his back yard with a sign that read, "You loot I shoot." There were no street signs and getting around was dangerous in Miami. We had reference points and radios, no one went out alone after dark; it was total chaos at night and curfews were put in place.

I and my team got Humanitarian Service Medals for our support efforts. The magazine won 3rd Place in the Keith L. Ware Awards that year for a special issue on this disaster. After this was over, I was working on a two week mission called Camp Wildcat. It was a drug awareness program designed for the children and teenagers of soldiers. It was at Fort Stewart, Ga. We stayed in these old center block buildings with no air-conditioning in August. We had to watch about 200 kids who were involved in the drug reduction program. This was an outreach program for the kids of soldiers, and the community.

I then got the opportunity to cover a few WWII reunions. These veterans are truly America's Greatest

Generation. Back then the country was going through a depression and then a world war.

The mission now shifted to Somalia; I had to cover stories about our commands support of Operation Restore Hope. I was slotted to go when at the last minute they sent Maj. Lawton the commander of the 300th MPAD. Maj. Simpkins said I needed to be in the office here in East Point. The postal units were called. Mostly personnel and transportation units were mobilized too. After Maj. Lawton got back, I was hoping he would do a story with some photos of Somalia. He had nothing, just a wasted trip for himself. I would have loved to have done a whole magazine about Somalia and told the Army story, but it was not meant to be. Maj. Simpkins killed my mission with a useless field grade officer.

I got to work again with the FORSCOM Color Guard during the NBA basketball season. I was able to go to 6 games and even got to cover a playoff game with the Atlanta Hawks against the Chicago Bulls. I got to meet Shaquille O'Neal, Dominique Wilkins, and even got to meet Michael Jordan. Another great opportunity was I got to interview the Sergeant Major of the Army, Sgt. Maj. Kidd, and he was also from Kentucky. I was able to sit down with him and the Sergeant Major of the Army Reserve too. Sgt. Major Younger. I did a two page article on both of them and it was also an honor just to be in the same room with them talking about taking care of soldiers. I also got command coins from them.

Next, I and a lot of other soldiers from the command had to participate in a change of command ceremony held at Hediken Field. This is the largest parade field in front of the headquarters at Fort McPherson. General

Reimer was taking command of Forces Command (FORSCOM). Most change of commands was done in a less than an hour, but this one took three days, including all the practicing. We were all in full battle rattle, which means we had weapons, pistol belts, canteens, ponchos, ammo pouches, first aid pouches, and suspenders. It was cold those days and we were not allowed to wear field jackets or gloves. We literally stood there at attention shaking our asses off for hours and it also rained two of the three days! The sergeant major in charge told us the morning of the ceremony, if any of you fall out there will be extra duty, no exceptions. Yes there were some soldiers who fell out. I was lucky I hung in there for the five hours it took for this change of command from start to end. The sergeant major was hard core, he kept his word and gave about 25 soldiers a week of extra duty that included staff duty which lasted for 12 hours on and 12 hours off in his company headquarters. He even went around to us while we were in formation and looked at some of us and said "do you feel faint and would you like to make my list." Yes he was a dickhead in the sense of the word. We were NCO's and we did not need to be treated like this, but assholes are assholes in the Army. I hate change of command ceremonies. It is just a pain in the ass to prepare for one. One general or commander toots his horn and the other takes over. Enlisted soldiers we just come and go and do our job, but officer's feel they have to be glorified when they come and go in commands. Most officers are pretty, very pretty, but they can't fight. Its one thing to stand and bullshit on a parade field, it is another thing to fight on a battle field commanding troops.

The bad part about most officers in the Army is, they can be put in any unit or be stationed anywhere no matter what their branch is. I have had commanders that were everything from Infantry to finance. None of them but a few were ever Public Affairs qualified. It is a shame when all the enlisted soldiers are qualified and the officers don't know their job. Sometimes it was like they were just there.

I made another good friend while I was stationed in Atlanta, Staff Sgt. Hayes; he was 20 years my senior and was not only a soldier, but also a Civil War Re-enactor. I always like books on the Civil War and I collector too. I have been to every major civil war battlefield in this country. I have taken trips to Gettysburg, Antietam, the Wilderness, Chattanooga, Shiloh, you name them and I have been there. I love the history and believe these soldiers are the true forefathers of this country.

Staff Sgt. Hayes was the real deal. He collected guns and I saw his collection once it was massive to say the least, with over 1500 rifles and pistols. He was also a Sergeant in his confederate reenactment unit. I use to go and take pictures for his unit and I enjoyed the reenactments. They were traditional and the soldiers wore the same uniforms, ate the same food, and slept in the same tents.

Staff Sgt. Hayes had a unique friend he introduced me too. He was called "The Wildman," I never knew his real name. He was from Kennesaw, Ga. and owned an old antique bookstore that sold civil war items. He had long hair and a beard and carried two .45 caliber pistols in holsters on his hips at all times. He looked like the sheriff of the town. In Kennesaw, there is a law that says if you do not have a pistol, you can be fined. That law is still on the books today. Hats are sold there with crossed pistols that say, "Kennesaw it's the Law." When I go through Georgia, I always make a point to stop in and say hi to The Wildman of Kennesaw. I don't know where Staff Sgt. Hayes is today, he was a good soldier and friend.

At the United States Army Reserve Command (USARC), I met a Col. Brumfield, he handled all the missions that were laid out for present and future public affairs operations for all the units. Some people just called him Scoop. He helped me get my next assignment. I did not get promoted here in Atlanta, but he knew I would be happier in North Little Rock, Ark. He talked to me about a position there in the 343rd Mobile Public Affairs Detachment. I also met Sgt. Maj. Starmer she was trying to clean up our field and wanted to make sure we got promoted. They both knew I was better than the assignment I was in and they helped me get back into a unit, where I belonged. I did not like being in a headquarters public affairs position. It was always about politics and the dog and pony show. Even though I had won two Keith L. Ware awards for third place writing and photographic awards for the Wildcat Magazine, I was not happy working for Maj. Simpkins, she was all about herself.

I was given the opportunity to be an instructor and Maj. Simpkins did not want to let me go and teach two weeks at the Defense Information School. She did not have a choice when my orders were cut from the USARC. Working for her took a back seat when it came to getting 25 soldiers MOS qualified in public Affairs. So I went to the school and helped soldiers get MOS Qualified as Army Journalist.

It was not until later, I found out that my real position was supposed to have been in the USARC, but it was given to Staff Sgt. Davis and this is why I was stuck working in the 81st ARCOM with Maj. Simpkins. Lester Miller and Bob O'Brien two senior DOD civilians told me this and they worked directly with the command section. Yes, as they put it I was the loser in what they called a drug deal with the USARC to maintain my position here. Word was they could not find anyone to fill the position so I got put in it. Also, no one wanted to work with Maj. Simpkins, because she was hard to get along with. She also, did not get along with Colonel Brumfield and she resented him helping me. Staff Sgt. Davis on the other hand was a little politician and moved in the position that was supposed to be mine.

During this time they were also offering soldiers in Public Affairs 15 years and out deal with 40 percent retirement to narrow our field with troop reductions after Desert Storm. A lot of soldiers took this. I was glad I did not have the time in because I probably would have taken it, but I stayed and retired with the full package.

After almost two years, Staff Sgt. Guthrie was brought in to replace me and once she met Maj. Simpkins, I knew that she did not want the job either. Unlike Staff Sgt. Elder, I worked with Staff Sgt. Guthrie for a month. I showed her the ropes and warned her about Maj. Simpkins ways. I found out she would not stay there long before transferring to the 81st Headquarters in Birmingham in less than a year.

Before I left, I did get an Army Commendation Medal, which took three months processing through the command. I actually got it when I was in North Little Rock, Arkansas where my next assignment was. I was now preparing for my next move to 90th Regional Support Command (RSC). I got my orders and I was making my move to where I was needed. I sold my house in the nick of time I was out of there and on my way to be with soldiers back in a real unit again.

Serving as a public affairs escort to CNN at the crash site of a shot down Serbian MIG in Tecak, Bosnia.

Capt. Harmon and I flipping the bird to the First Calvary Division in Bosnia, after a rough deployment as their bastard stepchildren.

Bob Williams and I at his retirement, he was one of my greatest mentors as a Soldier.

My son and I at my son's graduation ceremony from Advanced Individual Training as a 25B Information Technology Specialist at Fort Gordon, GA.

Me in Germany standing on top of the Berlin Wall near the Brandenburg Gate in 1989.

Myself in the winner's circle behind NASCAR National Guard Driver Greg Biffle at Michigan.

Myself Behind US Army NASCAR Driver Joe Nemechek at Kansas Motor Speedway.

Myself with Charllie Daniels and the Fort Campbell Air Assault Team during the PBR World Finals 2004.

Myself with the Laker Girls in Bosnia as their Escort.

Myself with "The King" Richard Petty.

Myself with Gene Simmons of KISS at Kentucky Motor Speedway.

Myself with Four-Time NASCAR Champion Jeff Gordon.

Myself with Dale Earnhardt Jr. on Memorial Day after he signed my Uniform.

Myself with lead singer of Lynyrd Skyryrd Johnny Van Zant.

Myself getting an autograph from former First Lady Laura Bush at Fort Jackson, SC.

Myself with General Schwarzkopf at the Desert Storm New York City Parade.

CHAPTER 6

90TH REGIONAL SUPPORT COMMAND
343RD MOBILE PUBLIC AFFAIRS DETACHMENT
CAMP ROBINSON
NORTH LITTLE ROCK, ARKANSAS
1994-1997

My new assignment in the 90th Regional Support Command RSC North Little Rock, Ark. and my new unit was the 343rd Mobile Public Affairs Detachment. I had to get an apartment in Jacksonville, because there was no housing at Camp Robinson. The post was an old WWI post and now belonged to the Arkansas National Guard, Navy and the Army Reserve. The unit was in the basement of the building across the street from the RSC and it had two rooms and the three supply cages were in back of the drill hall. I was the first full time soldier AGR in this unit. So this time I was not replacing anyone. There was a lot of work to do, but the unit was in pretty good shape for a unit that never had any full time support.

After reporting in and turning my orders over to the Public Affairs Headquarters in the 90th RSC Command Section. I met Mr. Bob Williams, I did not know it at the time, but, he would turn out to be the best friend I would ever have in the whole Army. He was like a second father to me. I really wanted to talk about him later in this chapter, but I will do it now. He was a special person not just another soldier and civilian employee. When I first met him I could tell right away he was there for me, his advice and help over the next three and a half years was always helpful. I could always tell where Bob was because he smoked a pipe. He loved his pipe and the smell was his presence. Bob had been in Public Affairs in the Army since its conception. He was in the second graduating class at Fort Slocum in New York. This is where the first Public Affairs School in the Army was located at the time. He was also the oldest man in Public Affairs, at age 72 when he retired in April 2007. Public Affairs was not only his job, he knew it and was the best in the field I had ever worked with. He was from Cyril, Oklahoma and was a commander of a Public Affairs Detachment in the late 60's in Vietnam. After that he came to work for the 122nd ARCOM in 1972, which was now the 90th RSC. Bob had close to 50 years experience in the Public Affairs Field and most of that was right here in the 90th RSC. He was the Public Affairs Specialist for the command a five state region, which was Arkansas, Texas, Oklahoma, Louisiana, and New Mexico. The commands and units in these states were massive, but Bob always had time for anyone. He also retired from the Army Reserve as a Lieutenant Colonel and even reverted back to the rank of Master Sergeant so he could stay until he was 60 years old. He loved it that much. He ended up retiring as a Department of the Army Civilian in Public Affairs. His office was like a walk through a history museum; If you needed any information about the 90th or Camp Robinson he had it all the way back to WWI. The post engineers even used maps he had kept of the post, which he had collected. He was a wealth of knowledge and he was always willing to share it. His favorite thing he had in his office was a picture of the 1957 World Series Champions New York Yankees with all their autographs. It was a great piece of baseball memorabilia and like me Bob loved baseball too. Even before Bob had been in the Army he had a chance to play some minor league ball. He played shortstop and third base and was even drafted by the Dodgers until he injured his leg. Every year Bob had season tickets to the Arkansas Travelers AA Division Team. He never missed a game and if he did he would always give me a few tickets here and there. Even with his failing health problems he was given season tickets by all of us who had worked with him the day he retired.

When we would travel on TDY together once in a while, we would always try and catch a game somewhere. Bob knew the sport, but what he really knew was Public Affairs. He used common sense, not just the Public Affairs Army regulations 360 series, he could quote them. He did things the smart way, not always by the regulations. Bob also would listen and we would talk out each step of handling every public affairs mission. He would not just look at you and tell you this would not work, if he thought it would work we would try it. This is what made him a great leader he listened to others, and then made a decision. He would weigh it out and everyone had a part to play. He was a great teacher and pupil. Anyone who ever worked with Bob Williams never had a bad thing to say about him. Also if it had not been for Bob I would not have made E-7 sergeant first class. The first board that met after I was stationed in the

343rd MPAD, I was promoted and he made sure my slot was valid. My slot use to be a 46R MOS slot, which is a broadcast journalist slot, but he did the paperwork and changed it to a 46Q journalist even before I arrived. He told me, "Sergeant Dunn, I know you can do the job and you should be promoted for it."

He helped me and always had time for me. I took care of the unit and he took care of me and this meant a lot, Bob and the soldiers in the unit where my Army family. He had faith in me and I was determined to fix the unit no matter what. He knew I had been screwed in Atlanta and he showed a genuine concern for me and my family. He did this with everybody he worked with and he always looked out for me and my soldiers in the unit.

We helped with recruiting quality soldiers for the Army. The Boys Club in Little Rock was looking for the Army to help them in the community. Bob had an idea to get kids off the street and clean up the parks in the area with support from the Army. Here's how it worked, the command supplied uniforms for the kids and the boys club paid the kids for the summer. The kids were broken down into a company and the Army Reserve leadership of Non Commissioned Officers (sergeants) headed up cleaning the parks. The kids got interested in the Army. It helped turn a lot of kids in the right direction. It was called Operation Boyle Park after one of the parks. Every day we would check on the teenagers and visit with them and the NCO's. After just 6 weeks, the city had clean parks, gang violence was down, and this helped recruit some kids off the streets and into the Army.

We were also involved in the cleanup of a series of tornados that hit Little Rock. We did not wait, we acted. I had already been involved with Hurricane Andrew a few years earlier and I applied some of what I knew to help. Water and food is what we collected first and with some help from our engineer units we moved out. Then we set up a family support center and helped the National Guard with helping the victims. I did a story and took some pictures of the 90th RSC soldier's support. We did not wait for guidance; Bob told us if you see something and you can fix it, do it. Bob let us do our job; we did not wait for the Army to tell us how to do it.

Later that year, I planned and went with the 343rd MPAD on my first Annual Training mission at the National Training Center (NTC) at Fort Irwin in the Mojave Desert in California. We needed to get all our equipment out there from Little Rock. My commander Maj. Bennett and Master Sgt. Ratliff wanted to know how we could do this. I suggested we take a vehicle with the equipment and drive it from Little Rock to Fort Irwin. This was not well received at first, but when I explained that you cannot drive a vehicle on Fort Irwin unless you are licensed and trained at Fort Irwin, they changed their mind. I could fly the equipment there, but we still needed a tactical vehicle once we got there. The best thing to do was take it there ourselves. I know this sounds crazy, but I and Master Sgt. Ratliff took it out there and me and Maj. Bennett brought it back after the two week mission was over. I cut our orders me, Maj. Bennett, and Master Sgt. Ratliff for 20 days each. This gave us enough time to come and go. We had so much equipment in the vehicle you could not see out the back window. We spent our first night in Tucumcari, New Mexico. We had to get two hotel rooms for all the equipment. The next night we stayed in Winslow, Arizona. The next day it was late at night when we arrived at Fort Irwin in the middle of the night, but we made good time. It was 50 miles from Barstow to Fort Irwin on no lighted roads in the desert. We finally arrived at the main gate.

After an hour of driving around with bad directions from everyone we met at Fort Irwin, we finally found the Public Affairs Office. The unit was there. They flew in the day before and now we were all finally together. We pitched in and unloaded the equipment at 0200 or 2 a.m. I was dog tired. Then news came that we were going to have to spend the night in the Public Affairs Office, because the buildings we were supposed to be in were locked and no one had the keys till morning. We slept under desks, on the floor, and putting chairs together, the next morning the place looked like Jonestown the day after. We put our equipment together and headed to the chow hall for breakfast. I and Master Sgt. Ratliff took care of our billeting situation. We got put in some old buildings on post with a few beds and some running water for showers. The buildings had been condemned and were scheduled for destruction, but we got them for two weeks. Then it was back to the Public Affairs Office to start our mission, Media on the Battlefield.

My first assignment was to take a four soldier team to cover a visit by the Secretary of Defense (SECDEF), William Perry. He was out in the desert being shown around and also being briefed by Brig Gen. Laporte. So I got our vehicle with a good map and headed out. We followed the SECDEF around and reported on his visit. I had to then brief the commander on our mission. One night I went out with the commander, Maj. Bennett and Master Sgt. Ratliff to get a few things at the commissary. I decided to stay with the vehicle and get some rest. I fell asleep, then all of the sudden I was awakened by blue lights right behind us. I said, "what in the hell is going on." I looked in front of me and saw a five gallon box of wine and a few six packs of beer. While looking back, I could see the Class Six (liquor store). I said, "Do not tell me you took a military vehicle through the drive thru window at the Class Six Store."

I looked to see if anything was opened. The next thing that happened was a Criminal Investigation Division Officer (CID) came up to the vehicle. Maj. Bennett and Master Sgt. Ratliff were lucky; he just followed us back to the billets and told us to never do it again. We were real lucky; CID Agents usually have a hard-on for soldiers who fuck up.

Fort Irwin is also the only place in the Army where true desert training is conducted to prepare units to deploy to the Middle East. Our job was to train commanders and soldiers about how to handle the media on the battlefield. We trained them on what to say and what not to say. Emphasizing, that nothing is ever off the record and you have to watch every word you say. Everything you say to the media can be quoted and scrutinized. I had one commander not show up to meet me in the desert. I fixed him, I went right into his operations tent and took a picture of his maps and put them in an article that was printed. The next day I showed up he was there.

We taught them that they had to talk to the media and tell the Army story. Unless you did not have firsthand knowledge about a subject, you did not talk about it especially to the media. The best answer is, "I will find out and get back with you." Make sure someone is always briefed before they talk to the media and never get into a battle with the media. You have got to think before you answer and do not be afraid to say "I don't know," this is better than trying to bullshit them.

We learned and we taught for two weeks in the desert in real live scenarios. The training was good and the unit knew what to do conducting real media on the battlefield and how to run a Press Camp Headquarters too. We credentialed and escorted civilian media in and out of an area of operation. Press releases, news stories, feature stories, and interviews, we did it all in an intense two weeks in the Mojave Desert heat and now it was time to go back to Little Rock.

Right before we left Fort Irwin, big national news also happened. On Wednesday April 19, 1995 The Alfred P. Murrah Federal Building was the target of a domestic terrorist attack. We saw it on the television in the Public Affairs Office that morning too. The Military Police on post started locking down gates and 100 percent ID check points were set up. No one knew who did it; all they wanted to do at this point was help the people in Oklahoma City who were dead or injured. My commander Maj. Bennett was from Oklahoma City, he phoned home and talked to his wife and son to make sure they were alright and he tried to find out more about what was going on. We were all briefed about the attack and told what we could and could not do on and off post.

I had to drive all the equipment back. This time it was me and the commander Maj. Bennett. I saddled up and moved out for the 2-3 day trip to Little Rock. We made our first stop in Winslow, Arizona. The next day we made it as far as Old Town in Albuquerque, New Mexico, where we ate lunch, and finally made it back to Oklahoma City. I dropped Maj. Bennett off at his house. Then I asked him if I could go to the memorial service and take some pictures of the Alfred P. Murrah building. I had all the equipment with me and I thought there might be a story and photos we could use for the command. After all Oklahoma was part of the 90th RSC's area. I was kind of surprised when he said I could do it. He also said, "be careful and don't get in the way of what's was going on." I said,"'thanks Maj. Bennett."

I proceeded to downtown Oklahoma City, the police waved me in when they saw I was in a military vehicle. I was careful not to get in the way of the rescuers after all they were still looking for people they thought might still be alive and trapped in some of the rubble. I noticed a lot of buildings in the area were damaged too, some even a few blocks away. I pulled over and started taking pictures. Then I walked to the building. Every floor was open and the damage was massive. It was like someone just ripped the whole face out of the front of the building and at least half of it was gone. I could see firemen up in the offices six floors high going through the damage. There were also two American Flags hanging at the top of each corner of the building. Policemen, Firemen, National Guard soldiers were everywhere digging and searching for anyone who might still be alive. Also the police were looking at each person in the area; it was like a massive witch hunt for whoever did this. There was a makeshift morgue in one building and everything brought out of the building was evidence and guarded over. They were still finding bodies and body parts and the smell of death was in the air. I got the pictures I needed and went back to my vehicle. I had seen enough.

I was now going to the Memorial Service. I got my camera and headed to the service. At the entrance there were secret servicemen and a metal detector set up. They asked for my ID card. I thought I was going to be turned away. Then this secret serviceman took me to the side and said, "We have a place for you sir, right this way." Well, he led me right in with the Press and they credentialed me.

While I was getting credentialed, in walked President Bill Clinton, with four secret servicemen surrounding him moving fast. I stepped to the side and he even brushed up against me on his way in. I got a program and was put right in the middle of the press stands. I was standing with cameramen from you name it CNN to FOX. They all had big beta video cameras and I had a hand held camcorder of my own. It was funny, no one knew me from Adam and I just played like I belonged. Then Billy Graham walked in and they focused on him.

This memorial service was one of the saddest things I had ever seen. There were the mothers on the front row of children who had been killed in the building's nursery by the bombing. They were all holding pictures of their children, and they were all given little teddy bears to hold, which represented their children. All of them were crying. At one point I could not stand it and had to go to the restroom. I took pictures and stayed for the whole service. It was something I will never forget.

Also I remember President Clinton saying it would be quick justice for those who did this, but it took more than 6 years for the justice system to ever kill Timothy McVeigh by lethal injection in Terre Haute, Indiana, which was a lot more humane than what he did to the people in Oklahoma City that day.

I started back to Little Rock late that night, still thinking about the memorial service. Once I arrived I had to stay at the Reserve Center to make sure all the unit equipment was unloaded and secured in the unit supply cages. Then I finally got home to my family about 0300.

The next day I was back in the unit at 0730. Doing an After Action Report on our Annual Training Mission and handling the units pay.

I gave my pictures to Bob that afternoon and told him the story of what I had seen. He said, "Don thanks, we can use these for the newspaper and I am sure the command would like to see them too." A story was done by another friend of mine, Capt. Chuck Prichard. I met Capt. Prichard, when he was brought in to do two weeks temporary duty to help Bob. He was from Louisiana and was working for a newspaper there. After his two weeks, Bob asked me what I thought of Capt. Prichard. I told Bob, "he is probably one of the best officers I had ever seen work out of this office." Bob told me he was going to bring him on permanently as a GS 9 DA Civilian and Army Reserve Officer. I said, "Great he is just the soldier to help you out in this office, Bob."

Now it was Me, Bob, and Capt. Prichard, all three of us began working together when I wasn't working in the 343rd MPAD across the street. I could go to him when Bob wasn't there and he was always a big help. I liked being able to help him and Bob in the headquarters and they used my pictures and stories I would give them for the quarterly newspaper called "The Tough Hombre".

Well, it was time to prepare for another Annual Training mission. This time the unit would be going to Fort Polk, Louisiana, to the Army's Joint Readiness Training Center (JRTC). The post once used for jungle training, Tigerland for Vietnam was now a place where you learned how to handle civilian town's people in a war scenario. It had makeshift villages and the local people played the roles of running a village and town. Then we would write about it, using video and telling stories. We also worked with Army Rangers; these are the elite special forces of the Army. We taught them how to do media on the battlefield, along with training their commanders on how to handle the media too. I remember this one cocky commander telling me to ask him some hard questions. So I just asked him where his next objective was going to be. He told me and I printed it in my daily closeout report. The next day, he let me ask the questions, because he knew I had burned him

While at Fort Polk, a female soldier showed up in an issue of Hustler Magazine naked wearing nothing but load bearing equipment LBE, with a blanket for a back drop. The funny thing was no one knew who she was. She was caught after the article and picture said she enjoyed riding her Harley Davidson on post. They checked all the Harley Davidson's registered to soldiers at Fort Polk, bingo. She was one of the Military Police on Post. They found her, matched the picture to her description, and she was one less MP at the post gate and also in the Army.

We finished up our two weeks at Fort Polk and headed back to Little Rock. Once again, I made sure the unit got on the plane for home and those of us who drove followed each other back to the unit. Like everything else I put away equipment, turned in vehicles, and made sure everything was cleaned and maintenance. Then the unit pay was done and the soldiers were happy to be back with their families.

No sooner than this was over, another mission for annual training came down again. This time it was back to Panama. I had just two public affairs teams to cover the rebuilding of schools and roads. My job was the schools in the Los Santos Province near Fort Sherman. It was about a half days ride from Fort Clayton.

U.S. Southern Command wanted us to tell the Army's story of how we were helping with putting the children of Panama back to school and helping rebuild the towns in the country. I

After the first week things were going along as planned. But in Panama things can change rapidly. We were on our way back from a video shoot at Fort Sherman near Colon and while on the road the traffic began to stop. Up ahead about a quarter of a mile I could see a huge crowd beginning to come out into the street. I asked a couple of the locals what was going on. They said there was a labor dispute over concrete and sand. It was starting to get ugly and out of hand. I was with Lt. Tiller and a few other soldiers in my unit; our driver was an Air Force Tech Sergeant whose last name was Waddle. We pulled the vehicle over into a field for about an hour to wait. Then Waddle told Lt. Tiller, "I think I can get us out of here." I said, "I would rather wait than get involved in something that could be dangerous and none of our business sir." Lt. Tiller agreed, but Waddle was driving and he finally convinced him to take a risky chance to get us back on time instead of being late. This was a mistake; Waddle drove us right into the middle of a huge street fight. I looked up in front of the van, and right in the front windshield was five fully armed Panamanian Defense Force PDF soldiers. Behind the van was a mob of people throwing rocks at the PDF. I was sitting behind Waddle on the driver's side of the van and saw a man throw a rock at one of the PDF soldiers. The soldier then turned and shot his right arm off with a shotgun. I then ducked when a rock came through the back window of the van not far from where I was sitting. I climbed behind a duffle bag still in view of what was going on. Next thing I know I started smelling tear gas. The PDF started throwing tear gas canisters into the crowd to disperse them. We were now in a grid lock and right in the middle of a riot getting out of control. I saw one kid come out of his house across the street with a sling shot. Then I noticed a small opening in the traffic where the PDF had came through. I yelled to Waddle and Lt. Tiller, "step on it lets get the fuck out of here now." Waddle gunned the van and we just made it through the opening before it closed with more traffic. Panamanian news crews started coming in and they were all wearing gas masks. I wished I had my mask, but when we traveled in Panama we did not even wear our uniforms, carry weapons, or sensitive items such as gas masks. We would go on our shoots as civilians as a way to not draw attention to ourselves as being American Soldiers. I also remember fires being set in the area by locals. The law in Panama and Central America is basically this, whoever has the biggest machete, wins. I told Sergeant Waddle, "You dumb bastard you almost got all of us killed and I hope you have a good story for the damage to this van when we get back you dipshit." Then Lt. Tiller came over to me and said, "Let it go Sergeant Dunn, so I stood down. We all headed back to Fort Clayton. Once we got to the main gate we got a lot of stares from the Military Police and others coming into the post. One of them said, "This van looks like shit, were you all in a war." I looked at him and said, "no, but we were in a battle." He laughed and waved us through. Everyone was looking at us and pointing as we drove to the Public Affairs Office. Upon arriving back at the Public Affairs Office on post, I saw Maj. Bennett our commander and Master Sgt. Ratliff, our first sergeant on the front porch their eyes said it all.

They ran to the van. Then Staff Sgt. Carl Legore a friend of mine in the Public Affairs Office came running out and said, "Are you all alright." I looked at him and said, "ask cheese head Waddle over there he drove us right into a combat zone." We had to all make statements on what had happened. Then we were called in to explain it again to Maj. Hillsboro and she told us she was glad we were alright. Then she talked to Sergeant Waddle behind closed doors and I could hear her yelling at him through the walls. The last thing I wanted was one of my soldiers and me in harm's way over not waiting out a dangerous situation. Some people are just idiots, they can't help it.

Well, the rest of the time we were in Panama, I made damn sure we did not go out with Sergeant Waddle. I found out from Sergeant Legore a few months later that Sergeant Waddle had got in some more trouble fraternizing with a female Navy sailor and was moved out of the U.S. SOUTHCOM Public Affairs Office for disciplinary action.

Another incident happened when Master Sgt. Ratliff had a wreck in one of the rental vans. He hit a big hole in the road on our last day out. The roads in Panama and all Central America are terrible, but luckily, no one was injured. I was in the back seat and we landed in a ditch. $5.00 got us out by a local Panamanian with a winch on the front of his truck. The van was alright and we did not report it.

Well, it was once again time for me to pack the 343rd MPAD up and go back to Little Rock. I had to coordinate all the equipment through customs and make sure it all came back. I and the commander did the After Action Report and it was turned in to our training section in the

90th Regional Readiness Command S-3 or Training Division for evaluation. I told Bob what had happened over there. He told me, "Don I'm glad to see you made it back." I told him I had my doubts at the time.'

Bob had another mission for me to cover the New Army Smoke Generator. I had done a story before with the old smoke system at Fort Chaffee, Ark with the 460th Chemical Brigade. This time I would be spending a week at Fort Bliss in El Paso, TX. I was now working with the 369th Chemical Company. I would go there with Master Sgt. Batey and Master Sgt. Rolf two other AGR soldiers from that command. My job was to get good pictures and do a detailed story on the Army going from the Humvee to the Army Personnel Carrier, laying down smoke for cover and concealment on the battlefield, in desert conditions. The personnel carrier was a more efficient vehicle and could lay down more smoke with a new multi-fueled smoke system. I would also work out at McGregor Base Camp just outside of Fort Bliss. We stayed in a center block building with no air conditioning. It was hot in July at Fort Bliss, over 100 degree temperatures every day. Also, the first morning I was there I went to put my boots on and a tarantula crawled out, luckily before my foot went in. After that I put my boots on my desk instead of the floor. There were also some rattle snakes outside our billets too. We got rid of a few of them by running over them with our Humvee. The story went well I also had help from Master Sgt. Batey and Master Sgt. Rolf who got me to the right training areas. These two soldiers were great and a lot of fun. Sergeant Rolf was completely bald headed and you could just look at him and laugh, he had that Uncle Fester look from the "Adams Family." He was always good for what we called shits and giggles. You never knew if he was crazy or serious. I remember back at his unit Sergeant Rolf created this make believe soldier called Private Houke. He put his name on every roster in his unit. His commander and first sergeant would always ask where is Private Houke? Master Sgt. Rolf would tell them he was in the latrine, PX, commissary, getting a haircut or whatever, this went on for months.

When I went to the National Training Center at Fort Irwin afew months earlier Sergeant Rolf asks me to write him back and tell him I was private Houke and had been reassigned. I went along with him and wrote him twice. When I got back from Fort Irwin, I came in to see him and there were my post cards right behind his desk on a bulletin board. His commander walked by and I said, "I see private Houke is at NTC, damn he is a good soldier." Sergeant Rolf just laughed and his commander just gave me a silly grin, I think by this time he knew what was going on. Sergeant Rolf took this private Houke thing so far that when the unit had an (IG) Inspection, they believed everything about this ghost soldier until they found out he did not have orders to be in the unit and had not been paid in over two years. Sergeant Rolf had to confess, after bribing them with donuts and coffee. The commander told Sergeant Rolf not to do it again.

Also there was Master Sgt. Batey, he was a old crusty NCO. He smoked, talked shit, bitched, and did not give a damn who heard it. He and Sergeant Rolf together were like crazy and crazier. Once Sergeant Batey was on the radio in the field and this young captain walked in and grabbed the radio from him while he was talking to another unit. Sergeant Batey turned and hit the captain in the head with the hand set and told him, "sir if you ever fuck with me again while I am on the radio I will beat you down with it." The captain looked at Sergeant Batey and before he could say anything Col. Glen Eddins, the commander came over and told him, "young captain if I were you I would stay away from that seedy NCO, because he ain't right." The young captain just stormed off and I never saw him again. The last day we were at Fort Bliss we went to Juarez, Mexico. We were told not to go to Mexico while we were there, but what the hell we went any way. Sergeant Rolf wanted to drink some mescal, a type of tequila in a bottle and he also wanted to swallow the worm in it. Going across the Rio Grande from El Paso to Juarez we looked like three outlaws heading over the border. Once across the bridge we walked to a few cantinas' (bars) and had a few drinks. We also checked out a few of the local vendors. Then on the way back this young girl came up to Sergeant Batey, he was smoking a cigarette and she asks him for a light. He gave it to her and we walked on thinking nothing about it. We were no more than a block away and the same girl came up to Sergeant Batey again and said, "My sister wants you." Sergeant Batey just looked and laughed and said, "I am too old for her." Then Sergeant Rolf said," I think we better get back to Fort Bliss now." So on our way back we had to go through a few rough neighborhoods. We were being eye bald by three or four local Mexicans. Sergeant Rolf said I will handle this so he picked up a stick and walked toward them and they ran off. Finally we made it back across the border with no incident

We finished up what we had to do at Fort Bliss and went back to Little Rock. I turned my pictures and stories in to Bob. He said," How was it Don?" I said, "It was great." Then I had to see Col. Eddins, their commander. He wanted me to give him a few of the pictures I took of the new Army Smoke Generator for training purposes. Col. Eddins, now he is another character I have to talk about. He is also bald headed just like Sergeant Rolf, one day they had a weapons inspection and they both looked at the inspector and put their heads together and said, "I hope we don't make an ass of ourselves during all of This." I never laughed so hard in my life, because their two heads together looked like an old man's ass. I remember when I was first assigned to my unit back in 1994. My unit was located in the basement in another building across the street from the 90th RSC headquarters building. I heard laughter and voices behind the door before I even opened it. Low and behold when I walked in there were Col. Eddins, a warrant officer and two other enlisted soldiers watching a porno movie on one of the units televisions. Instead of being startled Col. Eddins just looked at me with an unlit cigar in his mouth, twirled it and said, "Come on in sergeant Dunn and sit down, we are just checking out this new FM." Now in the Army the term FM means Field Manual, to him it was Fuck Movie. I just looked and laughed it was all I could do.

    Col. Eddins would walk around all week chewing a new cigar and never light it. Then once it got down to the butt, he would stir his coffee with it and walk around with it in his mouth for another couple of days, and then start all over again with another new cigar. He was your classic Army colonel, he worked smart, not hard and I learned a few things from him. He would say, "You have to separate the men from the boys." I remember once we were standing in a formation and he would call out a soldier's name in a humorous manner just to see the reaction. He called for sergeant Young, and the soldier's first name was Dick. He made it sound like young dick! He then looked at the soldiers with an unlit cigar and a shit eating grin and said, "Wow I wish that was my name."

Another funny thing I remember about him was once someone asked him what he was going to do on a Labor Day weekend. Col. Eddins, said, "I thought I might take the old lady and my corvette to Eureka Springs for a little sport fucking." The last time I saw him was a few years later in Kuwait City at the Central Command Headquarters (CENTCOM), during Operation Enduring Freedom, right before I went up into Iraq He was sitting right next to Gen. Tommy Franks, The Commander, and yes he had a new unlit cigar in his mouth and was briefing or bullshitting the general on the threat of Biological Chemicals in the area. It took everything I had not to burst out laughing in that meeting. He noticed me and said, 'By damn sergeant Dunn, what are you doing over here? I see I am not the only crazy son of a bitch in this sand box." I said, "Sir, I am in a Public Affairs unit getting ready to move out." He said, "Watch your soldiers and don't get your ass shot off." I said, sir, as hot as it is outside they would only be doing me a favor." Col. Eddins, then laughed, twirled the unlit cigar around in his mouth and said, "I will see you later sergeant Dunn, I got to go over and bullshit this general some more." It was the last time I saw him till I was watching a CNN special on the war in Iraq and there he was with that unlit cigar, it was a hoot.

Back to Little Rock, There was this headquarters supply sergeant who was a real dickhead to say the least and he was just counting down the days till his retirement. His name was Sgt. 1st Class Tilman and he always had a chip on his shoulder to go along with his half bald head. To hear him talk he thought he ran the whole command. I got into it with him once. I had a new soldier come in my unit, a Private. Noah, well he needed some unit crest for his uniform. I took him with me to see Sergeant Tilman to get them. Sergeant Tilman told me, "The only time you come over here Sergeant Dunn is to get something to create extra work for me." I said, "I got a new soldier in my unit and he just needs three unit crest for his Class A uniform." Sergeant Tilman said, "I will get to it later so come back, I'm too busy for this bullshit." He did not look to busy sitting behind his desk with his boots propped up on it reading a magazine. So I just leaned toward him and said, "Well why don't you retire now, you're not doing nothing anyway." Then Sergeant Tilman exploded, he started jumping up and down calling me a motherfucker and a son of a bitch. Then Staff Sgt. Spears walks in and says, "You need to chill out Sergeant Tilman, I can hear you all the way down the hall." I looked at Sergeant Tilman and then I took off my Battle Dress Uniform BDU top and said, "You fat overweight no good piece of shit now let's go, come on Sergeant Tilman." He just stood there and looked at me. I had called his bluff. I said, "What's wrong you talk the talk, but I see you can't walk the walk." Then Sergeant Spears said, "I will bring the unit crest over to you Sergeant Dunn". Before I left, "I told Sergeant Tilman, "you better never talk to me like that again in front of a new soldier and you better stay out of my way and go on retire while you are able dickhead!"

On the way back over to the unit private Noah looked at me and said, "Sergeant Dunn, he was a real asshole. I looked at him and said, "I want you to remember one thing while you're in the Army, and he looked at me and said, "What's that."

"Take care of your soldiers and do not let anyone stop you."

Well, Sergeant Spears came over and gave me the unit crest and said," He could not wait to get away from Sergeant Tilman." I also became pretty good friends with Sergeant Spears when he needed something I would help him too. It is ironic, but about six months before I retired years later at Fort Knox. I needed to have my computer worked on and guess who the computer technician was. Mr. Spears he had retired and he was a Department Of Defense GS-9 Information Technology Specialist. The Army is small.

School became more important as my career of being a soldier went on. I went to Fort McCoy in Wisconsin, I completed the Unit Administrators Course, Supply Course, Computer Course, and the one I remember most of all was the Unit Movement and Mobilization Officers Course, because they were the hardest. There was an incident that happened one night when I was out at a club on Fort McCoy called the Four Seasons. Inside the bar there was this table with soldiers and this asshole of a first sergeant was at the front. He started tooting his horn and putting this one soldier down at the table.

All at once I saw that soldier get up at the other end of the table. He took a drink out of everyone's glass till he made it to the first sergeant then he reared back and hit the first sergeant and literally knocked him out. I remember him saying, "Well I guess that's the end of your bullshit." Then some soldiers jumped on him and it was on, a real bar room fight. I just got out right when a beer bottle hit an MP coming through the door. I thought this was one of the funnies things I had ever seen.

Back again to Little Rock, one day I and Bob went to see Air Force One at the airport. President Clinton had come in to go to Hot Springs and we went over just to see the plane, not Clinton. So I started taking pictures, everything was alright till I started walking around the plane. Then low and behold the next thing I know, I was approached by two Air Force personnel who told me not to take anymore pictures especially behind the plane. Bob just laughed a little and told me it was time to go. Bob use to have this Bill Clinton doll with long legs. He put it in front of his door. When someone would ask what it was he would say, "It's my draft dodger." Unfortunately Bob had to put it away, some soldiers complained.

Bob once showed me a picture of this young soldier who had his hair cut by his commander for not getting a haircut when he was ordered to get one. Well, that young captain never made major. You cannot just get someone down these days and give them a haircut, like the old Army. The next few incidents that happened are even funnier. These two helicopter warrant officer pilots in Texas thought it would be cool to swoop down on an ostrich farm and scare the ostriches. Not only did they scare the ostriches they made them run until a lot of them were in barb wire fences and some stampeded each other to death. The pilots were court martial and they had to pay over $300,000 dollars for the damages to the ostrich farm.

Then there was this captain at Fort Hood who wanted to get the birds out of his chimney in his quarters. So he took an artillery simulator from his command and dropped it down the chimney. It worked, but it also destroyed the bottom of the chimney in his quarters and the idiot injured his wife and young son too! There was a master sergeant who was stationed at Fort Polk in Louisiana, one day his son got off the school bus and set off an artillery simulator. The Leesville police came and ask the kid where he got it. The kid said, "My father works at Fort Polk and he brings these home all the time and we set them off on Fourth of July too". The Army Criminal Investigation Department CID came and picked his father up. Yes he was court martial too.

Bob got a call from the Army Times one day and they wanted to know if our commanding general. Maj. Gen. James McDougal was the same James McDougal who was involved with President Clinton in Whitewater. Bob, said, "No, our commander is from Paris TX." It was funny Bob said, "The Army Times trying to make a connection with our commander and Whitewater, what will they think of next."

Sergeant Ratliff use to tell me, "Sergeant Dunn, I don't care how you do it just get it done." Believe it or not I liked this method, sometimes the regulations are just too difficult to follow and I did what it took especially when it came to making sure my soldiers were paid, trained, and personally taken care of. He would let me do my job and he would also take up for me if someone did not like it. He would get on me, but he would not let anyone else do that. The unit was like a family with only 15 soldiers we all knew each other's strength and weaknesses. He would ask my advice and he would listen, he knew what I put up with every day till drill weekends came around. He was like a coach he praised you when you did something right and he had strong convictions when you were wrong. He was by far the best first sergeant I had in any of my assignments and units in my career.

Readiness is the key to success in a unit. Vehicles, I had four, trailers I had three, weapons we had 20, protective mask 20, night vision devices 4, video equipment and camera equipment. Also there were laptop computers, desktop computers, field phones and all the soldiers Load Bearing Equipment LBE. This was just the supply area. Then there were personnel, training security, and maintenance. It is a hell of a lot of responsibility for one soldier and no one is ever happy no matter what you do for them. You are always the first to get blamed and then you try to fix it.

There was also my commander, Maj. Bennett, he was from Oklahoma City and would drive over six hours every weekend we had drill. He was a professor in Stillwater at Oklahoma State University OSU. He was great to work for and a good commander also probably the best commander I ever had.

There was a mutual respect between all of us. I was never in a unit like this. This was my favorite duty assignment. I know what you're thinking, Little Rock, Arkansas, but it was not the place it was the people I worked with and they were great. Like I said, nothing is perfect, but I really did like the 90th Regional Support Command. Also the commanding general, Maj Gen. McDougal, was a class act, he would even come around and see how you were doing, he believed in his full time staff and he liked Bob and knew me and him were working hard doing Public Affairs work for the command.

He also would ask our advice and listen. Most generals in the Army are politicians, but Maj. Gen. McDougal was all about soldiers. He would ask a private what was wrong before he would ask one of his Colonels. I would hear him say, "They will only tell me what I want to hear, but a private will tell me the truth." He also had a charisma about him; he did not want special treatment because of who he was. He just wanted what was best and however that could be achieved for the command. The leadership was far above the other RSC's and commands I was in before and after this.

One of my worst days in the Army came when I was received a call one morning in February of 1997 and told by Sgt. Maj. Starmer at the USARC, that I was being transferred to the 319th Mobile Public Affairs Detachment in Columbia, South Carolina. She told me the unit had been slated to go to Bosnia and it had to be ready to go. She said, "I know you like it where you are, but the mission comes first." You see in the Army the deal is you go where you are needed. You can't just quit like a civilian if you don't like your job. You suck it up and move on, and you deal with who you are stationed with good, bad and the cards you are dealt. I had this unit ready to go and now I had to go and start all over again and fix something else that was broken. In the Army it is always about starting over in new places. So I got my orders to report in South Carolina at Fort Jackson on 1 July 1997.

The unit and Bob took real good care of me, I received my first Meritorious Service Medal here and it was signed off by Maj. Gen McDougal, the 90th Regional Support Commander who I admired as a general officer. Also, I had the best first sergeant and commander. Master

Sgt. Ratliff and Maj. Bennett, they took me out to dinner and even gave me a plaque for my service for the three plus years I was in the unit. I did not want to move, but I had no choice. A move is not just hard on you the soldier, but also your family. My wife had to quit her job at the commissary and my son had to get use to a new place, school, and new friends. It is easy for a soldier he knows it will still be the Army, but your family has to go through the change too and it can be hard on them even more. I knew Bob was a phone call away. I said my goodbyes and like a desperado waiting for a train, I headed southeast to Fort Jackson SC.

CHAPTER 7

THE 81ST REGIONAL SUPPORT COMMAND
319TH MOBILE PUBLIC AFFAIRS DETACHMENT
FORT JACKSON
COLUMBIA, SOUTH CAROLINA
1997-2003

I was right back in the 81st Army Reserve Command, now called the 81st Regional Support Command. Same command, different name and different unit, The 319th Mobile Public Affairs Detachment. This time I was not alone, this unit had a unit administrator and his name was Clovis Dilbert. He was a Master Sergeant in the unit on drill weekends, but he was a GS-7 civilian during the week. Right away, this was going to be hard working with someone who already thought he was my boss. First, I got all my processing done and moved my family into post housing. I met with the new commander, Capt. Ronald Taylor and he told me. "Sergeant Dunn, I know you have been in other units like this one, we have a lot of work ahead of us before we go to Bosnia, and I know you can do it."

The first thing I did was fix the units supply. There was no one else who ever got their hands dirty before me.

Sergeant Dilbert was only there about 6 months before I got there and he only did pay and personnel. He did not do anything else and I could tell he was not going to be much help. He had a grudge about his own pay. He would always complain saying, "my little ole check." He also resented the fact that I made more money than him as a soldier. He always carried a chip on his shoulder. I was the training NCO and I was responsible for the arms room, physical security, supply, and the mobilization and movement plans. I was here to get this unit ready for Bosnia. Also we had a two week annual training mission in a few months. Yes, I was going back to Panama for the third and final time.

I was also sent to a Public Affairs Conference in Atlanta, Ga. Sgt. Maj. Starmer came up and asked me if Master Sgt. Dilbert was in my unit. I said, "Yes." Then I saw her walk over and the first thing she said to him was are you in the 319th MPAD and he said, "yes." Then she noticed he had the wrong rank on and said, "You. Master Sgt. Dilbert are not a First Sergeant, you are a Master Sergeant. I want you to get the right rank on by this afternoon. Those diamonds in your rank tells me you are a First Sergeant, but there are no First Sergeants in Public Affairs."

My first concern was the soldiers and I wanted to make sure they were trained and taken care of well before we go overseas for 270 days or 10 months to Bosnia. Right now my focus was back on Panama to make sure the unit got the most out of the two weeks training. I turned in all the old equipment and ordered the new equipment. I hated hearing things like, there's no money, or we have never done it like this before, and there is no schools to train the soldier right now. There is always money in the Army, especially training money. I got training money, especially for my soldiers who wanted to go to schools in the Army. I went to every school I could and I wanted my soldiers to do the same. I would rather be in a unit with five trained and highly motivated soldiers, than to be in a unit with twenty soldiers just to show the numbers on a unit manning report. I also believed if you did not want to be trained, you had one year to get your MOS or you found a new home. There is no room for soldiers who want to hide out and get paid. This unit had the bodies, but most of the bodies were not trained and needed schools. I made sure this happened, I scheduled soldiers for schools and they went. I refuse to go into a war with untrained soldiers, because it can only lead to disaster. Also I believed in cross training so everyone knew everyone's job if they had to do it. I was here for readiness; I put together short and long term training plans. I made out the next years training schedules and got them approved.

These plans are in detail from the time you get orders to move out till the time you get orders to come home. I made sure all the units weapons were maintenance quarterly. When I came in the unit, there were no keys to anything, except the arms room. When I asked Sergeant Dilbert where they were he pointed to a top desk drawer. The arms room keys from that point on were locked in the unit safe I ordered. I had 4 night vision devices, 20 M16A2 rifles and two M240 machine guns. I was responsible for four HUMVESS and three trailers. This did not include all the video equipment, print cameras, and laptop computers. Besides the commander; I was signed for it all. I made sure it was signed for by the soldiers who trained with it. If something broke I got it fixed. I made sure there was a key lock box and it was secure with keys to the unit supply cages. I made team rosters and it was time to go to Panama again. I had to make the flight and billeting arrangement.

There were vans, rental cars, billets and meals requisitioned. We flew into Tacoma Airport and once again the unit was picked up by my friend Sgt. 1st Class Legore. I always had a good time with Sergeant Legore. We also worked well together. He had been in Panama as a soldier for years. He knew the mission. He could also speak Spanish.

My team was going to Honduras to cover a school building and road construction. The second team was going to El Salvador to cover veterinarian operations. The third team was staying right here in Panama to cover local stories. The operation was called "New Horizons," meaning making a better Central America. We flew out to Honduras and once we got there we were picked up and taken to Base Camp Bravo near Soto Cano Air Base. We were briefed and not allowed to leave the camp without MP's. We were not even allowed to get near the fences of the base camp, because there had been trouble with identifying soldiers, especially at night, a few soldiers were killed previously by sniper fire. While in Honduras, I saw a young child get hit by a car. I tried to get out and help him, but I was told to stand down and get back in the vehicle. It was hard for me to watch this child die. Then a group of Hondurans came over and picked the child up and place him in a ditch. They left him and drove off like it was no big deal.

I saw a cow dead on the side of the road. On the way back the same day the only thing left of the cow was bones. The buzzards picked it clean. I also saw a truck load of Hondurans on the way to work in the fields one day. They hit a huge bump in the road and one of them flew out of the truck. The truck never stopped, one of the soldiers stationed there told me a joke. He said how many Hondurans can fit in the back of a truck, answer, one more. I also saw a dog eating one of our leftover tray packs out of the garbage. This mangy mutt looked like it had rabies; foam coming out of its mouth like Cujo. In this one particular street these Hondurans kept pointing to this small box. So I went over to the box and there was a newborn baby in the box which had been abandoned. The people there tried to give it to me. I called the Red Cross and they came and took the baby away. There were so many poor people that money would not do you any good, because there was nothing to buy with it. This place was filthy, dusty, flies were everywhere, and death in the air. We did our stories and helped who we could. I remember helping this lady back to her house. It was a one room mud shack with three families living there in one room. There were no cars in the whole town and if you owned a goat or a horse for transportation you were rich. The children would always come up to us and beg. I felt bad about even eating there and always gave most of my food to them. They even drank water out of mud puddles and off roof tops when it rained.

Americans have everything, I ate with the poor, I slept with the poor and I lived with the poor, as a soldier at times. I also slept in the streets when I had too. I remember living in a tent with Honduran soldiers and eating food from our mess tent. These soldiers thought it was Christmas dinner and when we got rid of our old shoes or boots they would pick them out of the garbage. I seen people literally strip naked and take showers from the rain water running off houses too. When I hear my friends and family cry about their problems in America, I just look at them and tell them. "You don't have a problem, you only think you do." Most Americans, bitch, bitch, bitch, while the rest of the world goes hungry. Then they want to bitch again about why we give money to third world nations. Then they use the line, "we have starving people right here in America." I have never seen anyone starving in America. Outside of our shell we call America, the rest of the world is not a pretty place. At night things are dangerous too in Honduras. I went into a town with Military Police escorts and we were not allowed to go anywhere without them.

The next day, I and Spec. Rowe, a broadcast journalist in my unit helped me packed the equipment up and we headed for the plane, nicknamed "The Freedom Bird."I said, 'I can't wait to get back to Panama. I do not care what bird takes me there," Spec. Rowe laughed and said, "You got that right Sergeant Dunn."

Back in Panama, we dropped off our stories and pictures, met deadline and got ready to pack up and come back to the good old U.S. of A. We spent ten days in Honduras. Like always I was tired as hell, you never ever get fully rested in the Army. We got to the airport and low and behold Sergeant Dilbert left my name off the manifest to fly home. Planes only leave on Tuesdays and Fridays at Tacoma Airport in Panama and this was Friday. I went to talk to the commander Capt. Taylor, and he and Sergeant Dilbert, were already on the plane. Spec. Rowe and Sgt. Keith Johnson, one of our other broadcast journalists came up to me and said, "Sergeant Dunn, I am staying with you, this is bullshit you know Sergeant Dilbert did this on purpose." I told them to get on the plane and not to worry about me." I will handle this when I get back." Then, Spec. Rowe watched the unit equipment while I called Sergeant Legore on the phone. "He said, "don't worry Sergeant Dunn I am on my way." He also said, "I will personally get you to billeting at Fort Clayton and I will help you get an extra room for the unit's equipment."

It's bad enough to lose accountability of a soldier, especially when he is the only active duty soldier and responsible for over $400,000 dollars worth of government equipment. One of the Army's Golden Rules is never leave a soldier behind. You make sure everyone comes and goes on a mission. The worst part was Capt. Taylor and Sergeant Dilbert did not even know I was missing. They also never got off the plane.

Sergeant Legore showed up and we had to use his personal van to carry all the equipment back to Fort Clayton. I had to wait until Tuesday to get out on the next flight, so I spent the next few days making damn sure I was on the next flight. In the Army if you don't have orders you are not covered as a soldier. I also made damn sure my orders were amended to include extra days spent in Panama.

I had extra money allocated for me to bring back the unit equipment as excess baggage. I went and talked to Maj. Knowles, Sergeant Legore's commander and he called the 81st personally to make sure things were done right. He said, Sergeant Dilbert told him that I got into an argument with the airline and they would not let me on the plane. "I looked at Maj. Knowles and told him flat out, "Sergeant Dilbert is a damn liar sir and I can prove it." Then Sergeant Legore walked in and said, "Listen sir. Sergeant Dunn is telling you the truth." he explained how he picked me up and how I was left me behind. I said, "Sir, here is my passport and it is not stamped. How could I have even gotten to the terminal without that?" Also sir, Sergeant Dilbert and the commander never came back to check on me or the equipment." He looked at me and Sergeant Legore and said," You got to be shitting me, what kind of a commander and master sergeant would leave one of their own soldiers behind."

When Tuesday came, I was on the plane with the unit equipment. Everything was smooth until I landed in Miami and had to go through customs. I had to pay $800 dollars of my own money to clear the equipment through customs. I kept the receipt, I thought wait till I send this to the 81st RSC for reimbursement. I made it back to Fort Jackson. All the equipment made it back to the unit thanks to Sergeant Keith Johnson one of the broadcast journalists in my unit who picked me up at the airport.

The next day, which was Wednesday, I went back into the unit and there was Mr. Dilbert sitting behind his desk like he always does, never smiling and never moving until the end of the day. He looked up not even surprised, I told him flat out, "I got my eye on you and as long as I am in this unit you will not fuck me over again." Then I walked out and got a call from the 81st Regional Support Command Public Affairs Office. "They said, Mr. Dilbert had called up there and said I was threatening him." I told Maj. Loring, "you know what happened in Panama, and she said, "Yes." How would you feel about this?" She said, "You're right Sergeant Dunn." Then Lt. Col. Trehan, the 314th commander who I knew very well called Mr. Dilbert and then called me and said, "I took care of it Sergeant Dunn and I am telling you this will never happen again, I don't think Sergeant Dilbert wants a personal visit from me." I said, "I appreciate this sir."

Next mission, Bosnia a 270 day rotation was just around the corner. The warning order came down and then the order to mobilize. It was August 1998. I made sure I was on separate orders. I was not going to be left in Bosnia by that moron Mr. Sergeant Dilbert. We also, got a new commander assigned by the 314th. Capt Taylor was out and Maj. McReynolds was in. Capt. Taylor now was only a Public Affairs Officer; he was not a happy camper. Readiness is the key and I started right away with updating the unit's mobilization and movement plans. I made sure the unit war trace was updated to where we were going. A war trace is a secret document and tells where a unit goes once orders have come down for mobilization. I made sure all of our four vehicles and trailers were maintenance and ready. I also ordered all the shortages and some extra equipment we needed.

I started making training schedules way in advance. I had to schedule ranges for weapons qualification which included night firing, NBC Firing in full mop four, which means you had to qualify with the M16A2 rifle in a full chemical biological suit to include wearing the mask while firing. I also needed to get two soldiers qualified on the M249 Machinegun and ammunition had to be ordered right away.

I had to schedule classes in map reading, combat operations, first aid, NBC, and MOS refresher training and cross training. We needed to get all our shot records and medical records updated. Everyone had to have a new current physical. I had to make sure everyone had a military driver's license. I had to get Government Bill of Ladings (GBL) complete to make sure our equipment was shipped to include three trailers that had to go with the HUMVEES. A packing list had to be completed to go on each trailer listing everything in them. I made sure every soldier had an updated family packet. You owe it to the soldier's family to keep them in the loop while he or she is gone. A Family Support Program had to be put in place.

We went to a two week operation called "Golden Medic" to help prepare for the Bosnia mission. I and three other soldiers went to the Combat Lifesavers Course. I wanted to make damn sure I have a soldier in each team that can care each other.

The second week of Golden Medic, we did stories and I ran the newspaper. I was the editor. We also had an unforeseen disaster happen, which no one was expecting. One of the Medical Units on the ground set up tents in an open field. There was a severe thunderstorm one night and lightning struck one of the tents and injured a few soldiers. No one was killed, but the unit had to pack up and return home.

Then the two weeks were up and we returned back to Fort Jackson. I arranged classes and did some MOS training and maintenance on our cameras and video editing equipment. We were now prepared to move out. Right before I left for Bosnia, my parents and my mother in law came up to visit me. My father had been diagnosed with Alzheimer's. This disease my father had was a real eye opener later in my career as I watched him slowly fade away. It was great to see them and we all went down to Charleston, SC. After we came back my mother said my dad cried all the way home in their car. He knew he was ill and was hoping I would make it back while he still had some memory. Family is always the hardest thing to leave behind for a soldier being deployed. It was now on to Bosnia.

BOSNIA
JOINT FORGE
AUGUST 1998 TO APRIL 1999

I made sure the buses were ordered for the unit movement. Arrangements had been made at Fort Benning, Ga., this is where we would go for two weeks, and it was our mobilization station for final preparation. I had to get all the units records. I was in the advance party, so me and the commander, Maj. McReynolds went down to Fort Benning to set up billeting for the unit and make sure all the training was a go. I made sure we hit the ground running and were ready for our physicals and shots too.

Then we went back to Fort Jackson to bring the rest of the unit forward. I remember a cartoon drawing one of my soldiers had drawn. It had a picture of Bill Clinton seeing a soldier off to Bosnia in full battle rattle. It said, "Don't do anything I wouldn't do." Then you could see the soldier looking over his shoulder back at Clinton and saying, "I am already doing something you would not do, Mr. President!"

I made sure the families had the soldiers insurance and wills were done by the Judge Advocate Office (JAG). The hardest thing was saying goodbye to our families the morning we left. I looked at my wife and son. Donald, who helped me load the last box of MRE's on the bus. He looked at me and said, "Dad I wish you did not have to go." It was hard; he was only 8 years old. I looked down at him and said, "Here this is one of my dog tags, I want you to keep this and I will give you the other one when I return." Then he hugged me and said, "I will take care of mom while you are gone." Then I kissed my wife Telena while she was crying and I said, "Don't worry, I will be back." She said, "I love you and take care of yourself." We kissed, hugged again and that was it, I got on the bus. Then I remember looking out the window with my son and wife standing right next to the flag pole and I waved one last time as we pulled out. It was a six hour bus ride to Fort Benning, Ga. We all were joking and laughing just to keep from thinking about the loved ones we were leaving behind for almost a year and the mission ahead of us.

We arrived late and were put in center block billets. The water worked about half the time and there was no air conditioning. It was night and we just wanted to sleep. A few soldiers started bitching about this and that, but a bitching soldier is a happy soldier. We had a lot to do before going to Bosnia and everyone was a little nervous each day leading up to this. All the days were long, 16 hours most of the time. It was hard to sleep in the heat; after all it was August in Georgia. I also made sure my soldiers had new boots and uniforms, but some things were just the way it is in the Army.

We had a captain who was attached to my unit named Capt. Brown, he was a former Army Ranger and he helped us with making sure we had a list of what was needed in each of the five duffle bags and equipment we were issued. He was a stickler; He was over bearing and hard to please. We just went along with him and stayed out of his way. I admired the fact that he was a Ranger in the Army, but, hell this was a Public Affairs Detachment, not a Ranger Regiment. My soldiers were skilled with cameras and video equipment. I did appreciate the fact Capt. Brown was hard core, but you also have to understand who you are dealing with in the Army. You can be a soldier without dramatizing it. I knew the difference between being a Tanker and a Public Affairs NCO. I had seen both sides of the Army. There is a difference in a field soldier and a technical soldier. But in the end everyone is a soldier first.

It was time to go at the Fort Benning Airfield on the tarmac. Tower Airlines a contracted airline was scheduled for our departure. I remember having two duffel bags with me to carry on, one on my back and one on my front. I remember walking up entering the plane with my weapon too headed for Bosnia.

The first stop on our flight was in Newfoundland. We stopped for fuel before heading over the Atlantic Ocean. Next stop was Ramstein, Germany seven hours later. We got off here before being bused to Tsar Hungary for more training, in processing, and briefings. The bus ride was long and grueling. Some of the soldiers were already getting sick with diarrhea and stomach aches. I was feeling it too, but I had to suck it up and carry on. We rode all night in that bus and early in the morning we arrived at Tsar. The place looked like a big flea market with carnival type white tents. The fun started with getting more shots and in processing. At this mobilization point we were all issued Stabilization Force Cards (SFOR).

You kept your weapon with you at all times, except when you took a shower. We watched after each other, and our weapons. I was once taking a shower and someone took my weapon; let me tell you it freaked me out. I was able to get it back without any real trouble. I was able to track down the soldier who took it and I was lucky he had not turned it in. After that I never let my weapon out of my sight. It was like part of my body; it stayed with me and remained with me at all times. General Order Number.One no alcohol, if you were caught drinking, your career was over, yes an article 15 and forfeiture of pay to boot.

Sure enough some soldier in another company lost his SFOR Card and we all had to report to our commanders and do a sensitive item check to make sure we all had ours. They later found the soldier's card in a wall locker he had used. You were accountable for every piece of ammunition issued to you. We were all issues 270 rounds of 5.56mm ammo for our M16A2 rifles. This was nine 30 round banana clip magazines and you had to carry it all everywhere you went. If you were caught without your ammo it was disciplinary action. So the three things you better have with you are your SFOR Card, M16A2 rifle, and 270 rounds of ammunition. This did not include wearing a heavy flack vest with LBE to include a Kevlar helmet, two canteens, two ammo pouches, first aid kit, pistol belt, suspenders, poncho, protective mask, MRE's, and field jacket. This shit was heavy and you wore it 12-16 hours a day. Going to the bathroom was a pain in the ass. You took it all off at night in your tent you dreaded the mornings putting it back on.

Also there are radios to be carried and when it came your turn you also carried an M240 Machinegun and a belt of ammo for it. Life was already getting real hard and this was for 10 months. Rest was a luxury when you could get it. You would just take what we call power naps when you could. You would sleep a little and work a lot.

Back to Tsar we were here about a week and everybody was already getting restless and ready to move out. We loaded up our equipment on buses and headed down range to Bosnia, Herzegovina to operation Joint Forge. We had to put a duffle bag in front of the window of the seat we were sitting in. We had to wear a heavy flack vest for the whole trip too. All a duffel bag and a flack vest will do is slow down a bullet and you are still going to take a hit. The duffel bag acted as cover and concealment. We were told not to remove the bags till we got to Tuzla. We only stopped two times for fuel and there were no other piss breaks. We ate MRE's till we either threw them up or we needed an ice pick to dig them out of our ass. I hate MRE's and I only eat them when I have too or I am starving. Too many soldiers have colonoscopies and bowel problems even after they leave the military.

We were now entering the main gate at Eagle Base, Tuzla. It was night and the base camp lights looked like we were coming into a Nazi Prisoner Of War (POW) camp. There were soldiers and dogs at the gate. The bus stopped and a sergeant walked on and said welcome to Eagle Base. "You are now in Bosnia." I looked over at Spec. Valentine, and said jokingly, did he say "Evil Base." Valentine was too tired to laugh but he grinned and said, "Sergeant Dunn, you are crazy." Then the sergeant said, "I need to see all you're SFOR Cards, so we showed them to him and then this barbed wire gate opened with two soldiers on each side carrying M60 Machineguns standing in a make shift wooden hut. Then everything was dark as the driver turned his lights off till we got to the base camp tents. Welcome to day 1 of 270.

There was mud everywhere and we walked on wooden pallets to get anywhere. We all looked like hell and felt like shit. Here we go again more in processing and more briefings. We were told about what to do and what not to do in Bosnia. Complacency was a word that was continuously used. They then kept expressing general order number one. No drinking. Who the hell feels like drinking after all this?

The base commander started talking about safety. I looked over at Specialist Rowe. He was asleep standing up. I thought I wish I could do that. I listened as best I could at about 3 a.m. they took us to our tents to get some sleep. We all just threw our bags on the floor and fell on top of them. I and the commander made sure everyone was accounted for, weapons were secure, and few hours to sleep.

My first morning in Bosnia, all I remember was waking up with freezing from rain and leaks in the tent. It was cold and then I heard over a loud base camp speaker echoing the song, "I'm Proud to be an American," by Lee Greenwood. I looked over at Maj. McReynolds and we both started laughing. It was one of those things that was not funny latter on when they played it every morning we were there at 0530. It got to be old quick, but it was one of Maj. Gen Larry Ellis 3rd Armor Division Commanders things he wanted to do to remind us why we were here.

We staggered down to the mess hall and then we were shown the building where we would be working, it was right next to the base church. Oh another thing to always remember when in Bosnia you stay on the hard top. Walking in the mud and the sides of the road there were mines. I saw a lot of one legged Bosnians and every story was the same, they stepped on a mine. The building we were in wasn't much there was a few windows and wires hanging down inside. It was now time to set up house.

Contractors from Brown and Root a Halliburton Company helped get us electricity, internet, and email. I nicknamed them, Burn and Loot; it just sounded better and made everyone laugh. We got together with the Coalition Press Information Center (CPIC) and learned more about our mission. Eagle Base was the main base camp in Multi National Division North (MNDN). We divided our unit into three teams. Each team would support other base camps. My team was assigned right here at Eagle Base in Tuzla and Comanche Base nearby. One of our teams was sent to Bedrock Base Camp. The Other team was sent to Camp Dobol. I had to go with each team and make sure they all had places to set up their equipment and tents to sleep in. The unit we were replacing was leaving in two weeks and we had to learn what we could from them before we took over. This was called the right seat ride or transition. Our mission was to do broadcast and journalism stories. We had a print journalism mission writing articles for the Talon, an Army publication about the peacekeeping mission in Bosnia. There were hand held radios, but no cell phones back then. We also used TA 312 Field Phones attached to communication wire and ran them to the places we needed to communicate. We had to do Guard duty too while we were here on the wire or outside the gates and check points. I remember stopping suspicious vehicles and wondering if these belonged to the Serbian Army. We had coalition forces always moving in and out. Russians, Italians, Swiss, British, French, Turkish just to name a few. You always had to be sure when you were pulling guard duty to watch for these vehicles and soldiers. Serbs were the enemy, but it was hard to tell them apart from the rest of the Bosnians, especially the ones that worked on the base camps.

I got the Flu twice while I was here; the first time was real bad. The second time I thought I was going to die. Being sick did not mean quarters or a few days off. The doctor would look at you and send you right back out into the elements with some aspirin. I remember running a fever and coughing until I almost passed out. The Bosnians who worked on the base camp were sick and it carried over to the soldiers. There were some cases of meningitis. Some soldiers were evacuated to Germany to hospitals.

Bosnia had over a million mines and even when I drove a Humvee I would only get out on the left hand side of the vehicle in the street. Anything off the streets could be mined. The roads were narrow in Bosnia; if I saw a vehicle coming I would let it pass. I never drove off the road, for the chance of hitting a mine. They were not just in the ground they were also in the walls of burned out buildings, and in the neighborhoods where ethnic cleansing had taken place. It would rain and you could see mines in the ground rise up out of the mud. The Army had cleared the area, but there were still mines. I also watched my soldiers and they watched me, safety came first. If it looked unsafe, it probably was. I saw a human skull off the side of the roads on top of a stick. This meant there were mines there and I sure did not want to be the next skull on a stick. I covered a story where they were demining an area. The Army paid the Bosnians to do this work, because they knew where the mines were. I took pictures from a distance and wrote the story. It was nerve racking, every day you had to walk on concrete or wooden pallets to get anywhere. Then sometimes you had to walk in the mud and you just prayed it is not your day. When I finished my tour in Bosnia, it took me a long time to get use to walking in the grass when I got back home.

We also went on many convoys, but never alone. You had to travel in four vehicle convoys at all times and they had to be up armored. We all had radios calling out every intersection, person walking, and even the dogs and cats in the road. If we did not hear from a vehicle we waited for it. This was a war zone and we were here to keep the peace and look for Serbian war criminals. All the towns and people carefully watched as we entered and exited. We respected the people of Bosnia and Yugoslavia, but we watched them too. We always had pictures and a list of war criminals we were looking for. If you saw something or someone suspicious you stopped them and asked for ID. If they could not produce it you made sure you found out who they were before releasing them.

The rules of engagement and use of deadly force was a thin line. We could only keep our eyes open and report anything we saw that was suspicious. Sometimes weapon caches were found instead of Serbian War Criminals and then the Army Explosive Ordnance Division (EOD) was brought in to destroy them. The Serbs would also give children fake guns and pistols to point at us, in hopes that we would shoot one of them to create negative propaganda against us being here. There were fake Serb checks points set up and poorly marked roads to deal with. You did not want to be out a night, we tried to do most of our business during the day. Another obstacle was poor visibility, cold weather with snow, fog and plenty of mud made it hard on us to get around in Bosnia.

Every Army in the coalition had their own sector, but the closest Army to the Serbs was the Russians. We worked with them to get to know what the Serbian Army was doing. We all worked together and every day we had to report what happened the day before. The headquarters had reports going out in the morning and at the close of each day. One of my jobs was to cover some of the morning briefings when my commander Maj. McReynolds could not be there. This all went on in what we called the White House, which was a headquarters building in the center of a five point intersection on Eagle Base.

The 3rd Armor Division was in charge until October and then the 1st Calvary Division from Fort Hood took over. It was already bad, but we had no idea it was only going to get worse. In the transition I myself knew we were dealing with the most arrogant division in the Army. Forget the fact we were here for a peacekeeping mission. Gary Owen was their hero and their Yellow Black Horse Patch was their mark. Everywhere you turned all you heard was "First Team." Their patch was like the mark of the beast, if you did not wear it you were just shit to them, especially by their officers. They put signs on every street that said, "Salute with pride you are first team." Well, I guess me and my unit were second string. They hated the Army Reserve and National Guard. In other words this was a fraternity instead of an Army Division. I hate talking about it, but this bunch thought they were Roy Rogers, The Lone Ranger, and Hop along Cassidy all rolled into one. They painted everything they could find with that Horse Patch and put in boot troughs to match. They even tried to make us take off our command patches. We had the lineage when it came to Army patches. Ours was the first and when they gave us our unit sign to hang with their patch on it. The first thing I said was "Hell no." I made sure our patch was on our sign. Our patch The Wildcat was the first patch worn and designated by the Army in WWI by General Black Jack Pershing.

I had no respect for the 1st Calvary Divisions officers. I respected the rank, but not the ones wearing it. Sergeant Dilbert loved them. They were like him all about themselves. The 1st Calvary Division was glory boys, wearing Stetson Hats, spurs and thought they were John Wayne.

Some of the stories they wanted me to cover was not at all about the peacekeeping mission in Bosnia. The reason why we were here to begin with was to help this war torn country and the people. They wanted me to cover a Spur Ride. Let me tell you what a Spur Ride is. It is a few days of treating soldiers like basic trainees so that they can earn a Stetson Hat and a set of spurs to show that they are worthy to be in the 1st Calvary Division. I remember walking down the street on Eagle Base and seeing their officers in their Stetsons and literally watching their enlisted soldiers duck in any doorway they could find to avoid them. It was like everyone clearing the streets in the old west before a gun fight. The Spur Ride, I flat out refused to cover it. My commander, Maj McReynolds let someone else do the story. The only way I would have given this media coverage is if I was directly ordered too. I also refused to cover a Grog Party for the officers at Comanche Base on New Year's Eve 1999. Lt. Col Coward, the Public Affairs Commander for the Coalition Press Camp Headquarters at Eagle Base was my commander's boss and I went to the party, but I never submitted a story. All the officers of the 1st Calvary Division got together and put an empty toilet bowl on an Army field table in the mess hall surrounded by sand bags. Then they emptied their canteens with who knows what in the toilet bowl and they dared each other to drink out of it. The ones who drink out of it are considered tuff or HOOAH!

Could you imagine if I had published the story? What would the American people think of how their tax dollars were being spent on this Army Division acting like this in a peacekeeping mission?

Also, I never thought much of Lt. Col Coward after that. He also abandoned his Forces Command Patch for the Horse Patch to suck up and get a good Officer Evaluation Report, so he could make full bird colonel when he got back to Fort McPherson, Ga. This bunch was all about ARME. He treated us just like the 1st Cavalry Division treated their enlisted soldiers in Bosnia. You had to also watch what you said about them. I know I was a marked soldier for standing up for Army Values. I was doing my job and taking care of my soldiers, this is what I do. Also I never could understand how Lt. Col Coward ever made his rank. He was the worst colonel I had ever seen in the whole Army.

Lt. Col Cowards's boss was Maj. Eaton, yes a Major. He was the 1st Cavalry Division Public Affairs Officer and he was a horse's asshole. He told Lt. Col. Coward what to do and he did it. He hated the Army Reserve and National Guard and he was very outspoken about it. I heard him tell Maj. McReynolds we were no help. I was an active duty reserve soldier my whole career and we are as good as any active duty soldier, because we are all one Army. Army Reserve and National Guard Soldiers in Public Affairs also have a lot of experience in the civilian sector and most are better than their active component counterparts. Also he had an E-5 Sergeant who thought she was my boss. As a Sergeant First Class, I did not take any shit off of her either. Lt. Col Coward might let Maj. Eaton tell him what to do, but there was no way in hell an E-5 Web Master for the 1st Calvary Division is going to tell me anything. She jumped on one of my soldiers and I told her if you have a problem with him, then you have a problem with me. He is one of mine and if you don't like it go cry to Maj. Eaton. She did just that and Maj. McReynolds told me to watch out because they were after me. I said to him, "sir I can take care of myself and I know you will back me if I am right." He said this to me, "Sergeant Dunn, I know one thing you are loyal. I said, "If it comes between them and this unit you know I got your back sir."

It started from their leadership. Their Command Sgt. Maj. Inama hated the Army Reserve and National Guard too and made it known. One of my soldiers got promoted to Staff Sergeant and he made the comment that the only reason he got promoted was because he was in the Army Reserve.

I heard this and said, "No Sergeant Major, the reason he got promoted was because he earned it and was a hell of a soldier." He also had us do extra duties, while his soldiers did nothing. He made us fill up water containers and refrigerators in the gym while his soldiers worked out. Also, he made us pass out towels to them and coalition soldiers too. I contacted the Army Reserve Command at Fort McPherson and talked directly with

Sgt. Maj. Starmer and asked her if this was our mission. I also talked to Mr. Haley; he was the director for Army Reserve Public Affairs. Nothing ever happened. Every day we had to rotate 12 hour shifts and do this stupid bullshit. Imagine you are a AGR Sergeant First Class in the United States Army and they make you do this because you belong to the Army Reserve. My soldiers were so tired they could barely do their stories. Master Sgt. Dilbert never stood up for our soldiers. It was up to me and the commander could not help us either, even though he tried. They also came into our Sea Huts where we lived and took our bunks and gave them to their officers. I signed for those bunks and had got them when the 3rd Armor Division was in command. All this without even asking or checking my hand receipts and yes Master Sgt. Dilbert helped them while he slept in nice bed in his own quarters in a trailer.

I came into my Sea Hut and caught one of their Staff Sergeants taking things off the wall that belonged to one of my soldiers. I asked him what he thought he was doing. He said there cannot be anything on the walls. So I told him to leave and he acted like he did not hear me. I said, "Staff Sergeant I am telling you to leave and if you don't I will personally throw your ass out." He left and went crying off to his Sergeant First Class. He walked up and asked why I told his staff sergeant to leave. I told him, "look you don't come in my soldiers quarters unless you talk to me first, get it." Now if you have a problem with this, we can go down the street and see my commander." He just looked at me and said nothing then he walked off mumbling to himself.

Once I was told to go to the Tuzla Air Strip and cover a visit by General Henry Shelton, The Joint Chief of

Staff. I had to meet with the driver, the four stars; red plate was on his vehicle. He was a civilian contracted driver. I know if I had to go and pick up a General there would be more than just me doing it. So I decided to have some fun. I told the driver to take me to the air strip. I got in the front seat, put my BDU hat over my eyes with my sunglasses on, then I told him to take me there the long way. I thought this would be funny and it was hilarious. We drove right past Maj. Eaton, Lt. Col Coward, and my commander Maj. McReynolds walking down the street together. They saw the vehicle with the red plate and four stars and right away they saluted me. They thought I was General Shelton. So I saluted them back. Maj. McReynolds realized it was me. Maj. Eaton and Lt. Col. Coward never had a clue. Everyone we passed started saluting me and I rendered a salute back. Once we reached the air strip, three full bird 1st Cavalry Division colonels came running over to the van opened the door for me and without even looking said, "we have been waiting for you sir, we need to take you to a briefing." I looked up and they said what you are doing here Sergeant Dunn." I said, "I was sent here by the Joint Visitors Center to pick up and cover General Shelton's visit. It was all I could do not to laugh in their faces. Then the real Generals convoy went right by us with a row of black Chevy Suburban's. The colonels rushed off and jumped in a vehicle and tried to catch up to him. When I got back Maj. McReynolds came running out and said, "Sergeant Dunn, I don't know whether to be mad as hell or laugh, just don't ever do that again."

Right then two of my soldiers came in Spec. Collins and Spec. Rowe and said, "We just saw General Shelton and he saluted us. I busted out laughing and they said,

"What's wrong with him Maj. McReynolds, and then he started laughing. Later I told them it was me having a bit of fun. They looked at me and said, "Damn sergeant Dunn you are crazy." I said no, "I am just a seedy NCO."

Let's talk about the 1st Cavalry Division Commander Maj. Gen. Kevin P. Byrnes. He was the commander of (MND). He would not allow us to take leave if we took a pass, especially if you were not in the 1st Cavalry Glory Boy Division. This only applied to all outsiders, especially the National Guard and the Army Reserve units. Yet he would allow his soldiers and officers knowingly to go on pass to Budapest to visit a whore house called Captain Jacks. Yes, this place was real and they would take soldiers in there for a good time. Flyers and maps were handed to the soldiers to tell them how to get there once they got off the bus in Budapest. An article was submitted to Stars and Stripes, but it was never published. I saw the pictures first hand of his soldiers and officers with the whores having sex and bragging about it. It was their way of saying it's alright to commit adultery in the Army. I just wish I had been given those pictures.

They would also go to Sarajevo the Bosnian Capital and the place where the Olympic Games were held in 1984 and drink. While we were told this was general order number one, no alcohol and if you were caught drinking it would mean severe disciplinary action or even Court Martial. It did happen to some soldiers who were caught drinking. Yet these glory boys of the 1st Cavalry Division would go whoring and drinking and nothing ever happened. To them this peacekeeping operation was a party on the taxpayers tab. Yes, it happened, later Captain Jacks was closed down after a hush, hush investigation. It was about the same time President

Clinton was having all his sex troubles. Why not if the president can have premarital sex with Monica Lewinski I guess the 1st Cavalry Division soldiers can do it too. Maj. Gen. Byrnes was promoted after Bosnia for a job well done. He later went on in his career to become a four star general over The Army Training and Doctrine Command (TRADOC). He finally got caught having an affair with another woman while he was married. He was ordered not to see this woman and he disobeyed a direct order by the Chief of the Army to stop his affair. He was then relieved of his command by The Chief of the Army shortly thereafter for sexual misconduct unbecoming of an officer and that was also kept hush, hush as to not embarrass the Army. I knew this general was bad news and could say nothing at the time, but yet he got two more stars before he gave the Army a black eye. I saw him at the 2005 All American Bowl in San Antonio, Texas. He noticed me and I told Lt. Col Paul Stamps my boss at the time, that he was no good. He believed me when one day we were back at Fort Knox and word came down that Gen. Byrnes was being relieved as the commander of TRADOC. Gen. Byrnes was one of President Clinton's boys, but he found himself in a world of shit when The Secretary of Defense Donald Rumsfeld sent him packing. No telling how many officers and soldiers would have lost their careers if they had exposed Captain Jacks back in Bosnia. It's a shame, also there were soldiers who were caught having sex at Camp Dobol with a cleaning woman who was a Bosnian contract worker and nothing was done. How, did I know this, my commander told me about it and there was an investigation going on into the matter.

The Deputy Commander of the 1st Cavalry Division was Brig Gen. Steven Whitcomb, but to his officers he was to be called Roy, period. No rank no last name, just Roy. He helped spend tax payer money on having a big rock with the 1st Cavalry Division patch on it placed right in the center of the main intersection at Tuzla Main called Five Points. One Brown and Root worker told me it cost over $50,000 dollars to make it and place it there. They also even brought a life size plastic horse they called Trigger to be placed in the entrance of the Command Headquarters. They gave the horse its own ID card and SFOR Card. There was also thousands of dollars spent on 1st Calvary Division signage all over Bosnia.

Finally a break, I and Spec. Tim Jones went on leave together. Capt. Barren his team leader did not like the idea of an E-4 fraternizing on leave with an E-7. especially me, but what the hell we would both be civilians for two weeks in Europe so we went anyway. It was great, we went to Germany first, then France, and even drank a little beer at Jim Morrison's Grave in Paris. Then we went to Belgium, where one night while I got locked in the subway. It was funny because the police there had to let me out and it looked like a crime scene. Everyone looked at me while I came out of the locked gate with about 5 Belgium cop cars there. We went to Normandy and visited the sites of D-Day WWII. Then we went to England through the new Chunnel, a train system that carried us and our rental car under the English Channel. In England we ran into some soccer hooligans after a game in a pub. They literally trashed the bar. One of them took a rare guitar off the wall hit his buddy over the head and threw it in the pub's fire place. We were lucky to get out of there before the Bobbies (police) got there.

I mean the place was trashed windows broken and beer bottles everywhere. After the pub fight, we did a little sightseeing and went back through the Chunnel to France the next day. Driving in England was a nightmare on the other side of the road. Tim drank more than me, because I did most of the driving. Hangovers are not my favorite thing and yes, I had a few. We listened to Jerry Jeff Walker, Johnny Cash, and Jimmy Buffett. Tim Jones use to be a country music disk jockey back in Alabama, I was more of a classic rocker, but we liked the same kinds of country music, particularly the Honky Tonk Music and Southern Bands. We topped it all off with a trip to Amsterdam. If it was illegal, it was legal here. I had never seen so much drugs, prostitution, and crazy people in all my life. We just hung out and laughed at all of it. It seemed like the party was over before it started and we had to pack it up and get our uniforms out. Get our LBE on and head back to Ramstein and then to lovely Eagle Base for the second half of hell. The trip with Spec. Jones later inspired him to write a book called European Confession, let's just say I read the book and thank God he did not do too much confessing about our wild two week trip in Europe.

Then came Thanksgiving, the best part about this was I got to go on the radio and talk to my wife Telena and my son Donald III with Country Music singer Lari White. The radio station in Columbia, SC., picked them up and brought them to the station for the call. This was special, since we had little communication with our families except by mail or occasional phone call. Lari White also did a concert for the soldiers while she was here too in one of the helicopter hangers.

Another good memory was having Mark Duper, a retired wide receiver for the Miami Dolphins visit the soldiers. He came over to Bosnia and watched the Super Bowl with us. Of course it was late Sunday night because of the time difference, but Super Duper signed autographs and stayed up with us for the whole game. That year the Denver Broncos beat the Atlanta Falcons.

New Years Eve 1998, the officers of the 1st Calvary Division, celebrated it with another Grog Party at Comanche Base. Guess, who was assigned to cover this?, yes me. It was a disgrace to the Army. Col. Coward our infamous traitor commander told Maj. McReynolds he wanted me to take pictures and cover this with a story. He wanted it to be published. Another fraternity party to bring in the New Year. The enlisted soldiers were separated to celebrate their New Years at Eagle Base with no coverage. The Grog Party was held at the mess hall on Comanche Base and the first thing I noticed coming in was this field table with a toilet bowl on top of it and sand bags all around it. It was surrounded on all four corners by tables and chairs. The ones in the front were for the command section, Maj. Gen. Byrnes and his good old Stetson Boys. They all sat down at the tables, each one of them had a big cigar. After everyone was seated, they all lit their cigars together. Then the ranking officer at each table took a canteen, with who only know what was in it and dumped it into the toilet bowl on the green field table. Then each table dared the other table to drink out of it with a steel canteen cup. This went around and around till all the lieutenants, captains, majors, and last of all the command section had a taste out of the toilet bowl. They all stood up and let out a big HOOAH.

I was ashamed to even mention I was there and I destroyed the pictures. When asked for the pictures by Col. Coward my response was, "sir I had some trouble with the camera and I could not fix it." He yelled at me, but there was no way in hell I was going to do this story. So without any pictures there was no story. All though I do wish I had kept a few for this book.

I did something else to piss first team off. I kept myself busy at night writing letters and collecting autographs from celebrities while I was here and it was fun to see who would write back. I wrote everyone, including the Army's top brass and the response was overwhelming. I wrote to see if we could get some celebrities to come over here and boost the morale and guess what, it worked. Right around Christmas we heard through the USO that Ricky Skaggs and Paul Overstreet was going to do concerts for all the base camps in the area. Spec. Jones called me up from where he was at Base Camp Bedrock. He told me he covered the first concert at that base camp. He said, "Sergeant Dunn, did you know Ricky Skaggs and Paul Overstreet were up here talking about a letter they got from you. I said, "Really, you're kidding me." Spec. Jones said, "No, they said they got your letter on a hunting trip in Montana and decided to come over here to do this for the soldiers as a Christmas present." I was glad I could do something for the soldiers, after all none of us would be home for the holidays. The next day Ricky Skaggs and Paul Overstreet came to Eagle Base in Tuzla where I was at. I went down to see the concert with Spec. Valentine and Spec. Lorrente. While watching the concert, right in the middle of their set, Ricky Skaggs stopped and said, "Is there a sergeant Dunn out there?

I raised my hand. Then he looked down at me and said, "look what you've done Dunn."

Then he talked about the letter I sent him and he said, "We knew all you soldiers were not going to be home for Christmas so we decided to bring a little of home to you." I was never more proud, I was able through one letter to the right person to give the soldiers here a real present." Also after the show I talked with Ricky Skaggs and a 1st Calvary Division soldier walked by and he said, "There patch looks like a big old guitar pick." I laughed and said, that is not all it looks like." The next day I was standing in Maj. Eaton's office at 0800 explaining why I wrote a letter to them and that this was a peacekeeping operation not a concert venue. I know what I did was right. Oh, but this was not the end of it. I was told not to right anymore letters to celebrities. I disobeyed this order and was then taken to the Inspector General's IG office with my commander Maj. McReynolds by my side and told my letters were being looked at as fraud, waste, and abuse. At first I was a bit scared of what might happen. Well, that did not hold water, because I bought all my paper, envelopes, and printer cartridges I used to write with. I had receipts for them all and they were sent to me by my wife. Then they tried to say I was selling autograph pictures I received in the mail. Another lie, because they could not find one soldier who said I had ever done this. Jealousy, this is all it was, but the 1st Calvary Division did not like it. I had been noticed and I worked for the Army Reserve as an AGR soldier and they did not like me at all. Then the IG told me I had to log all of my letters and give them the list of who I was writing. Then they asked my commander if he knew what I was doing on my down time. My commander Maj. McReynolds, then spoke up and said, "Some soldiers work out, others use email, Sergeant Dunn writes letters, what is the problem? It is his hobby and why should anyone care, he is not breaking rules. He has a right to his mail." Then the IG a Lt. Col. Barlow, "said OK don't shoot your foot off in the process." Then he admitted he had to answer this because of a complaint he received. I went back with my commander, he said, "Sergeant Dunn, you are right they really are after you." I thanked him for standing up for me and he said, "You might be a lot of things, but I was not going to let them mess with you on this, because you have a right to write to anyone you like and get mail."

Shortly after this, I got another important letter addressed to me from Gen. Henry Shelton, the Joint Chief of Staff. He told me he had read an article I wrote in Stars and Stripes and then he thanked me for my part in the Christmas Concert. He said, he heard I collected autographs and gave me his. Then he said in a separate letter to me he was coming to Eagle Base in Tuzla for a visit and wanted to see me. Then one afternoon I was sitting in our office and in walked a Marine Major she walked up to my commander and said, "I am looking for a Sergeant First Class Dunn, do you know where I can find him?"

Maj. McReynolds looked over at me while I was working on a story and said jokingly, "now what have you done Dunn?" The Major said, "Gen Shelton wants to see you." The whole room got quiet. So I went with the Marine officer down to see General Shelton. He was in the mess tent talking and visiting with other soldiers. I waited till he was done and then the Major took me over to see him.

He was a big man to say the least, then he looked down at me and said, "You must be Sergeant Dunn, I said, "Yes sir." He said, "I want to personally thank you and give you one of my coins. I appreciate what you and your unit are doing for the soldiers here, and that was a great Christmas Concert for the soldiers." I said, "Thanks sir, I try to take care of soldiers." He said, you are not only trying, you are doing it." Then he said, "I got to go and it was nice meeting with you and take care." Then he posed with me for a picture and shook my hand. He then walked away with his escorts and got into a black Chevy Suburban and left. I knew this was not going to go unnoticed; Maj. Eaton came over to me and said, "Who do you think you are interrupting the Joint Chief of Staff's schedule and visit? I'm sure he has better things to do than talk to you." I just looked at him and smiled. Then Col. Coward his side kick came over and they both joined in on me again, like two dogs on a three legged cat. It was a scene, but I just smiled again and said, "Anything you say sir." Well it did not end there; they went to my commander, "this time Maj. McReynolds looked at them and said, ".If Sergeant Dunn is summoned by the Joint Chief of Staff, well I am not going to stand in the way." Then they did not say anything and stormed out of our office. Maj. Eaton never did like coming to our office in the 10 months we were in Bosnia, He and Col. Coward only came in a handful of times and that was when they had too and it was never a social visit. The only other time I personally remember them coming into our office was to tell us if we took a pass we could not have leave. They both were always great for being the morale booster of shitty news and they enjoyed it.

Stars and Stripes got wind of my hobby collecting autographs and wanted to do a human interest story on me. You can guess how this went over, a story about a soldier in Public Affairs. I went to Maj. McReynolds and he said, "Do it and you have my blessing. This is your chance to really stop the 1st Calvary Division from messing with you." Stars and Stripes did an Article on me and guess what it landed right on the front page of their next issue.

It came out and it said in the Headlines, "Soldier Uses Bosnia Time for Autographs." you should have seen the faces when they all saw the paper. I had a blast being interviewed and telling my story and there was nothing they could do about it. I even got a letter from Bob Hope. In the letter he said, "I would come to Tuzla if I was not so old and knew where the hell Tuzla was." Then he said, "I am sending an appeal to the National USO Office on my behalf to get more shows and entertainment to come to Bosnia for the troops. At that point, almost every week, shows started coming to Bosnia for the troops, either by the USO or the Morale Welfare and Recreational (MWR). It was not long after that we got the Lakers Girls to visit the base camps here in Tuzla and I did not mind getting the assignment to escort them and do an article. Also Hootie and the Blowfish came and I and Spec. Valentine got to cover this and do interviews with the band. They were from Columbia, South Carolina and it was great because my unit and soldiers were from their too. Darius Rucker, the singer and Sonny the Drummer were always great and willing to help the soldiers and giving out autographs and CD's away. Darius even did a concert on Fort Jackson a year later and I got to cover it and interview him again. We also got some good local talent including comedy acts to come to Bosnia. I was glad I could make a difference in getting the morale up for the soldiers. As for the 1st Cavalry Division, the pin is mightier than the sword.

I went on an escort mission with Lt. Gen. Laporte, to Srebrenica. The III Corps Commander at Fort Hood, TX wanted to visit the war torn city. Srebrenica had seen some of the worst genocide and ethnic cleansing during the war by Serbian general Radislav Krstic and Slobodan Milosevic. The Serbs had killed thousands of people under him alone here. The dam leading into the city had bodies pulled out of it. So many that it had blocked off the water supply to the city. The men were taken to remote sites by buses, made to dig their own mass graves and were shot and buried by bulldozers. Women were also raped and killed and their own children were tied to them still alive like an anchor and drowned by the Serbs. The city still showed many scars of the atrocities and ethnic cleansing which happened here and unless you were there, it is incomprehensible. There was only one way in and one way out of Srebrenica and the United Nations could not help them at the time, even though they tried. When asked what was going on in the city, the Serbs replied "You know what is going on here." This city today is still a dangerous place with many land mines around the town. All that was left in this town was a few people and most of them stayed indoors because of snipers.

When they saw me with a camera, they hid. To them all it would take is a picture in the wrong place and there family could be next on the Serbs list. We were here as peacekeepers and I had to go with Gen. Laporte, on this mission. It took about 4 hours to get there up the winding roads and mountains of Bosnia. We were never met with resistance there, but, we were always cautious, observant, and ready. I was in a convoy with four vehicles and mine was right behind General Laporte's group. Anytime you move especially in this area you always kept your eyes wide open, because there is no room for complacency. I always packed 270 rounds on me and made sure my weapon was clean before each mission. We parked along the road right at the entrance of town. The reason was if we had to get out we were by the only exit. We were first approached by a lone dog and one of the soldiers kicked it. I told him to be careful, because some dogs belonged to snipers and we did not need trouble. We walked through the town and visited with some of the residents who still lived there. You could still see the war torn reminders of what had happened here just a few years ago. People's faces there told the story. Building were riddled with bullet holes some barely standing. The children are who I felt sorry for the most. They would come up to you and beg for food, while others would just stand off and watch. We had to watch everywhere we walked and you did not dare go off the hard top. Anything with grass and dirt could still be mined. There were also mines in the walls of the houses. A man ran out of his house with what looked like a bottle of Vodka. He was trying to give us some, but we just waved him off. I was with a general officer and he had to be guarded. The town was like coming back to the scene of a crime. We finished up with a visit to a church on the highest hill in the town and then we left.

Going back, we visited Camp Demi, Lt. Gen. Laporte wanted to see it because they were thinking about closing this base camp. There had been some security problems and he wanted to check it out. Upon our arrival he noticed a few buildings to close to the outer fences and the perimeter. There was a young Major who was the base commander. Lt. Gen. Laponte gave him a hard time when he noticed the security problems. I remember Lt. Gen. Laporte saying, "This is a fucked up place," then he looked over at me, laughed and said, "Sergeant Dunn you can quote me on that." Then Col. Johnson, who was the base commander at Eagle Base, looked at me and said, "You better not quote him." He was also asked by Lt. Gen. Laporte why he and the 1st Calvary Division had not given this base camp the proper support.

Col. Johnson just looked dumb founded and said nothing. While at Camp Demi a soldier was reenlisting and Lt. Gen. Laporte wanted to do his reenlistment. He looked at me and said, "Where do you think we can do it Sergeant Dunn to get a good picture." The soldier was a mechanic in the motor pool, so I said, "sir let's do it in front of a vehicle here with two soldiers holding the American Flag on each end. Also sir, you and the soldier reenlisting stand in the middle." Lt. Gen. Laporte looked at me and said, "That's a great idea." Then he looked over at Col. Johnson and said, "Go get the flag Col. Johnson." Col. Johnson did not like this and gave me a dirty look as he went and got the flag. I thought this was funny, because this was Lt. Gen Laporte's way of getting back at him for not supporting the commander of Camp Demi. After the reenlistment, we went back to the helicopter where Lt. Gen. Laporte had to go back to Tuzla to catch his flight back to Fort Hood, Texas. Before he left, he personally thanked me and gave me a commanders coin and said, "it was a pleasure once again Sergeant Dunn." I looked at him and said, "thank you sir." This was the last time I ever saw him, but I remember he went on to become the commander of South Korean Forces when he got his fourth star.

On another of my many media escorts we visited mass grave sites in Bosnia. This time we ran into some kids with what looked like real guns. We discovered they were not real after one of the HUMVEE gunners drew down on them with his 50 caliber machine gun. The Serbs had given the kids guns in hope that we would shoot one of them. This would create negative propaganda about the Army and our reasons for being here. Thank God, it did not happen.

I saw many burned out houses too with nothing left but the shell. When you would see a house untouched you knew that a Serb lived there or someone who helped them. Brchko, was especially a bad place and the Army was working on an arbitration to settle the ongoing violence in the area.

Also meeting with the Russians who were closest to the Serbs did not always go as planned and there had to be many compromises to keep the peace. I remember visits by Gen. Wesley Clark; He was the Commander of Allied Forces in Europe at the time. He and Maj. Gen. Byrnes were buddies; they always called each other by first names. Especially when officers call each other by first names in front of enlisted soldiers. I always called any soldiers by their rank and last name. This is how I was taught and trained to respect those over me and under me. These two generals were both President Clinton's boys, especially Gen. Clark. I remember him getting off the plane in Tuzla. He was as arrogant as they come. He looked down at everyone around him and had to be catered too. I also sat in the meetings between him and Maj. Gen. Byrnes ironing out the details of the Brchko Arbitration. I also set in meetings with General Montgomery Miggs, who was the NATO Stabilization Force Commander in Bosnia. I had high respect for Gen. Miggs, he would talk to the troops and listen, even if it was a private doing the talking. But, Gen. Clark, he was to me a turn coat who found his way out after President George Bush Jr. became President. Gen. Clark was in the Army as a politician and I was not impressed with anything he did, because he was doing it for himself. He was a true arrogant Democrat and not even good at that.

Enough about Gen. Clark, we had real issues after a soldier Master Sgt. Kelly, a civil affairs NCO killed a Serb. Word had it they were in a place getting something to eat in Tuzla and a Serb walked in and laid a big stick across their table. Sergeant Kelly and a few of his soldiers tried to exit the place without trouble, and then Sergeant Kelly was hit from behind with the board. He then turned and before he was hit again he shot the Serb with his 9mm pistol killing him right where he stood. He then came back to Eagle Base where a report was filed on the incident. I tried to interview him for a story, but it was too sensitive and I was told to stand down. Then Eagle Base Camp went on high alert and we had to go back to wearing all our LBE and Flack Vest everywhere we went. Later there was another incident, where a soldier got out of his Humvee after being pelted with rocks and shot the hand of a hostile demonstrator. Everything here rotated around the use of deadly force. Also there was a question of what deadly force was and when it should be used. I will tell you this if I am being pelted by rocks and someone comes at me with a two by four; I am going to shoot them too. The same goes if you are trying to hurt one of my soldiers. The way I look at it is the Army put me in Bosnia and if I have to defend myself or my soldiers. I think it would be better to be judged by twelve than carried by six.

Also, we were almost bombed a few times while we were in Bosnia. We had to build and secure bunkers at each base camp in the area. The first bombing came at night in early march in the late to early morning. I recall being woken up by base MP's and sirens going off at about 3 a.m., and told to take me and my soldiers to the nearest bunker. We stayed there and could hear what was going on over our radio. There were three Migs with Serbs set to attack Camp Dobol, Camp Comanche, and Eagle Base where we were at. Two of the Migs were shot down and one escaped.

The two Migs that were shot down by the Air Force after the Migs laid some fire down at Comanche Base and Camp Dobol. Then we heard the command "all clear." and we went back to our sea huts. After this Sirens were always going off at different times on the base camp.

The next day I went down to the Coalition Press Information Center (CPIC), I could not sleep after being up all night and wanted to find out more about what was happening with these air strikes. I was told by Maj. Hensley, the CPIC Executive Officer to go get Sergeant Holloway, a broadcast journalist in my squad and get right back as soon as possible to go to the site. I ran and got him and we took our cameras and headed out. When we got back we were told to saddle up and take a

CNN Press Team to the site where one of the Migs got shot down. We went on a commercial bus and headed to Tecak in the Russian Serbian Sector of Bosnia. We were escorted by two Humvees in front and back of the bus. Once we arrived there all we could see was smoke coming off a hill about two kilometers away. I also remember there was a lot of mud so much that even the Humvees could not get up the hill. We had to walk in two to three feet of mud in some places just to get up the hill. The CNN reporters wanted to be on sight before they started broadcasting the story and it was our job to get them there quick. Between the mud and the fear of land mines everywhere, we finally made it to the shot down Mig. There was debris everywhere from it. We even got there before Army Explosive Ordnance Team (EOD).

Looking at that plane with the bombs still attached to the wings smoking and praying that this Mig does not blow up while I am here. The CNN reporters rushed up to the plane, did there spot for the news and then we left the site. While on our way from the crash site this old Bosnian man with a bottle of vodka offered us a drink. Our interpreter said the man wanted to thank us for not letting the Serbian Mig hit his house which was about 50 yards from the crash site.

Then me and Sgt. Holloway got our pictures and some B-roll video footage and headed down the hill. I was so glad to get off that hill and away from that plane, because I knew it was a matter of time before it exploded. Also avoiding possible land mines getting back to the bus was no fun. I was up over two days with this story before I finally got to sleep. Again there is no rest in the Army.

The worst part came when all the Bosnians were told they were not going to be allowed on the Base Camp while the bombings raids were going on. So much for the 1st Calvary Division's Contingency Plan and Standard Operating Procedure (SOP) being in place. Without the Bosnians, there were no more haircuts, showers, or laundry service. Not to mention the mess hall was just filled with Meal Ready to Eat Boxes (MREs). Some soldiers would shit and piss in the showers. Uniforms were being worn for days and everyone smelled like the homeless. We all had to take a personal interest in our own hygiene to include giving each other haircuts. This went on for about three weeks till the 1st Calvary Division came out of their coma and said guess what we have a personal hygiene problem. No shit Sherlock, it took all this for them to figure this one out. So they let the Bosnians, who were not the cause of the bombings back on the base camps after many demonstrations at the front gate.

I had to cover a story at the Tuzla Morgue. What a gruesome place this was. The Bosnian people were still trying to figure out where all their missing relatives and friends were; the Army was still discovering mass graves and decomposed bodies in them. We had trouble there too, even though we were trying to help figure out who was who. The Bosnian people would grow very impatient with us and our efforts. Bodies and pieces of bodies in white bags would be brought in one at a time and the coroners there would try to figure out who each person was. Sometimes they would only have a body part of a person and it would be so decomposed it was impossible to figure out who it was. DNA did not work here. The coroner would lay out each body on a stainless steel metal table and try to put a skeleton back together. The smell was awful and even after you left the morgue you could smell it in your cloths; it is still something I will never forget. They also had all these wooden crosses hanging on the walls in the lab. There were wooden casket just leaning against the walls. There was another building with a tunnel about a hundred yards long and it had shelves on both sides with the remains of bodies in white garbage bags. Each bag was tagged and pulled in order. Sometimes all you would see in a white bag was a glob of human flesh and that was it. Imagine the pain these people must be going through to never know what really happened to their family members and friends. They only know that they were murdered by the Serbs and missing. This is all of whatever closure there is for them.

There were days when I thought I had had enough of this place and just wanted to be anywhere but here. To add to this, I had one laptop computer stolen out of my office and had to do a Report of Survey to explain that it was actually stolen.

I will start with how the 1st Calvary Division wasted taxpayer's money sorting out one missing lap top computer in a combat operation with no real place to permanently secure it or anything else we had in Bosnia. During my deployment I was told to go and get seven laptop computers by the commander Maj. McReynolds, so I made sure each of our three teams had two and the seventh one would remain in our office in Tuzla as a spare in case one of the others got damaged. It was locked in a closet and the keys to the office remained with Lt. Willard, the training officer, the only other set of keys was the commanders.

The 1st Calvary Division property book officer Col Bowers was determined to make me pay for it. I had done all my inventories every week and reported it missing in less than a day of it missing. I even double checked all the units hand receipts and I did the Report of Survey myself. Then I contacted the Criminal Investigation Department of the Army (CID) for further assistance. This was a big mistake. Unfortunately they were part of the 1st Cavalry Division and thought it was an inside job and started investigating and finger printing all the soldiers in our unit. They never thought about the Brown and Root Bosnian Cleaning Crew who was in and out of our office every day. They never took into consideration that the laptop was in the most secure place in the office and locked in a closet. To this day I hate the U.S. Army CID. They just want to find guilt and they don't care who they shit on as long as they settle their cases quickly. I was treated like a criminal and they lied about everything from not having laptop locks, which I had requested and never got. Also trailers, which were not temperature controlled and were all in a place with so much mud it was called a pig farm by the soldiers. Even before I left Bosnia to come back after the deployment they were breaking into my personal mail and even checked my quarters back at Fort Jackson. They even gave me and one of my soldiers Spec. Valentine a lie detector test after we returned home, which produced negative results.

My wife was continuously badgered by CID and they called her in and made her go to our quarters on post with them. They forced her to let them go through my quarters and search all my personal belongings. All this was going on, while I was on Temporary Duty (TDY), at Fort Benning after Bosnia, picking up one of my soldiers, who had just gotten back, and needed a ride to Fort

Jackson. Although they did not find anything, I went over to CID myself personally and asked them why they did not do this when I got back. Agent Hunley's response was, "we can do whatever we want to on Fort Jackson, because we are CID." I then asked him, "Well did you find what you were looking for?" He said, "no, but we saw your baseball card collection." I said, "I guess then you will not be coming back and I hope none of my baseball cards are missing." Then he got cute and threatened to arrest me, and I called his bluff and said, "Well do it if you have something to charge me with." He grinned and walked away.

They checked every pawn shop near Fort Jackson, after taking over $2500 dollars from me, out of my pay in monthly increments of $250 a month for almost a year. I finally had to go to the Army Board of Corrections of Military Records (ABCMR) who found me innocent of any wrong doing and finally stated, "Sergeant Dunn did what a prudent NCO would have done to protect unit equipment in a combat operation." I called down to Texas at Fort Hood to talk to the 1st Cavalry Division and Col. Bower. I got all my money back. They cost the Army and tax payers over $20,000 investigating over one lost laptop. He was still not convinced of me being innocent, but had to give me back the money out of the 1st Cavalry's Division year end funds. In the end it did not matter, because I got the satisfaction of knowing he was wrong whether he admitted it or not. Just because he was a Colonel, he still did not out rank the ABCMR Board. I later got a large packet from the ABCMR stating that this was the final action and my military record would never show this as ever happening. Then I also got the records on my case from CID at Fort Belvoir, Va., which outlined the whole investigation and everything was cleared from the record. Imagine all this documentation, over 200 pages, man power, and money spent for one Dell Laptop computer. This could have been easily written off as a combat loss.

Many soldiers told me not to fight this because I would lose, but I was taught if you are right, fight. I was not going to let the 1st Cavalry Division and their lousy command have my money, especially when they held the keys to our offices and were responsible for the lack of security for the whole base camp, to include not supplying locks for the laptops when I had requested them before I signed for them. It took me over a year to prove and win my case. The Army has no problem taking your money, but if they owe you money you know you are going to have to fight for it. They found out they could not piss down my back and tells me it is raining.

The only other time in my career that I had to deal directly with the CID, came when a window got broken by a football at my quarters, while me and my son were watching television. I heard a loud noise outside my sliding door leading to my patio and I noticed the window was shattered.

I saw two kids run off and I had to call maintenance and explain what had happened. I thought they would just come over and fix it and that would be it. Well, the next thing I know the Military Police were at my house making a report on the incident. I told them the same thing, I told the maintenance people. Then after they left, I got a visit from CID. I thought to myself, it's a broken window for crying out loud, not a break-in. Then the CID agent asked if he could talk to my son after I told them what happened. I said no problem. Then he said, he wanted to talk with him alone outside. I said, "Ok." Then about 10 minutes later my son comes in crying and I asked him what was wrong?

He said, "Dad they think I broke the window and then he started crying more." I looked at the CID agent and told him flat out, "get out of my quarters." I told them he was with me, "I said, what are you trying to do here make my 9 year old son tell you he did something when he did not, I personally know damn sure he did not." The CID agent looked at me and said, I have to look at all angles. I said again, "I trust my son and I know he is telling the truth, because he was right here with me when it happened."

"Does this make you proud using scare tactics on a child?" I simply have no use for CID period; to me they lack military bearing and want to clear up cases with fast blame.

Back to Master Sergeant Dilbert and the problems we had dealing with him in Bosnia. He did not like me because I would not put up with his bullshit. He did not care for the soldiers but he sure did care about Staff Sgt. Pepper a broadcast journalist in our unit. He and she even went on leave together for two weeks in Germany. We all knew something was going on even before this; they were inseparable when we had down time. It was nothing more than flat out fraternization. The Army frowns down on fraternization; we knew they were having an affair. Capt. Taylor, her team leader knew it too. Sergeant Pepper messed over a few soldiers in my unit and Spec. Lorrente, a journalist, and a good soldier let Maj. McReynolds, know it. I saw Spec. Lorrente walk into the office one day and physically tear his unit patch off his uniform and hand it to Maj. McReynolds.

He said, "I will not listen to Sergeant Pepper anymore," then right behind him Sergeant. Keith Johnson came in and said, "me too." She was notorious for making internal problems in our unit. She had also caused an Investigation, accusing Capt. Taylor of looking at pornography on his computer, which she could not prove. She got the 1st Calvary Divison to believe her and they took Capt. Taylor's computer from him and found nothing. I told Maj. McReynolds, "We have to do something about all this." I will take Spec. Lorrente and incorporate him into my team. Guess what Sergeant Dilber said, "I will take Sergeant Pepper," I thought to myself you already have had her you might as well move her in your quarters too! I spoke with the commander later that night and told him my view and what I thought we should do. Maj. McReynolds was a level headed commander and decided to let me have her soldier. He told me Sergeant Dunn, "I trust you and I know you are loyal and that is what I need right now, loyalty." I said, "Sir, I just wish you would not let Sergeant Dilbert have Sergeant Pepper, because if the unit sees them together it will only cause a morale problem." For now he let them play their game. He told me, "Sergeant Dunn it will all wash out in the end, I know what they are up to and this way I will have my eye on both of them while there with me in this office."

Yes, it did work out for now they were real careful how they acted around Maj. McReynolds. Guess what, when we got back to the unit at Fort Jackson after Bosnia. Sergeant Pepper and Sergeant Dilbert got married, also after all of this; she even got commissioned as an officer and went to a medical unit in the same building. Yes, they made her a First Lieutenant? The Army does not usually put married couples in the same unit. I was glad and our unit was glad to see her go. I only wish Sergeant Dilbert had gone with her. This was another case of what we called a Fuck up and a move up.

In Bosnia there were also incidents in other units. One story was of a soldier who shot and killed himself in front of his commander. Another story was of a soldier telling his first sergeant to get off his back or he knew what he would do with 270 rounds. The worst one came from Camp Bedrock. A sergeant got a video tape from home. He started watching it with a few other soldiers in his unit. It showed a woman with a bag over her head and she was having sex with three men. He thought it was a joke until the bag came off the woman's head and he realized it was his wife! She looked right at the camera and said, "Now will you give me a divorce." At that moment he lost it and had to be psychiatrically evaluated and sent to Walter Reed.

We were not the only ones who had internal problems; there were more at the Coalition Press Camp Headquarters. Maj. Hensley, who was the Executive Officer there, had problems of his own dealing with Lt. Col. Coward. He always yelled for him like a dog and never called him by his rank or last name. I personally use to hear him say, "XO get in here."

Maj Hensley also had a NCO, Sgt. Sellers who worked with him. Sgt. Sellers just did not think and was arrogant and it cost him a flight right out of Eagle Base, back to his command in the rear. Sgt. Sellers, as a joke wrote a story about the Russian Army. His big mistake was what he wrote and who he wrote it too. He sent the story to an Oregon Newspaper "The Oregonian." In his article he made fun of how the Russians were like mafia and liked to drink vodka. The other bad thing was Master Sgt Brier gave the article to the Russians before even reading it first. Then it was not funny, it almost caused an international incident right on Eagle Base. It all started in an early morning meeting with the Russian Brigade Commander. It was then Maj. Gen. Byrnes, told the Coalition Press Information Center (CPIC) to send Sgt. Sellers packing back to his unit in Oregon.

We also worked closely with the 82nd Airborne Public Affairs Office and helped them with stories for the weekly "Talon Magazine." I and my soldiers did at least two stories a week and made sure they had enough stories for their issues. I and Spec. Valentine were a two man team and we produced over 100 stories that were published. Later Spec. Valentine told me he heard it was a record, because no other Mobile Public Affairs Team before us had ever accomplished this. I liked working with Spec. Valentine he was a young soldier in his mid twenties. Even though I was his NCO, he was very talented and knew a computer like it was nobody's business. He was good with a digital camera and taught me the technical skills I needed. You see just because I was an E-7 and he was an E-4, I would listen to some of his suggestions, because unlike a lot of soldiers with rank who say it my way. I listened to one of my lower enlisted soldier if he or she had a good idea.

Another key to a successful mission was to have a good Sergeant Major. Well guess what we did not have a good Master Sergeant. Dilbert was not even Military Occupational Skill Qualified (MOS). I made sure the soldiers in my unit knew who they could rely on. I crossed trained my soldiers. This way if I needed a soldier he knew the job. The 1st Cavalry Divison had a Sergeant

Major, named Inama. He hated our unit, because we were not 1st Cavalry Division soldiers. He would find details specifically for us to do, like play water and towel boy for his soldiers in the gym after hours. I really do not want to talk about him, because it just pisses me off to think that someone who is as worthless as an oxygen thief ever made it to that rank. He was more useless than tits on a bore.

One of my many missions was to cover the visit of a congressman from Mississippi. It was my job to go with him as the escort from the Joint Visitors Bureau (JVB). I had to document and take pictures of his two day visit. I followed him and Maj. Gen Byrnes around to visit all the coalition forces and base camps. Our last visit on the second day was with the Russian Brigade Commander at Ugulvic a Russian base camp. We use to joke and call the place Ugly Dick. I was in one of the meeting with the congressman, Maj. Gen. Byrnes, and the Russian Commander and a female Russian soldier walked in and gave us some coffee. The Russian Commander started talking about needing money to pay some of his troops. The congressman joking said," if you can get her to see Bill Clinton you might get your money commander." I started laughing with him, but Maj. Gen. Byrnes did not think it was funny, because he was one of Clintons boys, who I personally would not let command a one legged nun walking a goat. Maj. Gen. Byrnes gave me a dirty look and the congressman said, "Lighten up General Byrnes, it's a joke," and the Russian commander laughed again after his interpreter told him what was going on.

After the meeting on the way back to the van the congressman looked at the photo album I made for him of his visit and said, "thanks Sergeant Dunn." Then he started talking to me about Mississippi and asked me if I had ever been there. I told him yes, then we started talking about a lot of places in Mississippi he had been and I had been too. Maj. Gen. Byrnes looked at me as if to say shut up, but the congressman wanted to talk to me more than him. Maj. Gen. Byrnes had had enough and about three blocks from the main gate at Eagle Base on the outskirts of Tuzla he said, "Sorry sir to interrupt you, but we will be dropping Sergeant Dunn off here, because I need to talk with you alone before you leave back to the states." The Congressman looked at Maj. Gen. Byrnes and said, "Is this a safe place to drop him off right here without a ride," and he replied, 'you will be alright won't you Sergeant Dunn." I looked at him and said, "I guess so sir whatever you say." The driver then pulled over and dropped me off. I could tell the congressman did not like it and on the way out of the van, he said, "nice talking to you Sergeant Dunn, I hope to see you again sometime." Maj. Gen. Byrnes just gave me an evil look and nodded to the driver to take off. The walk wasn't bad. What was bad was when I reached the main gate, the guards just looked at me and said, "don't you know it is dangerous to be walking out there alone sergeant". I looked at them and said, "Tell that to Maj. Gen. Byrnes, he dropped me off out here."

You see outside the gate it was unsafe, but I guess it was my lucky day and nothing happened. So I walked back to the unit where I was met by Maj. McReynolds, I told him what happened before he heard it from the horse's mouth. Maj McReynolds said, "Sergeant Dunn now I know the whole 1st Cavalry Division hates you." I told him, 'yes sir, but I am still loyal to you," he just laughed and said, 'let's go to the mess hall and get some of that good chow." I looked at him and said, "Surely you must be kidding sir."

I also worked with most of the coalition forces; my favorite was the Turkish Brigade and their commander Captain Idimir. Along with Spec. Valentine we created a great friendship with him, and his soldiers. When you approach a Turkish tent, you did not just walk in. They had two guards at the front and back of each tent, especially the one where the commander was or any of his officers. You had to gain permission to get in. Also in the Turkish Army, you did what you were told, there was no arguing, once you were given an order, you did not question it. They moved as a whole Brigade, when one soldier went to chow they all went in a formation. Their commander was versed in terrorism and Special Operation Tactics. I have to say I admired their discipline. Capt. Idimir, always ask for me and Spec. Valentine when he wanted a story. I learned a great deal from him and he gave us both his berets when he left Bosnia. I never served with a better coalition force in my career and they treated me and Spec. Valentine like we were one of their own.

I had a chance to work close with the Russians too. I was skeptical of them, but learned to get along with them and we even did a little trading once in a while. They were rough and sometimes even went beyond being tough. I remember going to one of their special forces demonstrations at Camp Ugulvic. It was in the middle of February and it was damn cold. There were about 20 Russian Special Forces soldiers and they all took off their shirts in sub zero weather. Then they set up their demonstration. They first lit stacks of bricks on fire with gasoline and broke them with their foreheads. Then they proceeded to take old vodka bottles they used to light the fires. When the bottles were empty they broke them over their head too. If that wasn't enough they did hand to hand combat with knives and pogo sticks. They would literally hit each other for real. Then they would take clay roof shingles and break them with their bare hands. They would put center blocks on their head and stomach while another soldier would break them in half with a sledge hammer. I saw one Russian soldier lay on the ground while two others dropped five bayonets in him. He literally stood up and pulled them out while blood was coming out of his chest and stomach. One Russian soldier walked right over to us and took two nine inch nails and shoved them up both sides of his nose. Then he picked up a light bulb and ate it. I know this sounds hard to believe, but I have a video of the whole thing and it was real. I looked over at another sergeant and said, "We are pretty good till we run out of bullets," he just laughed. I would never want to fight one of them hand to hand, it would be certain suicide. The Russians were war hard like the Serbs and you could tell it. They were in great shape, underpaid, and they just did not care. Killing and pain came natural to them.

The Turkish soldiers you did not talk shit to them either, because they could back it up. We have the advantage because of technology, but I would not want to get into hand to hand combat with them either. As an American soldier, I am glad we use our brains and not always our bodies.

The British were also good to work with. A lot of them had been to Northern Ireland and they said they would much rather be in Bosnia then there. I could relate to that after my short visit to Northern Ireland on leave when I was stationed in New York City. Most coalition forces had more freedom than we did. They were allowed to drink.

One of our soldiers a female, Spec Hester who worked for Master Sgt. Dilbert got into some serious trouble. I told him about her and her lack of accountability more than once. One night just clowning around, she pulled a knife on another female soldier over a male soldier they had both been seeing. I saw the incident and talked to her about it. What I did not know was Capt. Barren saw it too and he reported her to the 1st Calvary Division MP's. He was a rat and I never trusted him. He was attached to our unit, but would give you up in a heartbeat or as we use to say throw you under the bus.

She got an Article 15 and forfeiture of a month's pay. I tried to go to bat for her. They told me after making my statement that I might have to stay in Bosnia for three more weeks to see if they wanted to court martial her. They held her under base arrest after we left to go home. The sad thing about all of this was Sergeant Dilbert did not care enough about his soldier and Capt. Barren acted as a Judas in turning one of our own soldiers over to the 1st Cavalry Division for disciplinary action. After we got back, I personally took an interest in going to get her with Maj. McReynolds's permission. He told me to make sure to get her and her weapon and come right back. I was on permissive TDY and I used a government van to go and get her at Fort Benning, Ga.

After returning her to Fort Jackson, SC, she went to another unit, and guess who ended up at that unit too, yes Capt Barren. Boy what a double whammy for her. I heard she got out of the Army.

Another particular incident comes to mind. Maj. Hensley, who was dogged by Col. Coward, got his canteens pissed in and topped off by him. I was told by a friend of mine Staff Sgt. Tom Hovie at the CPIC. I knew Sergeant Hovie and he was a jokester too. I honestly think he was telling the truth, Col. Coward deserved it. I recently saw Master Sgt. Hovie in Salem, OR. He and I had a little fun rafting and talking about Bosnia.

As time was drawing nearer to leave this hell hole. I recall the 1st Cavalry Division sending home their big plastic Horse Trigger and their big rock they had put in the middle of the road before they sent home their own soldiers. The 1st Cavalry Division was only here six months and we were here for nine months. We saw them come and go. It was good to see the whole Robert Duvall Apocalypse Now production pack up and leave. The 10th Mountain Division from Fort Drum, New York was taking over and they brought in sledgehammers and knocked ever 1st Cavalry Division sign down they could see and painted over all of. They even tore up the cleaning boot troughs they left behind, with the little wooden cowboys on them and there wasn't a Stetson or spur to be found. I also pitched in and helped, I told them it was my pleasure. We battled them and now everything they left behind was being destroyed, what we could not throw away we burned. They hated them more than we did and they were ready to set up shop. I just wish we could have been with the 10th Mountain Division.

I felt I had been here so long it seemed like a prison sentence. Being the only Active duty soldier in the unit once we got back, I knew my work was cut out for me. I knew we had a lot of work to do just to get back home. I arranged for the buses which would drive us back to Tsar Hungary for our out processing. We also had to do what was called the "Right Seat Ride." This is where the next unit coming in was trained up to take over our mission.

They were a National Guard unit from my home state of Kentucky. Also the 314th Press Camp Headquarters our higher headquarters were there to replace those leaving the CPIC. They wanted to take over and we wanted to leave. We did a lot of good things and I could not help thinking about the children, the refugee camps, and how lucky we were to be American Soldiers. Kosovo was starting to heat up after all this, but, with all the internal problems we had with the 1st Calvary Divisions, we still were able to make a difference and this is what counted. Things were getting better for the people of Bosnia and now our soldiers were ready to go back to their families.

 I got off the bus back at Tsar and for the first time in a long time I felt really happy. One of the funniest things happened when I got there. I saw Capt, Harmon, he was a crazy and I liked him. He told, me "Sergeant Dunn, the 1st Cavalry Division may have cancelled our trip to Sarajevo, but they can't stop us from going home." He was referring to a time when we were going to get two days rest and relaxation R and R. Once they found out we were going together they cancelled it just for spite. I and he use to call the place Evil Base, because he had to deal with and hated the 1st Cavalry Division as much as me. We use to call them "The Dallas Cowboys." He told me he wanted me to see something. I knew it had to be funny. I said, "Ok sir lets go see it." It was a broomstick with a 1st Calvary Division yellow and black flag hanging on it. Their patch was circled in red with a red line right through the middle of it upside down. Below were the words written "The Bastard Step Children of the 1st Calvary Division?" We took a picture together with it and put up our middle fingers. We took it to his tent and hung it on the outside next to our unit guide on, so everyone in the camp could see it when they passed by. Maj. McReynolds even got a kick out of it, but said, "Sergeant Dunn you are a crazy NCO and I can't take you anywhere without some trouble happening." It caused quite a stir and we finally had to take it down when the Tsar Base commander didn't laugh. It was a good thing no one told who did it. The best thing about being in Tsar was there was no mud and the food was better, but I could not wait to get a real home cooked meal and see my bed, this was still my fantasy, just the simple things you take for granite.

Next it was Hohenfels, Germany, nicknamed "Hole in Hell." Unlike most of Germany, which is one of the best countries I had ever been in. This place was an isolated out processing base camp. We were out of Bosnia, but it would still be at least another week before we actually got home. I had over 110 days of annual leave built up and I knew I could not take one day until this was completely over.

Tower Airlines again and heading back to Fort Benning Ga for our final physicals and final out processing. It was a nervous time for all of us being away so long. There was Maj. Gen. Mayo from our command to welcome us home with some of his staff. All the sudden, I see Spec. Valentine come running down the stairs exiting the plane; I thought what's wrong with him. Then he fell on his knees right in front of Maj. Gen. Mayo and literally kissed the ground over and over.

Then he raised his hands like Willem Dafoe in "Platoon" and said "Thank God I am back in America." I laughed again and thought this is what it is like to truly appreciate the best country in the world. Maj. Gen. Mayo, who I knew from my days in the 81st ARCOM in

Atlanta as the chief of staff and my senior rater, thanked us all and told us how proud the command was of us. We stayed in the exact same billets we had right before we left. We were finally allowed to drink, and general order number one was over, funny thing was no one felt like it or thought about it, but me and Spec. Valentine did go out and get a beer.

We turned in LBE and equipment to the Clothing Issue Facility (CIF).If you lost anything they would make you pay for it. I had to go buy a $2.49 first aid pouch at Fort Benning Clothing and Sale before they would clear out my clothing record.

I also found out during my physical now that I was 40 years old, I had to have a rectal exam. Maj, McReynolds, just laughed when he saw me come out of the doctor's office. "Ok sir; laugh it up, bend over your next." I figured I had been taking it in the ass all these years in the Army, what made a difference now here at Fort Benning.

This was the final leg of the journey and we were finally on our way home. The bus driver asked us if we wanted to stop and eat on the way. We all replied, just stop when we get to Fort Jackson. This is how fast we wanted to get home. When our bus arrived back at Fort Jackson, we were rolling down Jackson Blvd., I looked up and there by the flag pole in front of the Floyd Spence Army Reserve Center was my wife, son right where I had left them nine months ago, and a lot of other family members to include the media. It was a magical moment with a lot of feeling I can't even explain it. I was the last one off the bus with the commander in front of me. Then I reached and grabbed one of my extra dog tags to give to my son. The day I left I gave him one and told him when I came back I would give him the other. I held it in my hand and ran to my wife Telena. We hugged and kissed for what felt like an eternity. Then I reached down and hugged my son Donald and handed him the other dog tag. It was a moment between a father and son. I left he was eight and now he was nine and had grown up some more. It was one of the happiest days of my life. We also had to turn in our weapons and gear. I was the last one to leave the center. I took all the weapons, locked them in the arms room. I then took my wife and sons hand and left the center, now I was home.

After 270 days a lot of things change and go through your mind, your wife, your son, and your family. The real world is in the rear and you have been isolated from that for a long time. It is a major adjustment and you can't just walk back in and take over, because you have not been there. It is stressful and it takes a lot of time. Some soldiers even got divorced; there are also those spouses who just can't take it. Soldiers and deployments are hard on everyone. My wife did a good job taking care of my son while I was gone. We made it through all this and I feel lucky to still have my wife and the relationship with my son, he is a great kid and I am grateful for them sticking by me. The Army is a lot of things to me, but my family is still the most important part. I called my parents and wife's parents too. They came up to see me and it was great to finally be back from Bosnia.

One of the greatest things happened after I was home. I got a call from a person named Tommy Devine, who I wrote to about trying to help get a few of the up and coming country music singers to go to Bosnia. He told me that he and Tommy Barnes, a song writer who has written songs for Willie Nelson, Hank Williams Jr., Little Texas and a lot of other country music singers wanted to host a Honky Tonk Heroes show for the soldiers still in Bosnia. He asked me if I wanted to go to Nashville and be a part of it. "I said, "why, hell yes," He laughed and told me it would be at the end of April and for me to bring my family. So I took some leave and headed to Nashville. It was great, not only did they have a show; they also sent over 10.000 CDs and T-shirts to Bosnia for the soldiers. They also sent over a video tape of the show to Armed Forces Network (AFN). They sent all this over for the soldiers to have, to show how much they appreciated what they were doing for peacekeeping mission.The show had a lot of local talent and created a big interest for support. There was not only Tommy Barnes and Tommy Devine. There was Tracey Houston, Jesse Wilson, Joni Denise, and many others. The show lasted over four hours and Tommy Barnes personally thanked me for writing him. I told him I was just trying to help the soldiers. He said, "Well I know you wrote a whole lot of people." He also joked and said, unlike those officers and generals in Washington eating steak dinners. I know you did this one on your own." I also made sure each singer and participant in the show got a letter of appreciation from the Army.

 Last, but not least, shortly after going to Bosnia, I had to go to Fort Hood to do a few things for our redeployment, the home of the 1st Cavalry Division. I like to go to the museums see them. While in the museum on Fort Hood, I saw a few pictures that I and some of my soldiers took. I also noticed below the pictures there were no credits to us. As an Army photojournalist, this is a slap in the face. They now have pictures in the Fort Hood Museum that we as a unit took and we did not even get credit for it. I brought this up to the museum director who said there was nothing they could do about it. I thought it was bad enough serving with these glory boys and now they take all the credit.

319TH MOBILE PUBLIC AFFAIRS DETACHMENT
FORT JACKSON
COLUMBIA, SOUTH CAROLINA
1997-2003
PART II

Two months after Bosnia, I took my family on vacation for a month in June 1999. I made sure the unit was back up to par. I had over 110 days of leave so I took 30 days and we drove from South Carolina to California in a rented Dodge Durango. This trip was also about being in Bosnia. You see when I was in Bosnia I wrote a movie star named Wings Hauser. He wrote me back and sent me his Sobriety Coin and told me to hang in there. He also wanted the coin back after the deployment was over. So instead of mailing it back, I thought I would personally take it to him. While, out in Marina Del Rey, Ca, I looked him up. He lived on a Yacht there. I did a little wheeling and dealing and talked the dock owner into calling him. It just so happened he was there. He wanted to know who I was and what I wanted; I told him it was something he wanted back. He reluctantly came down to the dock and met me, my wife, and son. He did not have a clue what to expect. I walked up to him and introduced myself and shook his hand with the coin in my hand. After shaking my hand he saw the coin. His eyes lit up and he then realized who I was. I said, "Wings, here is something that belongs to you." he said, "Sergeant Dunn, Bosnia."

"That's right; you wanted the coin back so I decided to bring it to you personally while I am here on vacation." He said, "Well I don't have to ask how you and your family are doing, I see you made it back." Then we talked for about an hour and he introduced me to his wife Daphne. He talked about his son Cole Hauser who is also an actor in Hollywood. It seems there is this movie where a soldier leaves for war and is given a coin and when he returns he gives the coin back. I don't know the name of the movie, but this was Wings reason for sending me the coin. I still write him every once in a while. I told him recently that I had retired and he said, "I guess the old dog had to finally give up his bone."

Back to the unit, it was now August 1999. When I got some bad news from my mother, Peggy Dunn, it seems my father; Donald Dunn Sr. was doing some funny things around the house. He also was forgetting a lot of little things, and he had a minor accident in the car. My mother started getting suspicious about his behavior when he got lost coming home from church one evening. She took him to his doctor where they did a series of test. The bad news came out; he was in the early stages of Alzheimer's. He was only 65 years old and just retired. Things started getting worse little by little. We started realizing he needed to be watched more and I started coming home on leave more to help when I could. For now, I was in the Army and had to make the best of it and help my mother, when I could.

The unit was also scheduled for another Annual Training Mission. We were going to the National Training Center at Fort Irwin Ca. Then to top it off, I was asked by Maj. Loring at the 314th PCH to cover the United States Army Reserve Small Arms Competition in Ottawa

Canada. I took the assignment for two weeks and went to Canada. The competition was between the U.S. Army and the Canadian Army. The Queens Medal at the end would go only to the Canadians, because it was their competition and the U.S. Army was invited to see how they would fare against them. We beat them. The competition was fierce and it included the best snipers and spotters the Army had to offer. It was hot on the ranges and I got stung by a few bees. It gave me the opportunity to work directly with Canadian Soldiers. We did a little trading with our Meals Ready to Eat (MREs) and their meals. I have to admit their field rations were better than ours. I also got to go into Ottawa the capital and see the Changing of the Guard. At the end of the competition the Canadian Small Arms Team took their best soldier with the Queens Medal and hoisted him upon a big wooden chair. With soldiers on both sides they carried him down the street to their headquarters, while bouncing him up and down along the way. It was like watching an Egyptian King being carried to a temple. I had a chance to meet some Eskimos from way up north in Canada. One Eskimo tried to sell me a polar bear skin. It was huge and the price was right, but I knew it would be trouble trying to get it over the Canadian Border back to the United States.

Another great opportunity came in the August of 1999. One of my soldiers was also an Artist named Spec. Denis was invited to bring some of his artwork to a three day Rock 'n' Roll concert for charity. He invited me and I jumped at the chance. The event was called Itchycoo Park after the famous Park in England. I was there as a photographer and they also liked the fact that two soldiers were there.

I was able to bring my son Donald III, who was nine at the time, the bad part was my wife had to work, but she did not mind us going together for three days. Talk about an all star line up of classic rockers. I met Christopher Cross, Doug Gray of the Marshall Tucker Band, Sammy Hagar, Eric Bloom and Buck Dharma of Blue Oyster Cult, Dave Mason of Traffic, John Kay of Steppenwolf, Iron Butterfly, Mark Farner of Grand Funk Railroad, David Clayton Thomas of Blood Sweat and Tears, Tommy Shaw and James Young of Styx, Dewey Bunnell and Gerry Beckley of America, John Entwistle of The Who, Mickey Thomas of Jefferson Starship, Buddy Cox and Mitch Mitchell who use to be in The Jimi Hendrix Band of Gypsy's, Paul Rogers of Bad Company, Pat Travers, Benjamin Orr of The Cars, Walter Egan, Joey Molland and Bad Finger. There was also a 1964 Tribute to the Beatles, others there were Mickey Dolenz, Peter Noone of Hermits Hernits, Felix Cavalier of the Rascals, and Joan Jett. It was almost like a Woodstock concert in a field in Manchester, Tenn. I remember sitting down to lunch and eating right next to John Entwistle of The Who. What a great Bass player, it was a shame that a few years later he was found dead at the Hard Rock Cafe Hotel in Las Vegas, NV. I also was invited into the tour bus with Benjamin Orr of the Cars and we talked about the Army. He was in the Army for a few years and wanted to do some shows for the soldiers overseas. I tried to help with talking to the USO, but nothing ever materialized. He had a new band and most of them were prior Air Force service members. We did stay in touch until he died from Pancreatic Cancer a few years later. I heard he played until he had to be carried off the stage at one point at a concert in Alaska. I also had supper with Mickey Thomas of Jefferson Starship, his drummer leaned over to me and said, "here you go Sarge have a couple of drumsticks on me." Pat Travers was real nice too; he invited us in his tour bus and talked with me and my son for a long time. Buddy Cox was great to talk too, after all he had served in the Army with Jimi Hendrix at Fort Campbell. We talked about the Army, Jimi and the legacy he left behind as probably the greatest guitarist who ever lived. I enjoyed the music and getting to meet some of my heroes, but I was also astonished at how they wanted to know more about the Army and how they could find a way to play for the soldiers.

Another great TDY assignment, the Army needed some public affairs soldiers to go cover Operation Northern Edge 2000 in Alaska and work with the Marines, Air Force, Navy and even the Coast Guard, in a joint services operation. The mission was working with Russian soldiers and Canadian Soldiers. This time the mission was a scenario was of the Russian Army coming over the Barren Strait and how this would be played out in Alaska.

I and Spec. Robert Valentine who I had worked with in Bosnia both volunteered in what proved to be a great three weeks. We arrived in Anchorage Alaska. The first thing we noticed getting off the plane was this huge 8 to 10 foot Kodiak bear in a glass case. We then found our contact; Air Force Tech Sergeant Howard and we went to Fort Richardson. He got us checked into our billets for the night.

The next day at Alaskan Command we met up with another Tech Sergeant named Neely. She showed us around and we had a few briefings on what we would be doing. Then we went and picked up some gear and winter uniforms from supply. She took me and Spec. Valentine to the Airport on Fort Richardson to show us where we would be working we met Maj. Monroe who was in charge. We walked into a big room already set up with Laptops, phones, and desks. Everything was well thought out and organized. Maj. Monroe showed me the vehicle I would be driving here. I was expecting a Humvee, but what I got was a new red Ford Explorer fully equipped with four wheel drive. Me and Valentine looked at each other and said, "Sweet.".

Our first day, we all got our assignments. Spec. Valentine was going to be working here and in Juneau, covering some off shore operations. I was staying here in the Press Camp Headquarters at the Airport, but I also got an assignment to work with Canadians, Russians, and I was going to cover the Iditarod, dog sled race. Later I was put on a Chinook Helicopter with a few Marines and we headed up to Wallah to cover a jump. Spec. Valentine got some great photos and I wrote the story.

Next, we worked with the Canadians. We went with them on one of their surveillance flights. They flew that plane every way but right. I started getting sick. I had never been air sick before, but this was not an ordinary flight. I had to go to the back of the plane twice and throw up. I could see Spec. Valentine and the crew laughing at me while they videotaped me. We landed I threw up one more time.

Back at the office, we heard one of the Marines in the operation got caught drunk driving up in Fairbanks. I and Spec. Valentine had met this young Sergeant Jenkins once and knew he was trouble. We were at dinner the first night and noticed he was drinking a pitcher of beer straight from the pitcher without a glass. I told Spec. Valentine, this Marine is headed for trouble. There is always someone who ruins it for everybody else. He thought he was on vacation, until they called his gunnery sergeant to come and get him all the way from Japan. The rest of the Marines were not happy. They pride themselves on being the best, but one of their own let them down. He had lied about why he needed the vehicle the day before. He told Maj. Monroe he was finishing up a story in Fairbanks. When he was really up there finishing off a 12 pack and got pulled over by the police and was now in jail. The next day on the accountability board in our office beside his name Spec. Valentine had put the word jail. It was a joke that got a lot of laughs, but the Marines did not think it was funny. They left the Marine in jail until his gunnery sergeant arrived a few days later. Then he was taken back to Japan and court martial.

Next, I got to cover the Iditarod and being it was the year 2000, it was special. They even brought truck loads of snow into the streets of Anchorage where the race was to begin. I thought this was funny, because I had seen snow many a time removed from the street, but I had never seen it put on the street. The race was going from downtown Anchorage, 1100 miles to downtown Nome. There were 85 teams and it cost each team at least $40,000 dollars with sponsorship just to get in. Every stop had to be calculated along the way. Each team had at least 25 dogs and they had to be watched over, taken care of, and fed. These team owners love their dogs and their dogs love to run. I had the opportunity to drive a sled team one mile and to ride shotgun for another mile. It was exciting and I got to do it. I fell one time. I did not get hurt bad, but I lost my watch and sprained my wrist. The rest of the way I made sure I did not fall again. The dogs know exactly who they are partnered up with and if you mix the dogs wrong, they will fight each other. The weather on these trails is unforgiving. If you make mistakes or get lost you can die, this is not just any race it is a race against time and the elements. I also got to eat some Caribou Stew at one of the check points, which was run by the Veterans of Foreign Wars (VFW).

I got to walk on a glacier. Also the days in Alaska never gets dark even at night. You can see for miles and the northern lights and all the stars are crystal clear in the sky. The sad thing was the three weeks here were coming to an end. I and Spec. Valentine did a lot of stories and we got to see America's last great frontier. I saw Spec. Valentine a few years ago. He was out of the Army. I was in his office where he works for Nissan, as a car salesman in Columbia, SC. On the wall was a huge picture of the soldiers jumping out of the plane in the Alaskan red sky. We both smiled and laughed; it brought back the memories of what we achieved working together as friends and soldiers.

A great story came while I was sitting at my desk back at Fort Jackson after Alaska; Mr. Grace who was a DA Civilian for a Civil Affairs unit asked me if I would do a story on a Colonel in his unit. He told me about Colonel Thomas Boland. He was an Army Reserve officer and a state attorney for South Carolina and he was going to go to jump school down at Fort Benning, Ga. What made this story special was the colonel was 57 years old. Jump school is hard and especially if you are that old trying to do it. I said "yes, I will do it." I called down to Fort Benning to the jump school and talked with one of the jump masters. He told me if Col. Boland makes it he would be the oldest soldier to ever to do it. I enjoyed working with Col. Boland. He ran over 100 miles a week getting ready. The young soldiers at jump school called him grandpa, till one of the instuctors said, "Well if grandpa makes it and you don't, then what does that say about you." Sure enough he made it through the one month course. Guess what, yes there were many young soldiers who did not make it. I contacted Soldiers Magazine and the Article was printed in the November 2000 issue. Jimmy Carter, the former President of the United States came down personally to Fort Benning and pinned Colonel Boland's jump wings on him. It was a big deal. Col. Boland was now the oldest soldier to complete jump school and I was lucky enough to have exclusively covered the story. I asked Col. Boland why he wanted to do it. He told me, "Well sergeant Dunn, I did just about everything I could do in my career. I thought I would go ahead and finally go to jump school. I wanted to finish my career off with something special." He also did charity work for the children in Bosnia sending shoeboxes full of small toys. As far as I know he is still the oldest soldier to finish jump school at Fort Benning, Ga.

Soon after George Bush Jr. was elected the 43rd President of the United States, his wife Laura Bush made a visit to Fort Jackson, SC. She was here to visit Hood Street Elementary School where my son attended. She promoted Troops to Training Program. Soldiers, who left the Army, could also be used as teachers. I took a four man public affairs team from the unit to cover it. She went in every classroom to include my son's sixth grade class. He said he was nervous when she talked to him.

She then spoke in front of the school; she really cared about education and soldiers. I had the opportunity of having my picture taken with her and she signed an autograph card for me, what a great classy lady.

I was a stringer for some upcoming concerts on Post. I got to meet the Commodores, Bad Company, and Tanya Tucker. I did not mind helping the post paper and it was a fun. They also appreciated the stories.

I am a huge fan of stock car racing, and I decided to do what I could on my own to get involved in what I think is America's greatest sport. NASCAR, and they heavily supported the military. I started getting around the garages of tracks and talking to the drivers about the Army. It was amazing and I was able to work and do some stories and they wanted to get involved with the military. One of the first drivers I had an opportunity to work with was Ward Burton. He was the only NASCAR driver who had a commission as a First Lieutenant in the Army and was a graduate from Hargrove Military Academy in Chatham, Va. He was also the school's top rifle marksman. He recently won the 2002 Daytona 500. I ironically also worked with a supply sergeant named Ronnie Brewer and he told at one time he raced with him and his brother Jeff Burton.

I got a great idea for a story, I called up Heidi Stoddard, Ward Burton's Public Relations person at Bill Davis Racing and seen if I could do a story on him and Sergeant. Brewer. It was the race in Darlington, SC; I set up the story myself and even took some of my personal leave to cover it. I also persuaded Sergeant Brewer's unit to let him go with me for the story. We went to the track and I got the credentials we needed. After that I met up with Ward in his hauler. He looked at Sergeant Brewer and right away he knew who he was. Then they talked and I did the interview with both of them together. One of the questions I asked Ward was, "if you were ordered to active duty and told you had to go to Afghanistan today, would you leave NASCAR and go?" his answer was, "You damn right I would Sergeant Dunn. My biggest regret is when I came to NASCAR was I never got to go on active duty and become a true American Patriot. There are a lot of my classmates who I still talk with today who are serving. It is something that was built into me." I then looked at him and pulled a new black Army beret out of my pocket with a 1st Lieutenant Silver Bar on it and gave it to him. He thanked me and looked at me like I had given him a race trophy. He put it on and headed out of the hauler for afternoon practice. The funny thing was he got into his #22 Caterpillar sponsored car and still had it on till a NASCAR official told him he needed to put his helmet on. He went out to practice with the beret still in the car. Sergeant Brewer looked over at me and said, "He will always remember you giving him that beret Sergeant Dunn." I told him, "I was glad you came with me and did this story." On the way out of the garage we ran into Bobby Labonte and Sergeant Brewer knew him too. They talked for a while; they both had gone to Trinity High School together in Trinity, NC. The story was put in the upcoming edition of Army Reserve Magazine and got a two page double truck spread. I remember Sergeant Brewer coming over to me back at the Army Reserve Center and telling me how much he appreciated me doing the story. I told him, "I'm glad you like it, it is not every day I get to meet a true celebrity in the Army." He just laughed and went back to his unit's supply room. The last thing he said to me was, "it was a sweet ride while it lasted."

    I had the chance to work with Mike Skinner another NASCAR driver; he drove one of the first Army cars at Lowes Motor Speedway in Charlotte, NC. The #31 Lowe's Chevy, the car had eagles, Army tanks and stars and stripes all over it. It was very patriotic looking. When it came off the hauler; I was the only soldier there. I was surprised and disappointed, because after all this was a big deal and a lot of people will see this car on Memorial Day. I talked with two news reporters by from The Charlotte Observer. The questions were just about the car. My interview was seen on the 6 p.m. news that night.

Another young NASCAR Busch Series Driver I had a chance to work with was Brian Vickers. Just barely out of high school. He was also at Lowes Motor Speedway. He was only18 years old, but he was already showing promise as a good young driver. At the time he posted a top ten in qualifying. I was doing a story for the newspaper at Fort Jackson, "The Leader." Upon entering the garage I saw him driving a number 40 car, it was black with eagles and the word Army written in gold on the rear quarter panels. So I went over and checked it out. I ran into his Public Relations person named Dave Goodman. While I was talking to Dave, a woman came out and told me she was his mother. Her name was Ramona Vickers; she introduced me to Brian after practice had ended. He told me he had some sponsorship, but wanted the Army to help if they would come on board as his primary sponsor. Another words he was helping the Army without true sponsorship. I admired this about him. He also told me his grandfather had served in the Army and he wanted to do his part by racing this car. I thought another great story; after all we are always trying to recruit kids between the ages of 18 and 24.

This kid was clean cut and very nice and he fit the description for what could be a great story for recruiting.

So I talked with him a while, took some pictures and started working on a story. I thought this kid could be just what we needed to attract good young people to enlist in the Army. I was able to get the story in "The Leader." A few weeks later, I got a call from Mr. Goodman, who was also a master sergeant in the National Guard. He said, "Sergeant Dunn, Brian wants you to take some pictures for his website. Then he asked me to meet him at Bristol, TN for another race. I was overjoyed, because I loved NASCAR and this was another opportunity to tell more about his involvement in the Army. I took some more of my personal leave. I did not mind using my leave, getting to do Army stories at NASCAR races.

I was then asked to go to Darlington and take more pictures. This time I was able to get one of my soldiers Spec. Remson, who also worked at a local television station in Columbia, SC., to come along. He had missed a few drills and I was able to get him to come with me to make up some of his time he owed the Army Reserve. Spec. Remson was a broadcast journalist and we took one of the unit's beta video cameras to do some interviews. After I took some pictures for Brian's website, it started to rain; I knew this would be a great opportunity for me and Spec. Remson to get some good stand up interviews on tape. I talked to Kerry Earnhardt; he is the oldest son of the late great Dale Earnhardt. I remember him saying, "I wish I could be there with you guys, but I want you all over in Bosnia to know we are thinking about you, and want you all to come home safe." I talked with Richard Childress, the man who owned Dale Earnhardt Sr.' cars, He said, "I want to thank all of you for letting me do what I do. If it was not for you I would not be able to be in NASCAR as an owner." I also talked with many other drivers, to include; Jeff Gordon, Dale Earnhardt Jr.,

Jimmie Johnson, Ryan Newman, Kevin Harvick, Tim and Johnny Sauter. Another great interview was with Richard Petty's son Kyle Petty. He said, "We use to just look at soldiers, now we know they are our protectors. We just drive around in pretty painted cars; they drive around in Humvee's taking care of our freedoms. I want all of you to know that we appreciate what you do." Another great quote came from Morgan Shepherd, he said, "This is the greatest country and it is because of the soldiers. Also I want you all to know God and Jesus loves you and I am proud of you." I sent the tape to Bosnia for the soldiers the next day. I wanted them to know they had the support of NASCAR.

Like all good things this had to come to an end. I was told I could not cover NASCAR on my personal leave, because let's just say some false accusations were made about me and how I did it. I was told if I was not on orders then it could not be done. Of course Sergeant Dilbert and his new buddy, my new commander Maj. Strickland were all over me. You see good ideas are not always met with good results in the Army. There is jealousy. I was told if I did it again, I would be disciplined. Specialist Remson, said, "I think it is a shame sergeant Dunn, "I'm sorry they feel like that, I thought it was a great idea and story and the soldiers loved the tape you sent them." Well, I told him, what can they really do to me? After all it is like Sgt. Brewer said it was a sweet ride while it lasted."

After all this, America was attacked by terrorist on 9 September 2001. I was sitting in my office looking over my emails for the day. I started hearing loud noises in the other room, I heard this banging on the wall and my name being called. It was Staff Sgt. Spears. He had an old black and white television in his office, which he rarely used, but it was on that day. I went over to see what was going on. I saw several soldiers around the television talking. I said, "What's going on sergeant Spears," He looked at me and said, "An airplane just hit the World Trade Center." I said, "What! let me see." It was right then that another plane came into view and it hit the other tower. I had been stationed in New York City and I had been in the World Trade Center many times dropping off things from public affairs at the 77th Army Reserve Command. I could not believe what I was seeing; both World Trade Center Towers were engulfed in flames. Then the phones started ringing all over the Army Reserve Center. It was like, "Oh shit." I had two phones and I could hear both of them ringing. It was Maj. Perez at my higher headquarters the 314th Public Affairs Press Camp headquarters. "He said, listen carefully Sergeant Dunn, The country has been attacked and we are in the process of trying to figure out what to do next." I said, "Ok sir, what do you want me to do." he went on to say, "don't talk to any outside media if they call you, till we get a plan together. Then I got word that the Pentagon had been hit by another airplane. Then word came to us about a plane that had gone down in Shanksville, Pennsylvania. America had never been attacked before on our own soil, except in WWII at Pearl Harbor in Hawaii. Outside I could see soldiers running to the gates of the post and MP's were everywhere. We locked down our building and posted guards at all doors. I went to the unit safe and got the arms room keys, just in case I needed to get in there right away. Later we watched as the World Trade Center Towers fell. I could not believe what I was seeing on the TV. We watched as people ran and others jumped to their death out of those towers.

We were told to go home and see about our families and to stay by the phone for further instructions. Then come back the next day. I ran to my truck and headed to my wife's work and sons school. All the students were all outside waiting for someone to pick them up. I picked Donald up and explained to him what had just happened. My son said to me, "does this mean you will go to war." I said, "It is possible." I also explained to him about terrorism what had happened.

After just coming back from Bosnia a couple of years ago, I knew it would not be too long and I would be in the Middle East. I went and got my full American Flag. At the Floyd Spence Army Reserve Center where I worked on Fort Jackson, there was a flag pole with no flag on it. We were told a year before that we could not fly the flag, because the post commander at the time in his infinite wisdom said the only flag to fly on post was the one at his headquarters. There was also this memo put out by the JAG and it was in the Reserve Center Standard Operating Procedure (SOP). The flag at one time was flown, but there were complaints about it being a burden on the ones putting it up and down every day. A female civilian where we worked had this done. I always thought this was plain and simple bullshit. If there is a flag pole in front of an Army Reserve Center, then by damn there ought to be a flag on it, period! Well, you should have seen the faces the next day when I personally went out to that flag pole and put a new American Flag up. After all Floyd Spence, who the center was named for, was a retired Naval officer and congressman. I thought it should have never come down. Some of the Department of Army civilians did not like it, but I did not hear one word out of the soldiers. Staff Sgt. Spears, Staff Sgt. Tolley, and Sgt. Haig were the first to come up to me and say, "Sergeant Dunn, it looks good and it should have been put up a long time ago before this." I thought to myself, it was a shame that it took this to realize it.

All went well for about two months, and then a few of the civilians. They went to none other than Mr. Dilbert who thought he was my boss. He also told me as a civilian he was equal to a 3rd Lieutenant. I told him, "Can you show me this in the regulations." Of course he could not show me this, because there are no 3rd Lieutenants in the Army. He might have been a Master Sergeant on drill weekends, but other than that he was in a civilian capacity. I was always a soldier, and he is not my boss when he is not in a uniform, But at drill or AT. Mr. Dilbert did not know shit about shit, I was an active duty soldier period.

Mr. Dilberts's first mistake was when he came up to me in front of Staff Sgt. Spears and Sgt. Haig, who are good NCO's and also my friends. He started popping his mouth off about the flag and then he ordered me to take it down. "I told him no, I will not take the flag down till the end of the day." Then he threatened to give me an Article 15 for disobeying a direct order. I flat out told him, "You do not have the authority to give me an Article 15." Mr. Dilbert said, "we will see about that Sergeant Dunn." Then I walked away. Staff Sgt. Spears and Sgt. Haig, both wrote me sworn statements on what he said to me. Then, two officers in the 360th Civil Affairs unit signed them as true documents.

Mr. Dilbert went crying off to the commander, Capt. Strickland, his buddy. Now I got along good with Maj.

McReynolds when he was commander, but Capt. Strickland and Mr. Dilbert were tight. I did my job and I was trained in Public Affairs, these two were just infantry and chemical soldiers who thought they knew public affairs. It took Mr. Dilbert two times at the school and four years just to get trained in a two week short course in public affairs to even justify his slot in the unit. I also never cried to officers as an NCO. Nothing is worse than a soldier crying up the chain of command. Capt Strickland was put in the unit because he was separated from his Infantry unit at Fort Benning. He was put in the unit because our higher headquarters the 314th Press Camp could not find a quick replacement for Maj. McReynolds who was promoted to Lieutenant Colonel and moved to another unit.

When I came to work in the morning there was Capt. Strickland in his office waiting for me. Well, I was not going to be intimidated, he called me in with Mr. Dilbert and shut the door. He looked at me and told me to stand at attention. "I said yes sir." Then he started listening to Mr. Dilbert tell his part. I just stood there, because I knew it was not going to matter what I said, him and Mr. Dilbert they had decided on their own what they were going to try and do to me. I was well prepared, He then turned to me and said, and "Did Mr. Dilbert tell you to take down the flag"? I said "Yes." Capt. Strickland then said did you do it, I said, "No." He, said well that's it, Mr. Dilbert give Sergeant Dunn an Article 15 and also put on his counseling form to Bar him from reenlistment in the Army."

Capt. Strickland looked at me with an evil grin and said, "You know Sergeant Dunn when I was at Fort Benning back in Georgia me and another officer in my unit use to give Article 15's to soldiers just to see how many we could give out in a month, and tally then up to see who the winner was. But you will make my first one with a Bar to Reenlistment to boot. Also this will be reflected on your Enlisted Evaluation NCOER."

I looked at him and said, "Sir you might want to take a look at these two sworn statements I have from two other NCO's who were there when this happened. He looked at me and said, "I don't care what you have, I am the commander and I have made my decision on what to do." I looked at him and said, will that be all sir?" He said, just get out of my face and get out of my office." I said, "No problem sir.

I always let someone in the Army who thinks he has the upper hand shoot first. Then I know how to adjust my fire and hit the target as they say. Capt. Strickland was the commander, but he did not know the regulations governing this. He acted irrationally, but I had rights too and now I was going to the Inspector General's Office (IG) on post and talk to them.

Before I went to the IG formally, I just went and talked to them first. I wanted to see if he was bluffing and he wasn't. I got a call from the senior civilian in our command, his name was Mr. Fields, and he was Mr. Dilberts's civilian boss. Now I had met Mr. Fields a few times and he was a fair man. He wanted to hear from me on what was going on. So I told him what had happened and his reply was. Sergeant Dunn, "don't worry about this; I will have Col. Marks square them away. I had also met the colonel and he was a good officer. Later in the week Mr. Fields called me back and said, "nothing is going to happen to you, but what I want you to do is check with the post sergeant major to see if you can fly the flag and if he says yes then by all means keep the flag on the pole in front of the center."

Most people before 9/11 looked at the flag like it was just a piece of cloth and went through the motions during the singing of the National Anthem. Me, I always looked at it as a symbol of freedom for this country and everyone who fought to preserve it. Capt. Strickland was not happy; he had to drop the whole ordeal. Col. Marks told him, "Mr. Dilbert has no authority in his weekly civilian status to give Sergeant Dunn a direct order." Also to Bar a Sergeant First Class from reenlistment with over 10 years active duty takes the approval of a one star general in the command. I knew Major Gen. Mayo, and he would question this whether it was me or any other soldier in his command. Capt. Strickland was told by Col. Michaels, "If you give Sergeant Dunn a bad Enlisted Evaluation Report it will reflect on your evaluation. At this point, I wanted to be transferred from this assignment. I liked the unit and the soldiers, but the leadership was terrible and I had had enough of spanky and buck wheat.

I had support from the Sergeant Major at The Army Training and Doctrine Command (TRADOC) he agreed with me and said, "Sergeant Dunn, I fully support you. The flag should be on the pole in front of that center." Unfortunately the Fort Jackson Command Sgt. Maj. Martinez, said, Maj. Gen. Barno the post commander did not want a flag anywhere but at his headquarters. My response to this was then why is it flying at the schools and post office on Fort Jackson. Also the 81st Regional Support Command owned the building, but the post commander owned the property. I was ordered to take down the American Flag. I did and I flew it in front of my quarters on post.

The thing about all this is when Congressman Floyd Spence, who brought about the Thrift Saving Program into the military died. They flew the American Flag at the center, but as soon as he was buried it came down again. To this day there is not a flag on the pole at the Floyd Spence Army Reserve Center on Fort Jackson, SC. Recently, being retired and staying at the post on vacation I brought this to the attention of Maj. Gen. Milano, the Fort Jackson Commander and he called me a smart ass. After also talking to post Sergeant Major Stall's secretary he said he would look into it, over 12 years the flag pole is empty and in my opinion they don't care!

Back to 9/11, everything about the way we did business in the Army started to change. It all started with more security. Before then you could just ride on most Army Installations and never be stopped. We all started pulling guard duty. We checked ID cards in and out of all of our buildings. Also every building now had military vehicles in front of it, and barriers at the entrances.

It would not be long and the Army would be in Afghanistan fighting the terrorist groups Al Qaida and the Taliban, the war on terrorism began. We all started finding out real quick, which Osama Bin Laden was. Before this no one knew much about him. I had heard his name in Bosnia after the Embassies in Africa were bombed. President Clinton had the opportunity to get him, but blew it. Now my Commander in Chief George Bush Jr. was going after him and his terrorist network. I was glad we had President George Bush Jr. to spearhead this war. We had to do something about this and I don't care what anybody says about finding weapons of mass destruction. It was a weapon of mass destruction that attacked our country in those airplanes. It was now time to go to a different kind of war and I knew down the line my name would be on a set of orders. I fully agree with President Bush either you are with us or you're with the terrorist, this bunch have no regard for life, liberty and the pursuit of happiness.

A decision had to be made and President Bush Jr. made it quickly and I commend him for this. He told everyone this was going to be a different kind of war. You see we were not fighting an Army we are looking for groups of evil insurgents who want to destroy everything we believe in. Most Americans think everything should be quick and easy, drop a bomb, kill them all, but when you deploy 300,000 soldiers to a region of the world it takes time to do what is right.

By October 2001 the Army was on its way to Afghanistan. I sat in classified meetings we were told what to say and what not to say, especially to the media. My unit was now preparing for war. I had the commander's checklist and it was my job to make sure it was complete. The 314th Press Camp Headquarters sent down soldiers from each section to support us in getting ready. We knew a warning order was coming but we did not know when. Guess what, during all of this, we were additionally task to do a three week mission in Korea.

I had to plan Korea first and then the orders came down saying we were going to support Team Spirit. We were going to Camp Walker in Taegu. The mission was to support South Korean forces with public affairs. I got all our billeting and airline tickets and we were ready to move out. Our job was to provide pictures, stories, and video. Also we did media escort.

The flight took over 2 days just to get there. We made stops in Atlanta Georgia, Tacoma, Washington,

Fairbanks Alaska, and then we landed in Seoul Korea and the unit was bused to Taegu. One of the reasons the flight took so long was while we were in Atlanta we were given specific orders not to drink alcohol. Like always there is some soldier who does not obey the rules. This time it was a Staff Sergeant, who was so drunk when he got on the plane he started making sexual passes at one of the stewardesses. Then he started getting loud and out of hand. Well, this got the attention of one of the unit commanders on the plane. He was restrained till we got to Tacoma. The MP's came on board and zip locked him and dragged him off.

It was February 2002 and outside the plane it was damn cold in Tacoma, especially on an open run way. All of us had to get off the plane and stand in a formation and do an accountability check. We were not allowed to go back onto the plane until our names were called and military ID's were checked. Of course out of 250 passengers I would be one of the last ten to be called freezing my ass off. This took over 2 hours and delayed us. We also were held over due to bad weather for 4 hours before takeoff.

Next stop Fairbanks Alaska, a colder place. We got in and out of there a few hours more. We finally landed In Korea and bused to Taegu from Seoul. We met with our contacts from U.S. South Korean Command and briefed on everything from the Korean culture to the do's and don'ts. It was hard just to keep our eyes open after two days of no rest. We then set up all our video and print equipment. We had to go to a huge warehouse where a few hundred other soldiers were staying to set up our bunks.

All of us were given a briefing on assignments to various locations to cover stories and do media escort. While all this was going on I noticed we were missing a monitor. It was my job to track it down. A unit up in Seoul had it. So I had to make arrangements to get this equipment back.

Me and Capt. Halas, one of our Public Affairs officers got on a train and went to Seoul. We got up to Seoul, found the equipment and brought it back. While there I saw one of Republic of Korea (ROK) commanders; hit his next in command for making a mistake in a formation. Then I watched that soldier hit another soldier. I mean they would just walk up and literally smack the shit out of each other in their whole chain of command if that's what it took to get it right. When something happened it happened to the whole chain of command and no one was left out. The ROK soldiers would also stand on small platforms in front of each of their military headquarters for hours and would never flinch, before being relieved. I was amazed at their discipline. Back in Taegu we met with Korean politicians. A lot of time we were in civilian attire as to not let them know we were American Soldiers and just the civilian press during their briefings.

We got a little time off one day and I went with Capt. Halas, at this market I noticed something I had never seen before. There was this Korean woman whipping her daughter for something her son did. I asked one of the soldiers who was with us why she did not discipline her son. He told me, the man child is the future ruler of the family and his sister is not. You never saw a woman talk back to their husband; he was always in charge and made the decisions for the family. Korean culture was all male dominated.

I later had to deal with repacking equipment and personally getting it through customs. This is different in every country and the movement and paperwork alone would stress you out. After all this we waited on the curb by the command in the cold and caught the bus back to the airport in Seoul. Korea was a great experience and my first time in the Far East. Soldiers that get stationed there are here for one year and cannot bring their families over with them.

Back at Fort Jackson we had been given our next assignment to go and train for two weeks at the National Training Center in Fort Irwin Ca. My second time out here with a different unit, we had to support the 1st Cavalry Division again. I had to make a four day trip to good old Fort Hood again. I found out the only support we would get was a tent and MRE's to eat. Well I listened to four days of their bullshit and came back with a plan of my own. I was not going to submit my soldiers to their stupid shit again. So I got together with my higher headquarters at the 314th PCH in Birmingham, Ala., and we had enough year end money to put us up in the hotel on post. I justified it with the fact we would have sensitive equipment and needed to set up and store it there for security purposes.

We set up our press camp headquarters in one of the hotel rooms. We did our stories, video, and escort missions and we were ready to saddle up and go back to Fort Jackson. Back at the 314th PCH Lt. Col Joe Trehan was leaving and being replaced by Lt. Col McGrew as our new higher commander. I liked Lt. Col Trehan and I had known him before being assigned to the 319th MPAD. He was Commandant at the Defense Information School at Fort Benjamin Harrison, Indianapolis, IN. I worked with him during Operation Golden Medic too. I was the editor of the two week newsletter. He once saw Sergeant Dilbert giving me a hard time about the newsletter and he told him flat out. "Sergeant Dunn, reports only to me. He is the editor, what he says goes and any changes will be by me." I also respected Lt. Col Trehan, I learned from him and he let me teach a two week course at Fort Benjamin Harrison to help get soldiers MOS qualified. He knew the big picture. The sad thing was he was popular like me with the command. They used travel vouchers and his travels back and forth to Fort Benjamin Harrison to force him out. He was not a yes man and I admired that more than anything about him. He just left and took a reserve position at the school, closer to his home. He knew Army Public Affairs and could also teach it. To me he was only one of a few officers in Public Affairs that really knew the job. I like Lt. Col McGrew, but he was no Lt. Col. Trehan, he had little experience in Public Affairs. It was their loss not Lt. Col. Trehan's.

October 2002, my wife walked into my office crying and told me her dad, my father in law was dying. I got up immediately put in an emergency leave request and left. I told Mr. Dilbert, I was taking two weeks leave. He did not say a word. I did not even call Capt. Strickland, I just left. To me family is more important than the Army. All this talk about God and Country, My belief is this God, Family, and then country. Also if any of my soldiers had to be with their family, I always went out of my way to get them home in emergencies. Unfortunately it was my turn; I rushed home as fast as I could. I picked my son Donald III up from school and we were on our way back to Louisville, Ky. It was a nine hour drive and I I made it in seven. I went straight to my wife's house and everyone was at the hospital. So we rushed over to the hospital and my mother in law, Mable Shimfessel was in tears and a nervous wreck. I was close to my father in law, Frank Shimfessel. He had served in the Air Force during the Korean War and being a soldier I could talk to him and we had common ground. Frank was like a second father to me, we always talked about everything and I use to go out with him for coffee to a cottage restaurant he liked to hang out at. Even before I married his daughter he was always good to me and today I still miss him. He had a lot of mental problems, which he never got over after losing his oldest son in the Navy. Michael Shimfessel was about to get out of the Navy in the late 70's, when he was killed in a ship wreck in Barcelona, Spain. I never met him, but I remember Frank talking about him. Frank never got over this and I guess I would be the same if anything ever happened to my son.

He had a heart attack in the hallway of his house. Mable was there, when he fell. He was rushed to the hospital and was now on life support. The doctors told Mable there was no hope and she had to make the decision to take him off it through a Living Will. She asked me what I thought she should do. I told her, I see Frank, but Frank is gone. I just looked at him lying there in that hospital bed for over three days and I was hard. My mother in law made the hard decision. Me, Donald III, and Telena were all there holding hands in the hospital room along with Mable, David Shimfessel, her other son and his wife Kim and their daughter Tiffany. I watched as they unhooked everything from him and the lines on the heart monitor just went flat in less than 20 minutes. He was now gone. I was also a pallbearer at his funeral and it was an honor to carry him. He lived to be 67, but I knew him over 16 years and he was a good man.

Also during this exact time a friend of mine became very ill. Staff Sgt. Haig, he was a supply NCO for a Civil Affairs Unit. I worked with him off and on and we helped each other in getting supplies for both of our units. He was back in his supply cage, when he suddenly passed out. I thought he may have been in the heat to long, because the supply rooms were always hot in the summer with no air conditioning. I looked at him and he was turning yellow, so I called for an ambulance. Hewent directly to the post hospital, they ran tests for a few days. It was discovered that he had Leukemia.

Sergeant Haig was later moved from Fort Jackson, SC to Fort Gordon, Ga. He desperately needed a bone marl transplant. He was a good soldier and helped me with everything from ordering supplies to getting ranges for my unit. He was always physically fit and believed like myself in helping soldiers. The last time I saw him I brought him a card to Fort Gordon signed by Kerry Earnhardt and Brian Vickers, two NASCAR drivers. I told them about him and they even called him. It was no time after that he started losing more weight and hair. The last time I saw him was before I was deployed to Iraq he was in real bad shape. While I was in Iraq, I heard he died.

Now to add to all this my own father's Alzheimer's getting worse and I had to start helping my mother more with him. This was all a bad trying time because I knew in a few months I would be in Iraq. You see the Army is about mission, but we as soldiers all have families and it is hard, because you cannot always be there for someone who truly needs you. You do what you can and you deal with the cards you are dealt. The years you're in the Army, time goes by without family and everyone like yourself gets older, it is a sacrifice a soldier makes.

After all this, I got orders to go to the 367th Mobile Public Affairs Detachment in Columbus, OH. It was January 2003 and I had been at Fort Jackson for over five and a half years and now it was time to pick up and move again. My Permanent Change of Station (PCS) was I thought a welcome change. I had had all I could deal with, especially with Maj. Strickland and Mr. Dilbert. I only wish my replacement Sgt. 1st Class Hudson good luck, before I left. I did not even get a thank you or any awards from my command. I had good soldiers, but piss poor leadership. Oh, well every dog has his day. In the Army we use to say your worst assignment is the one you are leaving and your best assignment is the next one. I just hoped my next assignment was good. One thing was for certain it did not matter where you went the Army was always the same only the place was different.

I had to clear housing, it was not a problem for me, but there are a few stories about Fort Jackson housing, some are funny and some are sad. There was this NCO who lived right down from me and when he left to go to another duty assignment, he was 50 miles down the road and realized he forgot one of his kids. I watched his son until he made it back to pick him up. I said, "Sergeant Hernandez did you forget something, he just said, "very funny," and thanked me for watching his son. Another incident was an NCO right next door to me abandoned his cat. The maintenance people came over and found it living in the wall. They had to tear out the whole kitchen wall to get the cat out. Also after one deployment I saw a soldier's bags on the front porch of his quarters and his wife was gone back to Korea with his kids. The worst thing I ever saw was a kid who was just 10 years old and taking care of everything. His dad got deployed and he was separated from his wife. Well, he left his 10 year old son the check book and told him to take care of everything until he got back from a nine month tour in Bosnia. This did not go over well when he was brought back and court martial for neglecting and abandoning his son three months into the deployment. There was also domestic violence. Once I had to pull an NCO off his son for stealing a bicycle. He was beating his son right out in the front yard with a garden hose, because the incident got him kicked out of his quarters. Fort Jackson had some of the worst housing I ever lived in the military. Soldiers would also put up their whole families like a refugee camp. This place in itself was bad enough without all I had been through trying to be a soldier here.

I was now all packed up, my household goods transferred and my son was with my wife in Louisville, Ky. I had friends I would miss, but it is always a duffle bag and time to go to where something else needed to be fixed in the Army.

I would later find out my new commander and master sergeant were no bargain either. You see in the Army you are sometimes stuck with assholes you can't get away from for years. This is not a civilian job, you can't say I have had enough and quit, you have to deal with it no matter how good or bad it is. I made this unit better than it was before I came here and this was the end of my mission.

CHAPTER 8

THE 88TH REGIONAL SUPPORT COMMAND
367TH MOBILE PUBLIC AFFAIRS DETACHMENT
COLUMBUS/WHITEHALL, OHIO
PART I 2003-2004

In Ohio, I had to get housing at Wright Patterson Air Force Base in Dayton. I would have to drive over 160 miles round trip each day to work. I could have lived in Columbus, but my wife Telena wanted to work at the Commissary and I wanted my son to go to school on the base. So I sacrificed my time on the road to make sure they were taken care of. My family is more important.

I met my new commander and first sergeant in Whitehall, outside of Columbus Ohio where the Army Reserve Center was. I in processed and met the new Unit Administrator I would be working with too. His name was Mr. Lamb. He showed me around the command and I met with the key personnel in the 88th Regional Support Command. Capt. Flint and Master Sgt. Jennings both seemed nice enough and told me what they expected. I had to get the unit ready right away for a two week annual training mission at Fort Polk La. The unit was going to the Joint Readiness Training Center (JRTC) in less than a month to do Media on the Battlefield Training and all the equipment needed to be shipped out right away.

Next, I was also in charge of training and I started working on the units training schedules and supply records. Mr. Lamb was alright, He was a Sergeant First Class on the weekend drills, the same rank as me. He handled the unit personnel and pay. He did his thing and I did mine and we got along fine. I don't know what went on in the past in this unit. I never blamed any of my predecessors, this is my job now. My job was making sure this unit was ready for the next deployment; I knew it would be Iraq.

The equipment all got down to Fort Polk alright and the mission was a success. I started out on Temporary Duty (TDY) a least twice a week. I was in Ohio, but I was going to Michigan, Minnesota, Indiana, and Illinois were units were moving out to Iraq. A lot of media escorting had to be done.

Well, we got the call. The worst thing happened before we got the call; Our Commander Capt. Flint and Master Sgt. Jennings got taken away from us by 318th Press Camp Headquarters in Illinois and were assigned to another unit. Now we had no commander and first sergeant. After taking them away one month to the day we got mobilized. I had been mobilized before, but now we had to get a new commander and first sergeant and this was not good for the unit and me as the full time AGR soldier.

We had orders to go to Fort Campbell, Ky., our Mobilization Station. We had to be validated at Fort Snellen in Minneapolis, Minn. I had been here less than two months and now we were going to Iraq. My wife and son were devastated and I still had boxes to move in my quarters.

I got the buses, the rooms and off to Fort Snellen we went. I and Sgt. First Class Bellows a reservist in the unit were sharing the duties of first sergeant. Sergeant Bellows and I were getting it together and we got the unit in processed and validated. Mr. Lamb, he did not have to go because, he did not have the 46 series MOS and he was staying back to take care of the unit's functions in the rear. I and Capt. Willard a public affairs officer in the unit were on our way in the advance party to Fort Campbell. We drove down from Columbus, Oh to Fort Campbell, Ky in one of the units HUMVEES. We had to get

Barracks, food, unit training schedules, supplies, you name it had to be done and quick. We were attached to the 101st Airborne Division. I and Capt. Willard had a lot of reports to do and a whole lot of other paperwork to do too. It was day and night for three days. There was so much going on we never slept.

Then we met the new commander Maj. Kate who was from the 345th Public Affairs Detachment in San Antonio, TX. I and Capt. Wolfe introduced ourselves and told him where we were at in getting the unit ready to move out. I could tell when I met Maj. Kate that this was only going to get worse. He was kind of big, lanky, and walked like he had shit in his pants; all he ever talked about was Texas A&M University and his old ROTC Class there. Everything in his room resembled an Aggie from College Station, Texas. I thought this is not a football game this is a war and we need to prepare for it. He was arrogant to say the least and thought his shit was sweet. He was here to get bragging rights after it was over and he only worried about getting medals. I could care less, my job was to make sure these soldiers knew their job and hopefully we would all come back safe to our families. This commander did not know shit about shit. I had worked with his old unit the 345th Mobile Public Affairs unit in San Antonio and me and Bob Williams back then knew their officers were lacking in training and skill qualifications.

There was even one officer there a Capt. Morris, who Bob told him, either you get qualified or find another unit. I had worked with the 345th MPAD and I knew the officers in the unit were eaten up and Maj. Tillman was the worst. He was a do nothing, I had seen officers like him before, but I wanted to get this unit ready even if I had to go around him to do it. He was just one big obstacle for me to overcome. Fort Campbell and getting this unit validated in the next six weeks was my mission for now.

There were physicals and dental exams. The worst was the shots, typhoid, tetanus, hepatitis A, B, C, and small pox. Also the six series anthrax shots and we were given one every week. They burned and they left bruises and knots all over your arm. I saw soldiers go to their knees taking shots. It was like a cocktail of shots all the time and you usually felt like shit for at least 3 days afterwards. If you had bad teeth, the one dentist they had would just literally pull them out. It was nothing to see soldiers walking around with gauze in their mouths, bleeding everywhere.

There were ranges and ammunition. We qualified on night ranges, Nuclear Biological Chemical (NBC) ranges, and many other ranges. It rained most of the time and it was one hell of a mess in the field. Shooting targets in a thunderstorm and cleaning weapons, equipment, and picking up brass. Everyone had to qualify and it took some soldiers two and three times. I was responsible for the ammunition and arms room too.

Everything really got bad when we got a new Master Sergeant named Margie; he was from the 318th PCH. I thought Maj. Kate was bad; this idiot was the worst. I just looked at Sergeant Bellows and said," were fucked." Sergeant Margie started kissing Maj. Kate's ass and he let him treat us like shit.

Sergeant Margie did not want to be here and we did not want him here. He would not listen to anything me and the rest of the unit did to try and help him. He would undermine me at any chance he got and yes he thought he was always right. He thought he had the answer to everything. After his first week in the unit, all the soldiers hated him. He had the personality of someone who could walk in a room and it took everything you had not to get up and just smack the shit out of him and leave. How he made it to Master Sergeant is beyond me, but he kissed the commanders ass and hated all of us. It was evident this was going to be a long miserable deployment. After eating chow one day, which tasted like hot shit on a griddle. Sergeant Margie popped off to Staff Sgt. Bender, a journalist in the unit. It took me and another NCO about 20 minutes to persuade him not to kick his ass. As a former airborne soldier, Sergeant Bender was squared away and helped me a lot. Looking back now I should have let him kick the shit out of him and helped. I and Staff Sgt. Catlet, a broadcast journalist who was another good NCO I worked with in the unit; we started referring to Maj. Tillman as buckwheat and Sergeant Margie as spanky.

It was the fourth week of our validation and we were told we would be deployed to southern Iraq. I knew once

I got to Iraq, I would do my best to get away from spanky and buckwheat. These two could not cross their legs and cut a beer fart to clear their minds. I was starting to worry about the soldiers and I had made my mind up to take care of them myself. These two only cared about themselves and their evaluations and awards. I cared about soldier and I did not want to see anyone get planted because of them two dumb fucks. While here I had to make a trip to the port in Charleston, SC., to make sure our equipment was ready to be shipped to Camp Spearhead in Kuwait. I had given Maj. Tillman and Sergeant Margie the shipping labels for our two conex boxes, the four Humvees, and three trailers. The day they put the labels on the equipment I was drawing ammunition for our last range. They told me the shipping labels had been placed on the equipment. Two days later I had to go to Charleston and make sure the equipment was loaded, and ready to go on the cargo ships. I headed down to Charleston on TDY, and checked in at the port. There were thousands of vehicles ready to be shipped to Kuwait for the war. I found our equipment, but there were a few major problems. Maj. Kate and Sergeant Margie had put the shipping labels on the wrong equipment. I had a trailer with a Humvee label and another one of the trailers was not even marked. To make this nightmare worse, I could not find one of the Humvees. After looking for three hours through hundreds of vehicles, I decided to call Maj. Kate and tell him we had a problem. I called him and he was drunk off his ass. I could tell in his voice Friday had came early for him and his beer drinking. He told me while laughing, "Oh, Sergeant Dunn, I forgot to tell you that one of the tractor trailers broke down from Fort Campbell on the way and the other Humvee would be there tomorrow." I said, "Sir this is information I needed to know," his answer was, "don't worry about it and go out and get something to eat and drink." At that point I did not say anything and hung up the phone. I thought to myself, this idiot did not care if we were missing a $40,000 dollar Humvee.

Upon entering week six, we had orders to move out. We knew we would be going with the 101st Airborne Division. Lanes training was last, we had to go out on a two day war game mission and I had to draw flares, smoke canisters, and blank ammunition from the Ammo Site. Maj. Kate and Sergeant Margie got back before me and I ask them to put all the unused simulators, left over ammunition and canisters in the arms room for turn in. I gave them the keys and combinations to the locks. Once I got there I found all the canisters and ammunition just lying in the hallway of our barracks. I knew from that point on if I had to do something, I either needed to do it myself or get someone more responsible to do it. Also, the night before going to the last range, they stored the M16A2 Ammo under my bed without me knowing. It was suppose to be in the Arms Room with all the weapons. So the next morning, I issued all the weapons out. I did not see the ammo so I thought they must have put it in the Humvees. I should have known better, while on the way to the range, Maj. Kate asks me if I had the ammo and I said, "No sir," He said, "what we don't have any ammo." I looked at him puzzled, he said, "It was under your bed. I said, "What was it doing there." He said. "Since the arms room was not open last night, I had Spec. Charles, put it under your bed." Once I got out to the range and dropped the soldiers off. I sped back to the barracks and got the ammo from under my bed. Then I raced back to the range, where Sergeant Margie was waiting to start shit with me. The unit was waiting for another unit to fire before we could take the range. So there was no time lost in qualifying. He said this was my fault and Staff Sgt. Bender came over in my defense and then he started on both of us about how we were all incompetent. I just looked at him and nodded and thought to myself, what a dickhead.

After getting through this ordeal at the range, Maj. Kate, who liked to drink a lot thought it, would be great to have a unit party, a Toga Party, since our deployment was delayed a few days. I highly advised against it. I told my soldiers if you join in on this it will only be a bad thing. Maj. Kate had his party, his butt buddy Sergeant Margie was there to make sure he got his brownie points while he sat with the commander. I went to get something to eat with Spec. Charles, when we got back to the barracks the party was going in full force. The first thing I noticed were two under aged females in the unit drinking with the commander. They were both dressed in Army bed sheets and dancing around Maj. Kate as he laughed and made sexual advances toward them. Then I saw other unit soldiers dressed the same way. Some barely had anything on at all. In another room a few soldiers were playing cards and gambling. I and Spec. Charles looked at each other and I said," this has gone too far." I got out my video camera and shot the whole thing. If I was implicated I wanted the Army to know we had nothing to do with it.

Then it started getting way out of hand. Maj. Kate rounded up the unit and took the party out of the dayroom and into the hallway. There it got even rowdier and louder, they went down the steps and out of the barracks into the courtyard. There they started running around and acting like they were fighting each other with mops and brooms from a cleaning closet. The soldiers in the next barracks came out and Maj. Kate let out a big laugh and said, we are coming to get our porn. He had given all his porno magazines to the soldiers in the 318th PCH the day before. He came back to our barracks raising so much hell that one of the senior NCO's in another unit came out of a very important training meeting and looked at Maj. Kate who burped and laughed at the same time in the NCO's face. The NCO could not believe his eyes. He said, "We are having a training meeting in here sir." Then Maj. Kate said, Oh fuck that we want to get drunk."

The next day, that NCO, a Staff Sgt. Wilson looked at me and said, "Sergeant Dunn, your commander needs to be relieved for cause and conduct unbecoming of an officer. The rest of the unit should also be held accountable for their actions in this toga party. I said, "you are right," then I told Wilson, I advised them against such behavior here on post. The 3397th Garrison Support Unit in charge of the barracks did nothing. The next morning in formation it was funny when Maj. Kate came out of his room hung over in front of the formation wearing this female's specialist hat with her rank on it. That female specialist was right next to me in my squad wearing his hat with the majors oak leaf on it.

KUWAIT/IRAQ
OPERATION IRAQI FREEDOM (OIF) I
FEBRUARY 2003-JULY 2003

We had orders for the 23rd of March to move out, even though we had been here at Fort Campbell since early February. We went to the Airport on Fort Campbell and started the hurry up and wait routine. We flew first to Rome, Italy for our first gas stop.

It took over 12 hours to get to Italy and we had equipment everywhere, along with all our weapons. I woke up to the smell of a shit leaking lavatory, where the soldiers had stopped it up on the way. The whole plane also smelled like feet and ass. We were not allowed to get off the plane and we just laid there in misery waiting. I was so tired I used my protective mask carrier for a pillow, why? Because I had my gas mask on so I would not have to smell shit.

Our next stop was Kuwait. I then heard an Arabic voice come over the plane speaker and we were told to close all the airplane windows. I heard the voice in English say, "Let us pray, the voice said a prayer for freedom in English told us good luck on our mission. A sergeant major from the 101st came down the aisle and said we are here, grab you shit and get off my plane. He said, "I want a single file line and then I want every swinging dick to move to the tents across the runway.' This was day one of 365. Unlike the Air Force and the Marines who do 6 month deployments or less. This is a year for the Army.

It was noon in Kuwait and the temperature was over a 120 degrees. I actually thought I was going to die. I had been to Panama in the summer, but that place was air conditioned compared to Kuwait. I could feel my skin burning in my uniform and sweat running down my back.

After in processing, we got on two buses, with the shades closed, duffle bags in the windows for security purposes, and we moved out. It was an hour to Camp Virginia, for more in processing and being told where we were going. This was the true Army Cluster Fuck! We were given bottles of water for the trip and they were as hot as a cup of coffee, but you had to stay hydrated. We all smelled like a group of homeless people. When we got to Camp Virginia, through a field of old blown up vehicles and tanks left over from the 1990 Gulf War. It was like traveling back in time or returning to the scene of a crime. The road was all the blown up and the burned vehicles looked just like it just happened yesterday instead of over 13 years ago. At Camp Virginia we gathered up our gear and weapons and moved to yet another in processing tent for pay. We were headed for Camp Commando, our final stop. Here we were to support the 1st Marine Expeditionary Force.

The place was in the middle of the desert there was a gate with two Marines in two machine gun shacks. We all had to get out and show our ID cards, get back in and go through another gate with two more marines and two more machine gun towers; a double check point. We proceeded to the Marine Public Affairs Office to meet our points of contact, Maj. Kelly and his NCO a Master Sgt. Ball. They were glad to see us, but we sure as hell were not glad to see them. They showed us to our tents and then we finally got some chow. The mess hall was a tent and it was hotter in there than it was outside. I thought to myself great now we get to go eat with the devil. It was food, but it looked like homemade shit. We went back to the Public Affairs Office and started our mission plans. I was more tired than three son of a bitches." we finally got to sleep after the training meetings, but how could you sleep in this heat, with fly's, and little brown mice running around on our floor. Camel Spiders were also on the prowl. I dozed off for a few hours and then I woke up so dehydrated that I drank two 32 oz. bottles of hot water. No bed, no shower and in the desert. The first few days, taking a good shit in a hot ass portal potty was a luxury. The mess hall, tent, no laundry facilities, just heat and sand was all we had to walk in. There was some idiot in another unit smoking a cigarette outside his tent and instead of putting it out in the sand. He flicked it on another tent. This one cigarette started a fire that burned down over 25 tents with everyone's gear in it. Luckily no one was not burned, or killed. Everyone was at chow when it happened. The fire department was in Kuwait City two hours away, and by the time they got there a fourth of our base camp was in ashes. Those soldiers had to sleep outside under the stars till they got new tents and equipment. I only saw a few building that had air conditioning, but they were not where we were. You could walk past a tent or a building and feel the heat off of it and there was no shade to be found.

Sand fleas, flies and scorpions were another problem to look out for and everyone got sick. If you threw up and dry heaved for days you had what we called Sadaam's Revenge. Also there were sand storms to deal with, some lasted for hours.

I had to take a team to get our four Humvees, two trailers, and three conex boxes. All of this equipment needed to be picked up at Camp Spearhead in Kuwait near the Persian Gulf. The ship was called the Palmeroy. I had put new tags on the equipment in Charleston and I knew what I was looking for. I also knew the staging lots where the equipment would be. I, Sgt. Chalk, and Staff Sgt. Bender, went down to get it. I would get the Humvees, Sergeant Chalk would find the trailers and Sergeant Bender would park them. It took three days to get everything. Getting the equipment was easy, getting clearance to move it was another story. With a little help from Sergeant Bender, we were able to trade a couple of pair of Wilex Sunglasses to the movement NCO, who then bumped us up to the top of the list.

I was just glad Sergeant Bender had some extra sunglasses or we would still be there. There were some units grabbing equipment they even caught an NCO painting his unit insignia on someone else's equipment. He found out real quick when he got an Article 15 and forfeiture of pay for a month not to steal other unit's equipment. I was glad to leave with our equipment; Camp Spearhead was an environmental disaster too. There were two factories. One was a Sulfur Factory and the other was a Cement Factory. Both in the middle of all this were the soldiers. At night you could not see 20 yards in front of you. All the chemicals and smokestacks from those two factories filled the air. There were soldiers stationed there who had series medical and lung problems, even cancer after redeployment.

After getting everything back to Camp Commando we were given our first mission, with the unit being broken up into three 5 soldier teams, we all headed for three different locations. My team was sent to Al Kut, another team was sent to Ah Hillah, and the last team was left in Kuwait at Camp Commando. Our mission was to provide video, broadcast, and print journalism stories in support of the 1st Marine Expeditionary Force. We were all task to do media escorting when needed too. The unit was just like infantry soldiers, but with cameras and weapoms. I and Staff Sgt. Chalk were sent up first to recon for our team. We went with a Marine Civil Affairs unit and proceeded in a convoy to Iraq. We were in the back of a M1008 Army Pickup Truck, there were no up armored vehicles and we were exposed with just a canvas covering us in the back, sitting on two green benches. Two Marines had M16A2 rifles in the front and two in the back; I was in the middle right across from Sergeant Chalk with our M16A2's. It was Full Metal Jacket. There was a sand berm at the border into Iraq. The first town we reached in Iraq was Safwan along the "Highway of Death." This is where the cease fire negotiations between Gen. Norman Schwarzkopf and the Iraq delegation led by Lt. Gen. Sultan Hashim Ahmad took place after the Gulf War in 1991. All these Iraqi civilians dressed in gowns were coming up to our vehicles begging for anything we had. Some looked friendly and some looked hostile. It was real hard to tell who was who, we did not stop. I also could hear people saying No Sadaam, Sadaam is a donkey. Some soldiers threw them a few things to eat out of their MRE's. One kid almost got hit by a Humvee. We were radioed and told not to throw anything else to them. I heard gun fire off in the distance. You could not tell where it was coming from.

 The next town was Al Basrah, which was being controlled by the British. There was some fighting here and a few buildings were being targeted with Rocket Propelled Grenades (RPG). I looked through a set of binoculars and could see people running out of certain buildings trying to get cover. It was bad, we had wounded and hungry Iraqi's coming up to us and taking off everything from cloths to weapons for money or food. Another thing I remember them saying was "mister mister do you have a dollar." They also would try to sell you anything from old Dinars, Iraqi money to weapons, flags, bayonets, and anything they had. It seemed like everything you wanted could be gotten in Iraq for a dollar. We again gave some of them MRE's and they followed us down the street. There were parents hitting their children for approaching and trying to befriend us. I remember this little girl. I gave her some peanut butter and crackers. As we were riding away, I saw an adult knock her down and take what I had given her. I always watched everything around me and would put my back against a wall or vehicle. I did not want anyone coming up behind me. I also made sure my soldiers were in my sight at all times.

Next was the town of Ah Nasariyah. I felt different physically in every town. I got sick on a number of occasions and I was only eating MRE's. I was afraid to eat anything anyone would try to sell or give me. I remember some of my soldiers in Al Kut eating something called the Mix. They asked me if I wanted some and I said no. I also suggested they stay away from it. The next two days I had some sick soldiers. We joked and called this sickness the Al Kut Skoot. They had diarrhea and were also vomiting for three days and running a fever. I also got sick in Al Kut, but it was not from the food. It was no Joke when I dry heaved for two days and almost dehydrated from the heat. It was so hot, I drank sometimes eight two liter bottles of water a day and was still thirsty. The worst part was there was no cold water. If you were lucky to find a haji, another name we used for an Iraqi civilian. Especially one selling ice, you jumped on it. You could buy a decent block of Ice for a dollar. You also never used the ice in your drink, because it was just like drinking their water. You put the ice in a box with your water bottles and hopefully before it melted you had a cold drink. We never went near the water in the Tigris and Euphrates Rivers. It was beyond polluted. I saw a young Iraqi floating down the Tigris River holding on to a dead cow and waving at us. I saw one of the soldiers get some water splashed on him and in a few days he had to be treated for Ring Worm. Leishmaniasis, was a new disease we had never seen before. If you were bitten by a sand flea with the disease, you had to be treated right away. One of my soldiers Sgt. Catlett had to be flown to Walter Reed Hospital in Washington D.C.

If you are bitten it sets up into a scab which leaves a scar. If it is not treated is can spread into your blood and into your vital organs. If this happens you can die. Also the mosquitoes and fly's in the towns and near the rivers carried all kind of other diseases. I seen another soldier, Spec. Lowe who did not use his mosquito net one night near the Euphrates River and he had so many mosquito bites he looked like he had the chicken pox. I had to get him to a hospital back in Kuwait City. I made damn sure I had the mosquito net over me and my soldiers had theirs over them every night. Even then you would find these little bite marks on you. We did not have showers being on the move, so we used bottle water to wash off. Sometimes it would be three weeks before we would find a field shower, another luxury. Camel Spiders another threat, they can make you very sick. I use to walk around in these Iraqi towns and see thousands of people with permanent marks and scars all over them from sand flea bites and camel spider bites. There were so many flies I could be standing right next to a haji and he would not have a fly on him and I would have them all over me. I remember reading a book and putting fly paper on both the arms of my chair and in less than an hour they were completely full of flies. Another rodent was mice and rats. We had to get some mouse traps sent to us, because it was nothing to go into your field pack and find that mice had been in you MRE's. One night we were playing cards and we had set up a just a few mouse traps with MRE peanut butter on them. We could hear the traps snapping up the mice. There were so many, that we would hear a trap snap every 5 minutes after we reset them. Iraq is a shit hole. Speaking of shit holes we had to burn our own shit in diesel cans and stir it with big sticks. Filling sand bags was always fun too in 130 degree heat. Not to mention we were in a war. One day we picked up some canned cokes and they exploded in the back of a Humvee. The heat was so hot it actually set them off. I thought we were being shot at till I looked back and seen the cokes popping like pop corn.

Back to Ah Nasahriya, this was where a lot of Marines got killed because the Iraqi's came up from the rear and flanked the convoys as they moved through the town. We were lucky; we came in after the initial surge. It was also hard getting through the sand storms.

I was ordered back to the rear in Kuwait to write my stories and head out again. My photographs were sent to the Central Command (CENTCOM). I was glad to be out of Iraq for now, but my time in Kuwait was short lived. Maj. Kate told me and Staff Sgt.Chalk we had to go back up to Ad Diwaniyah.

Before we left we visited the 318th Press Camp Headquarters in Kuwait City. Talk about a bunch that had it made. My buddy Sgt. First Class Zeile, was the AGR soldier with them. They were in the Kuwait Hilton. Yes, while we were sweating and getting shot at this group of soldiers were staying in a luxurious hotel, with three great meals a day. I looked at him and said it must be nice. He said, "We eat MRE's only once a week, because the commander said we need to know what it is like in the field." I had to laugh." I saw their plush office and some of their rooms, it was a joke and the Army was paying the bill. On deployments I have always been a field soldier. This place looked like a news station studio. I told them, how are you going to write stories about the war in here? "There were even some of them complaining about it. I said, "You got it made." When I offered to take some of them up to Iraq with me, let's just say I did not see any volunteers. Hell, we did the job and they got the glory once it was sent up to CENTCOM. I seen all I wanted to see here. I and Sergeant Chalk headed back to Iraq.

This time it was our baptism, which means your first time getting shot at. Anything, to get away from Maj. Tillman and his side kick Sergeant Margie, even being shot at was better than being with them two sorry sons of bitches. I asked about our mail and the first thing out of Sergeant Margie's sewer was. "I don't want to hear about the mail, this is all you all care about. I am sick and tired of hearing about the mail." This asshole only cared about ARME. I told the soldiers don't worry I will get our mail. Listen. "I don't care if you are my rater or want to give me a bad evaluation, my job is to take care of soldiers. I will get mail for our soldiers and I don't give a shit about your pissing and moaning. He use to point his finger at me and called me out. I flat out told him, "The mail is important to the soldiers and I want to make sure they hear from their families." He also hated the mail because I wrote celebrities in my spare time and sometimes I would get letters and autographs in the mail. It was a little hobby of mine to kill some of the down time and I had some fun with it. The mail was free up to 13 ounces and there was no limit to what you could mail out, especially letters. This pissed him off, because when I was away he had to go get my mail. Sergeant Margie was always pissed down our backs and told us it was raining, He was an asshole.

It was now April; Operation Enduring Freedom had been going on now for over month. On the way to Ad Diwaniyah we stopped for the night at an old abandoned warehouse where the Iraqi's use to make turrets for their tanks. I and Sergeant Chalk decided to do a little exploring. We came across an old tank and I found a tankers helmet inside. I was careful, because things can be booby trapped.

Just when we thought there was nothing to watch out for. We were walking in a mine field. I noticed an anti personnel mine sticking up out of the ground, so we back stepped our way out. If this was not enough we got a radio message back at the warehouse that three Marines had been killed trying to arm a Rocket Propelled Grenade Launcher (RPG) it backfired on them and blew up.

Also, nights were more dangerous. This was when wild dogs come out. I remember hearing them all night fighting, fucking, and killing each other. It got so bad one night a Marines I was with picked up his night vision device and went on a dog hunt. I went with him because we never went anywhere alone. While we were out he said, "Look Sergeant Dunn do you see those dogs." I said yeah," he said, "watch what happens when I kill one of them." He shot and killed one of the dogs. He laughed and said, "look at this, you see they can't' resist their buddies guts." Then the Marine shot a couple more and said now let's go get some sleep while they feast on each other's guts." Once a wild dog came out of a sand burrow attacked one of the soldiers in our Humvee. The dog grabbed on to this soldiers boot and he tried to shoot it with a 9mm pistol, but the dog fell and went under the back wheel of the Humvee. The dog was killed instantly and we remembered looking back and seeing a pack of dogs make lunch out of him. You don't want to sleep on the ground in Iraq either. I carried a cot with me no matter how it added to the weight of what I had packed. I don't know what would be worse; getting ate up by a pack of wild dogs or having a Camel Spider, or scorpion on you. I had my mosquito net around me every night too. The sand flies and mosquitoes are worse than the enemy. Sleep was short every night and you always had a buzzing in your ear from some kind of insect always waking you up.

The next day we had to let The Explosive Ordnance (EOD) soldiers blow up some of the RPG's we found. Also, a bridge had to be taken out; the Army Apache Helicopters did a number on it with Hell Fire Missiles.

While I was here a Marine Staff Sergeant named Rickett saw me with a camera and said, "Sergeant Dunn do you work for Public Affairs? I said, "Yes." He said do you happen to know a Maj. Kate. I said, "Yes he is the commander." Then He said, "I have got a real problem with him." Here we were four hundred miles north in Iraq and now I was hearing about our Maj. Kate who was down in Kuwait. The Marine looked at me and said, "This Maj. Kate was in Baghdad a week ago and he jack fucked one of my young Marines. Maj. Kate also stole some items from the Palestine Hotel and traded them to him for his flag." I made him take it back to the hotel and Maj. Kate kept his flag." I said, "this sounds like something Maj. Kate would do, he is your typical souvenir hunter." The Marine said; when you see your commander again, tell him he is a Cock Sucker for screwing one of my Marines over. Also tell him, he is a piss poor officer for not giving back the flag and fucking one of my Marines over." I thought to myself, hell I can't go anywhere over here without hearing about Maj. Kate and his dumb shit deals.

Later in the week it was hot, but luck had it, I and Sergeant Chalk found this water bladder not being used and we jumped in it to cool off. It was like a field Jacuzzi. There was this one stupid soldier who climbed up on a Water Buffalo, and opened the lid and took a bath. He was given an Article 15, because the Water Buffalo was for the soldiers to use for drinking water. He even left his towel and wash cloth over it to dry. His First Sergeant had a shit fit; the soldiers had to wait a day to get more clean water.

I and Sergeant Chalk were then dropped off at a base camp in Diwaniyah, the fighting there was still going on. I had to take some pictures and he had to use the video camera and get some B roll. We were there for two days and we ran into a group of helicopter pilots who were with a unit called the Purple Foxes. They offered to fly us back to Kuwait. We packed it in for the night and sat around a camp fire and burned left over furniture we found in an abandoned building. It was a night to remember, these Pilots and their crews were crazy. They used some of their personal video cameras to film each other dancing in the fire. The next day we flew on a CH 46 Sea Knight helicopter, which looked like the Army's Chinnok, which we all called a shithook. I had to give up an AK 47 I had to the Marines. I heard it was given to a unit after it was bronzed. Hell, it is probably hanging in a colonel's office somewhere in Camp Pendleton.

There was also an Emergency Call to the Helicopter while we were there. They had to fly off and see about a soldier who was injured. They came back and told us they had found a dead soldier on the road to Baghdad. It seems he had fallen off a vehicle in a convoy; he had broken legs and was beaten to death by Iaqi's and left for dead. His unit caught hell for lack of accountability.

Changing subjects, right before we left one of the crew had to take a shit. This is not important, but it was funny. He was sitting on an end table with a toilet seat nailed to it so his ass would not be in the sand. While he was sitting, the rest of the crew was throwing rocks at him and the only thing he had to protect himself was a shovel coving his face. It was hilarious. He just kept saying paybacks are a bitch.

I was glad they let me use the toilet, because up until now I was using empty MRE Boxes to take a shit in. You see all you had to do was empty out the MRE Box, stand it on its end and use it to take a shit in. Then you left it in the sand, a soldier has to do what a soldier has to do.

Before take off one of the pilots on the helicopter handed me a card that read, it leaks, it squeaks, but at least you're not walking. It also had a picture of a purple fox giving you the middle finger. Another unique thing was believe it or not this was the last CH 46 Sea Knight Helicopter used in Vietnam during the fall of Saigon. How do I know this, I actually looked up the numbers on the rear wing of the helicopter and yes they matched an article in Time Life Magazine in April 1975.

I and Sergeant Chalk were riding with Capt Lumpkin, nicknamed "Lumpy." He was a character to say the least.

We followed Capt Lamonte a pilot in another helicopter back. While in the helicopter we got a call from Capt. Lamonte. He said, "Look at our blades I think we have a problem." We looked out the window and all I could see was four Marines in the windows of the helicopter with their pants down mooning us, one even had a lit cigar hanging out of his ass. One Marine had a tattoo on his ass that said, "Fuck Haji." Then we heard Capt. Lamont come over the radio. "How do you all like the view? Then I saw, the end table toilet seat go flying out the rear of the helicopter. Down below in a village we could see Iraqi's scrambling as it hit and one of the crew said, "Oh well there goes the shitter."

If this wasn't crazy enough, I looked out the window and noticed we were landing on an Iraqi concrete aircraft hangar. Then I looked down and could see Capt. Lamonte landing his helicopter on the run way so he could take a picture of Capt. Lumpkin landing on top of this hanger. Later, we landed on an abandoned airstrip and the tail gunner and co pilot got off with a tool box and took the back blades off a downed Iraqi helicopter. They said they were going to give them to a sergeant major that was getting ready to retire in their command. Then we went helicopter drag racing down the run way on the way out.

Last stop, Camp Commando, me and Sergeant Chalk reported and turned in our stories and pictures to the command. Two days later, I had to report to my team at Task Force Tarawa back in the Iraqi in the city of Al Kut. My team was already there and I had to catch up to them. The worst part was I had to go on a flight up there with Sergeant Margie. He tried to bump me off the flight, but I talked to the pilot who I had flown with before and he said. "Don't worry about that dickhead, this is my aircraft and you're going Sergeant Dunn." Sergeant Margie had also taken one of my best soldiers Private 1st Class Sosa, he was a young soldier and I was watching out for him, because Sergeant Margie had made him his personal pack mule. The only reason he wanted him to go was to carry his shit. Sergeant Margie was also a lazy bastard and used soldiers. Worst of all his breath smelled like what we called camel breath. I told Pvt. 1st Class Sosa, "just do what he says and try your best to get away from him." Once I got to Task Force Tarawa, I asked Sergeant Margie, "who is our point of contact?" He looked at me and said, "you are an E-7 figure it out yourself." Then I went on my own. I found a public affairs officer; Capt. Flowers and she hooked me up with a ride. I headed up to Al Kut with this Navy Captain who was headed that way too. The Navy Captain did not waste time; we got in his Chevy Suburban and moved out, like a bat out of hell. He said, "Sergeant Dunn, hang on." I could hear gun fire in the streets out of the gate. The captain said, give me my pistol." I handed him the pistol and I grabbed my M16A2 and away we went right through the gun fire. We were racing through the streets and when we reached the Tarawa hotel in Al Kut where my unit was. I remember getting out in the middle of all these Iraqi's. The Captain said, run as fast as you can to the guards at the entrance of the hotel and don't stop." I jumped out in the middle of the street and ran like hell. The Army MP's seen me, opened the gates and let me in and then they shut them like closing the doors to a subway train. Once inside, I could see Iraqi's with white paint on their children's faces hoping to fool the MP's into letting them in for protection

I had been here a few minutes and I thought I was in the Alamo. Then I saw Sgt. Catlet, one of our soldiers. He said; "let's go Sergeant Dunn; I will brief you upstairs with Capt. Fenney on our mission." Then I went upstairs to the headquarters office. I had to pull this big steel plate out of the way. I said, "What's the steel plate for." Sergeant Catlet said, "At night when we write our stories they like to shoot at us from the street. So this steel plate keeps the bullets from going through the door." I said, "Great, I get to hear bullets hit the plate in front of the door all night. Then I saw Sergeant Mooney, Spec. Loyd, and Spec. Andrews. We had one vehicle and it was a two seated Humvee with a canvas over the back. So much for up armored vehicles, also we could not turn on any lights while we were there at night after dark. I had a sense of fear just being here. A few days later Lt. Col. Zangus got killed along with some others at a fake check point. We were told never stop after that and if we saw someone holding a white parlay don't stop either.

Terrorist were using civilians as shields and Sadaam had put a price tag on killing American soldiers, I don't think I slept for a week there, at night I could hear gun fire, and screams outside. Also, there were the dogs to deal with again and the damn heat, the place was like 'Night of the Living Dead." We were attacked a few times and I could hear bullets at night hitting that steel plate door. A few days before that one of the rooms got hit by an RPG. We cleaned it up and were told by the Marine Commander Lt. Col. Farley that this was going to be our public affairs operations room. He said they probably won't strike here twice. I said, "Thanks sir, I hope you are right." We were now working out of a bombed out room and all our equipment was set up and working. Then into the streets we went doing stories every day, at night we had to go out a few times. Also a few soldiers were killed on a bridge.

I caught a few soldiers trying to buy alcohol off the street. This shit was in a bottle and it looked like tea and smelled like shit. I told one soldier, you are lucky I caught you. If one of these Marines would have caught you, they would probably court martial your ass. I made him pour it out and he said, "Damn sergeant Dunn that cost me 10 dollars." I told him damn, I probably just saved your life, besides not giving you an Article 15 for drinking, I said let this be your warning." There were soldiers who had died from drinking this homemade brew. Some soldiers are not smart enough to realize if they can't shoot you they will poison you too. Also the soft drinks came in bottles and cans. I would drink out of the cans, but the bottles were never safe and a lot of soldiers got dysentery and diarrhea from street eating.

Al Kut was a bad place and I always felt uneasy about being there. Many of the Iraqi's were targeted, especially if they befriended American soldiers. Jihad was always a problem, and we kept the citizens of the town at bay, no one was to be trusted and everyone outside the gate was a suspected terrorist. One night at the Tarawa hotel, we got a radio message at about four o'clock in the morning it came from Task Force Tarawa. The message was clear, get out of here as soon as possible it has been targeted. We packed up all our shit in that one Humvee in less than an hour and moved out. We did not know where we going, but we knew we could not stay here. As soon as we pulled out less than a block away, it got hit. We heard it was overrun by the town's people and burned to the ground. Talk about perfect timing, I had my baptism.

Next, I was told I was going to another team, this time in Babylon, near Ah Hillah, the ride there was at night. Like I said, I hated to travel at night in Iraq. The haji's all come up to you bumming and saying mister do you have a dollar. I remember this one kid came up to this Marine and the he threw the kid the accessory pack out of his MRE, which only had gum and toilet paper in it. The kid caught it looked at it and gave the Marine the middle finger, it was hilarious. The next morning we somehow reached Babylon and guess who was there, Maj. Kate and Sergeant Margie. I thought I would rather be back at Task Force Tarawa being shot at or blown up. Then we found out they were only going to be there for another week. Hell, a week with them two dip shits was a long time. They did not like me, because the soldiers would come to me instead of them. These two idiots wanted me to be their spy and tell them all about the soldiers. I told them if they did not have the soldier's respects it was their problem. I care about soldiers and I don't give my soldiers up to nobody.

Now, I had to go up to Baghdad and meet with the 318th PCH. It was June 1st 2003 and President Bush announced the end of the war and the reconstruction of Iraq was beginning. Terrorist were just starting to implement road side bombs and on the way we saw a tank on fire. We stopped at the Parade Ground and took a few photos of the Cross Swords. I noticed the speed bumps leading up to it. They were Iranian helmets buried in the concrete and other helmets cemented into the base of the cross swords coming out of a basket. It was a reminder of the Iran Iraq War.

We were here to go over story ideas. The next day we went back to Babylon. Early in the morning, I heard a gunshot. Then I saw a few Marines run by looking for a medic. What had happened was a Marine on guard duty had nothing better to do than try to open up a 50 caliber bullet with a Gerber (pliers). The bad thing was the round exploded on him. It burned the whole left side of his face he lost one of his eyes. In the same day there was a helicopter crash. One of the CH 46 Sea Knight Helicopters belonging to the Purple Foxes crashed in the Euphrates River. It seems the helicopter got to close to some utility wires and the propellers hit them. The helicopter was in two pieces in the river. On board was two Marines door gunners, a combat medic, and of course the pilot and co-pilot. Then another bad thing happened. A Marine who was driving his Humvee alongside the river saw the crash and jumped in the river with all his equipment on to try and save any survivors, and he drowned. This day there were a total six casualties. It was now my job with Spec. Kent to cover this at the crash site.

    The next day divers were brought early to try and find the bodies. It took those five days to find them, I also had to document it and take pictures for the investigators. The first thing the divers found was ID Cards and equipment. While I was standing there on the shore one of the divers threw an ID card on shore. I looked down and right between my boots was the ID card of Capt Lamonte. I had just flown with him and Capt Lumpkin "Lumpy" a few days earlier. It was one of the hardest things I ever had to look at and take a picture of. He was the only one I knew in the crew. I thought, we had just laughed and sat around a camp fire a few weeks ago and now his body was in that stinking river somewhere. I did not know Capt Lamonte real well, but the time I spent with him is still in my memory. Later, that day I saw Capt.

Lumpkin and he looked like he was in shock. We talked, but I could see the tears in his eyes, because they were friends and in the same unit and had flown together on numerous missions. Also, that night the divers stayed in my tent and no one talked about it that night and I could tell they were not looking forward to going back in that shitty river and recover more bodies and belongings.

I got my camera and Spec. Kent and I headed back down to the Euphrates River early in the morning. They had to lower the water in the river so they could find the section of the helicopter where they thought the bodies were. After they removed all the wreckage, they found the bodies about 200 yards downstream. I was there when they brought all the bodies out including the Marine who had tried to save them and drowned. It was something I will never forget. The bodies were all white and disfigured from being in the water.

On that Sunday there was a memorial service for them right there at Babylon. Yes, unfortunately I had to cover that too! All I could think about was their families back home. I remember seeing Capt. Lumpkin one more time before he left and was sent back to Kuwait. He gave me one of his purple fox patches and said don't forget us. I watched him take off in a helicopter it was the last time I saw him.

I was now on another convoy and another story. This time I had to cover the building of a new school in Ah Hillah. We had a briefing and expected trouble. You see the Bathe Party did not want us helping even the children get back to school. Sometimes they would destroy the engineer's construction sites at night when they left. We stayed at the schools until they were finished. On a convoy if there was trouble, we stuck together, we lived by a code and it was this. If one of us has to do something like kill someone. All of our lives were in danger or threatened. Our motto was this; they can judge me by twelve rather than carry me by six. We were like brothers; we had each other's back. We did not want trouble, but if trouble came to us we backed each other's play.

We never did take female soldiers with us on convoys, because groups of Iraqi's especially men would always come up to them, because their faces were uncovered. I had to also go to the Iraqi Police Station in Ah Hillah to cover a Psychological Unit passing out flyers to the people. It was one of the ways we told the towns people what we were there for and doing to help them. We always had pictures and a list of war criminals we were looking for in the towns. Once in a while they would show up and we could tell who they were, because they would grab the flyers from the Iraqi's. One day out in Ah Hillah, I had just got in the Humvee and closed the door; I started to hear gun fire. The gunner on the turret right above me said, "I see where it is coming from." Then a bullet hit off his barrel and another one hit the door where I was sitting. I made sure my weapon was locked and loaded with a 30 round banana clip. Then the gunner shot a sniper in a building across the street from us. He kept yelling, "I got him move out." When we got back to Task Force Tarawa, I got out and took a look at the door. The bullet had gone through the first layer of the door and there was a dent where it did not go through all the way. I thanked God; I had a hard time sleeping that night, because all I could think about was my family and what if I had been shot. I and Spec. Kent turned in our story and pictures and I saw Sergeant Margie. I was in the Humvee with Spec. Kent and I said to him, "Watch, this dickhead is going to say something about the way we look, our uniforms, and tell us to get a haircut." Sure enough Sergeant Margie came over to me on the passenger's side of the Humvee and said, "You two need to get into new uniforms and get a haircut, do you hear me." All at once Spec. Kent started laughing and Sergeant Margie said, "What's so funny Specialist", Kent said, "Oh nothing, just something Sergeant Dunn said." Just seeing Sergeant Margie reminded me of a pile of shit on the side of the road, I was so tired I did not care what he said. He just walked away and kept looking back at us on his way to his air conditioned office. I looked at Spec. Kent and we both started laughing, hell we were too tired to let that shithead ruin our day. Then Spec. Kent looked over at me and said, "Sergeant Dunn, I knew he would not say too much to me, because I am just a small penis man in this outfit." I looked at him and we both started laughing again. Then we went to chow before we did anything else.

While we were in there Maj. Knightner the Public Affairs Officer from the 1st Marine Expeditionary Force came in and dumb ass Maj. Kate pointed his pistol at him in a joking gesture. Maj. Knightner exploded! He told Maj. Kate, "If you ever point a pistol at me again major, I will make sure you are brought up on charges and run off this base camp, do I make myself clear." Maj. Kate did not say a word. Later, Maj. Knightner saw me and said, "Your commander is an idiot. I said," yes I know that sir." He said I feel your pain being under him, Sergeant Dunn."

My next mission was to cover a town hall meeting in Najaf. I went there with some Marines and Civil Affairs soldiers to help with the unrest in the town. While I was there, out of nowhere a small group of Hajji's came up to me and started handing me these pieces of paper. So I went over to one of our interpreters and asked him. He then went with me back to talk to them. He said they wanted me to get them a job, help pay for their house, and give them money for their families. Tell them I do not have anything to do with this. I am here to write about what is going on with the reconstruction of their town. He then, went back and explained to them what I was there for.

Once returning from Najaf, I went on a few medical medicine runs with this Navy officer named Capt. Christopher. We would run the medicine to the hospital or clinic, literally throw it to the first medical person who come out the door and then we would run like hell back to the Humvee and take off. There were still Sadaam Bathe party soldiers lingering around the hospitals and if they saw you trying to help the sick they would shoot at you. A few times we did hear gun fire, but luckily we were not shot.

Mean while the engineers were clearing a road in Ah Hillah, they came across by accident a mass grave site from the Desert Storm war. I and Spec. Kent had to go cover it. When we got there all you could see were plastic bags, bones and ID Cards stacked up everywhere. So we started taking pictures while all these Iraqi's were crying trying to find out which bag of bones were their relatives or friends. Some of the bags did not have any ID; also there were sandals all over the place. It was estimated that over 10,000 Iraqis were buried here. The smell was awful and some of the birds were picking around the bones. Also, dogs were carrying away some of the bones. The engineers had to finally give up the search to finishing the road. They could not spend the time it would take to dig up everyone they thought was there. It was now up to the Iraqi's in Ah Hillah to get shovels and look for their people.

On the way back, I stopped the convoy, because I saw something suspicious. There was an Iraqi behind a building and I saw his head briefly go up and down twice. The convoy commander came back and told me, "Sergeant Dunn, there better be a damn good reason for stopping us." I said, "Come with me," and he walked with me. We slowly sneaked up on the Iraqi behind the building. I drew my M16A2 on him and he started to run. I was going to shoot him, but the commander said no. Then we found three RPG's on the other side of the corner of the building. I told him you should have let me kill him. He said, "Maybe your right, but we did not know the RPG's were there until he was gone." Then we proceeded back to the base camp in Ah Hillah. This was luck; he was going to used those RPG's on us.

The next day back in Babylon, I had a little time off before we had to go out and cover some more stories. I decided to take a little tour with one of my soldiers Pvt. 1st Class Sosa. He wanted to see the old ruins of Babylon and so did I. We met up and got a tour from one of the locals. Having gone to church a lot, I had heard the stories from the Bible of Daniel in the lion's den. Now I was standing right where it happened. The guide was very informative and told us about the prophets Jeremiah, Ezekiel, and King Nebuchadnezzar Also this was where Alexander the Great supposedly died. Then the guide showed us where the three Hebrew children were cast in the fiery oven. We then saw the old Babylon walls which were built in 650 B.C. there was a statue of a lion with his head gone still there. The guide said the head was taken off during World War I. There were still palm trees and some of the hieroglyphics remained on the walls of animals. The old road and the gates were still at the entrance to Babylon. Down the road a few meter were some remnants of the Tower of Babel. Right next to old Babylon was a new Babylon that Sadaam was trying to build. The amazing thing was the new Babylon Sadaam tried to build was like a maze. I never thought being in the Army would take me to Babylon in Iraq.

Later that day it was back to work and guess what it was Pvt. 1st Class Sosa's turn to empty the latrines and burn the shit in the diesel cans, so I helped him. You see, I would not ask any of my soldiers to do anything I would not do. While we were doing this a few soldiers walked by and laughed when they saw me as a Sgt. 1st Class doing this. I looked at Sosa and I said," they probably think I am being punished with extra duty. I always worked with my younger soldiers; I felt it was important to be an example. After all one day they will be leading and I want them to understand it is all about teamwork no matter what the task.

At least the Navy Engineers had finally set up field showers. For three weeks we had only taken showers with bottled water to clean ourselves.

The next day was one of the hottest days I remembered and it was just the end of June and we ran out of water that day too. When the Water Buffalo's showed up, soldiers were on it like a pack of wild Iraqi mad dogs on a three legged cat. We chased it up the hill. You would have thought as a kid it was the ice cream man. I started getting real tired of everyday at noon hearing the theme song from the movie "Lawrence of Arabia." I felt like I was going to see Peter O'Toole come over a sand dune on a camel with the British Army behind him. Armed Forces Network played this every day in this hell hole.

One day I got to ride my first camel, then getting off the camel, it breathed right in my face. I thought to myself this is almost as bad as Sergeant Margie's breathe then he approached me to ask me what I was doing. "I told him I wanted to ride a camel." He said, "get back to work this is not the zoo."

The heat was getting worse every day. There were jokes about the heat. I heard one soldier say it was hotter than a French Whorehouse on Nickel Night. I started to feel sick one day in late June. I passed out; when I woke up I was in a tent somewhere in Baghdad. I remember hearing helicopters and seeing someone with a laptop computer on my stomach with a needle sticking strait up in me. I saw a doctor giving me an Ivey. Then I passed out again, this time I woke up and there was this Iraqi next to me with one arm in an intensive care unit tent. I looked at all my body parts and thanked God everything was there. I could also hear this other Iraqi across from me breathing through a tube stuck in his neck like a tracheotomy. I thought I was captured until I saw a soldier checking my pulse. He looked at me and said, "Do you know where you are Sergeant Dunn?" I said, "No." He said you are at the 25th Combat Action Support Hospital, 25th CASH in southern Baghdad. "I said, "Where are my soldiers?" Then I started to get up. He looked at me and said, "you are not going anywhere for a few days." Then I said. "Am I alright, he said, "You have heat exhaustion." I said, "How long have I been here, and he said, "Almost two days."

I had not heard from Sergeant Margie and Maj. Kate, not that I cared. There was a soldier next to me who had been brought in with me. I saw his commander and first sergeant with him. They said where's your first sergeant and commander? "I smiled and said, "I am on my own." They both said it was a damn shame my chain of command did not care or knew where I was. Two of my soldiers emailed me and I talked to them over a computer I borrowed. I just rested there for a few days and was released. Before being released the Iraqi across from me died and his family was there crying and mourning over him. It was sad, because he was one of our interpreters and was shot for helping us by his own people. I had no way back to my unit and no one to get me. My last email said, they were trying to get together a few Humvees and were coming to get me, but Sergeant Margie had not approved it. Too hell with this, I will get back on my own. So I went looking for a ride, but there was not one to be found. Then a helicopter landed and I saw a purple fox painted on the back of it. I went over to it after they dropped off some soldiers. I looked in and there was Lumpy. I said, hey Capt. Lumpkin, can I get a ride. He looked at me and said, "Get on Sergeant Dunn you old desert dog." I said, thanks sir," and we went back to Babylon."

In Babylon at the mess tent, I saw Maj. Kate, he just looked at me and said, "how did you get back, we were going to come up there and get you." I just looked at him saluted and walked on. I thought to myself, what a dickhead. Then I saw his side kick Sergeant Margie. He started giving me a hard time about some story I did not finish. I looked at him and said," thanks for the ride and so much for never leaving a fallen soldier behind." That night while I was sleeping on the floor of the Palace in Babylon, a chandelier fell, damn; I thought we had all been hit. It woke everyone up and it was a miracle it didn't land on anybody.

The next day I had to go with Maj. Kate to Ah Hillah to pick up something at a school. I did not know what it was till we got there. Spec. Kent was driving and I was in the back of the Humvee. After leaving the school, I saw Maj. Kate get in with an Iraqi flag. I said, "Sir where did you get the flag." He said, "I took it from the school, they won't miss it and by the way it is a good souvenir and I don't have one like this yet." I thought to myself, he put us in harm's way just to steal a flag from a school. Maj. Kate was only here for him and to loot whatever he could and when this was over get whatever medals he could say he earned and brag about it back home in Texas. Oh, by the way he got a Bronze Star for his service in Iraq, kissing up to the active component. Also his butt buddy Sergeant Margie got one too. Awards are so common now in the Army. I remember when you had to earn one. A Bronze Star for what, soldiers have died in WWI, WWII, Korea, and Vietnam and never got one. The Army must think they are candy

It wasn't but a few days after this, those two misfits got called back to Kuwait to work at Camp Commando. The unit was glad to see them go. Now we could finally get back to the mission. The next day I went back into the streets of Ah Hillah.

Next, I had to cover, a soccer game between the Marines and the Iraqi's in Al Kut. Like in the movie "The Boys in Company C." The only people invited were soldiers and Iraqi men and male children. Females were not allowed. It was a fun game and thank God there were no incidents. I felt very uncomfortable on the field with the stands full of Iraqi's. The Iraqi's won 5-3, they could play soccer.

Soon after that I began working with the Army Engineers and was covering stories on roads, bridges, and more school building projects. Helping the kids get back to school was rewarding. These schools were just basically concrete buildings with a few chairs and tables, and no desks. The engineers did the best they could with the building materials they had. I felt sorry for the children. I gave the children some of our MRE's to eat. It was all about winning over the hearts and minds of the Iraqis.

We got a little break in the action when we were visited by some celebrities; I got a chance to meet actors John Stamos and Gary Sinise, best known for his part as Lt. Dan in the movie "Forrest Gump." They both were real supportive and it was nice to see them care enough to come over here and see the soldiers. I remember walking up to Gary Sinise and asking to see his magic legs, he just laughed and put his arm around me and said, "Sergeant Dunn, you are a character."

Back to the mission, I still did not feel well and it was starting to show. I pushed myself in the heat to carry on. I tried not to show it, but I could tell that I was wearing out. I was almost 45 years old. I could tell I was not the young soldier I use to be. The long hours and the stress of dealing with my command were taking its toll too. Also my father was dying with Alzheimer's and he was entering the late stages of the disease. My mother was especially worried because of his condition and me being in Iraq. Then at the end of June 2003, Maj. Kate, said he wanted me see a doctor again. So I went back to Camp Commando in Kuwait and went to the doctor at Camp Doha. Col. Stevens, an internal medicine doctor took one look at me and said, "Sergeant Dunn, I think you have had enough, you have lost over 25 pounds and you have already been hospitalized once. I don't want you to have a heart attack over here." He said, "I think it is time for you to go home." I told the doctor, I wanted to stay with my soldiers. He called in another colonel who was a doctor also and he said, "We will have to see, but I am leaning in the direction for you to go home too."

While all this was going on Maj. Kate busted in and said, "Are you all done with him, because I need him to go back to Iraq tomorrow to do his job." The two colonels looked at him and said, "we have made our decision, Sergeant Dunn you are going home." Maj. Kate was furious and they could see it. The doctors then asked him to step outside and they both told me. "We see your commander does not care about you or your health. You need to go home and get well and try to get a compassionate reassignment to help your mother with your father. If your commander gives you any flack, you let us know. This war is over and you have done what you came here to do. You don't owe anyone Sergeant Dunn, especially Maj. Kate." The two colonels arranged for me to be medically evacuated out of Camp Wolfe in Kuwait. It was Monday and my flight was leaving on Thursday. I called my soldiers together and told them personally and they said, "Forget all this shit Sergeant Dunn and get out of here." Gunny Hemphill, a friend and Marine came by and said, "When you get home get a roll of nickels and throw them in the backyard for your son that will give you enough time to chase the wife around the house. I looked at him and said, "You Marines." They all supported me, but this was not my decision, it was the doctors. I had to wait until Thursday to fly out. The worst was yet to come. Maj. Kate and Sergeant Margie did not feel the same way as my soldiers and doctors. That night after we returned from the hospital, Maj. Kate called me into his tent and told everyone else to leave. He then looked me right in the eyes and said, "I want you to tell me what you told those doctors to make them send you home." I looked right back at him and said, "sir, it is not what I said it is what you said." Then he exploded and said, "you might be out of here, but this is not over Sergeant Dunn, I will get you for this." He just walked away and threw back the tent cover and went to the Public Affairs Office mumbling to himself.

Now it was Tuesday and I was called in to see Sergeant Margie. He was sitting behind his desk and said, "Sit down Sergeant Dunn, I got something for you." he said, "I and the commander have decided once you get home, you will be transferred to another unit. I have contacted the United States Army Reserve Command (USARC) and have talked with them. I also have this counseling form for you to sign." In the Army a counseling form is one sheet of paper front and back, but here I was holding six sheets of paper.

Then I looked at Sergeant Margie and smiled, who had looked like he had been up all night enjoying writing this and said, "you have got to be kidding right," he said, "hell no, I am serious." I said, "can I read it first and he said no, you will sign it." I looked at him and left it right on his desk and walked away. "He called for me, but I just went back to my tent. I thought about how they were treating me and came to the conclusion that they were just jealous because they were not going home. I decided to wait till I got back home to do what I had to do about these two jerk off's. I was determined they were not going to upset me and make me do something they could use against me here. I did not care what these two dickhead morons had to say. I respect their rank, but I don't have to respect them. To me they were just a couple of oxygen thieves who would not get the pleasure of issuing me an Article 15 or a Bar to Reenlist. So, I went to see the base Chaplin. He said, "Sergeant Dunn, you are under doctors care and all of this will play out in your favor." At that precise moment, Maj. Kate who had been following me walked in the tent where I and the Chaplin were talking. He reached down in front of the Chaplin and grabbed my weapon and said, "You won't need this anymore." and walked out of the tent. The Chaplin looked at me and said, "Is that your commander?" I said. "Yes sir." Then he told me he had been on a convoy with Maj. Kate and he had caused an incident in one of the towns with some Iraqi's. The Chaplin, said, "Sergeant Dunn, I don't like him, he is trouble, I will do something about this." I said, "Don't worry sir; I will just let him hang himself." He said, "I will report this to the command anyway, you do not need to be around him, because I fear for your safety." I said, "don't worry sir I can take care of myself." I left the Chaplin and went to the mess hall, on the way out I happen to see Maj. Kate waiting for me; he came over and said, "Did you and the Chaplin have a nice talk. I also want your ammunition." So I went and got my ammunition. He counted every bullet and tracer as if he was looking for something missing. He looked up at me and said, "You can go now." I said, "I would like to have my original hand receipt for the weapon and my ammo." He went to his desk and got it. I was not going to let him say I lost a weapon and ammo without my original hand receipt in my possession. He and Sgt. Margie were on me like a shark attack. They both should have kissed me before I left, because I like getting kissed when I am getting fucked. The funny thing was after this deployment the 88th RSC made Sergeant Margie the Sergeant Major of the 318th Press Camp Headquarters and soldiers jumped out of that unit like rats leaving a sewer. A fuck up who moved up.

While, I was there Maj. Knightner came in to see me. He looked at me and said, "Sergeant Dunn, just be glad you are leaving those two idiots." then he asked me if I needed anything and I said, "no thank you sir," he said, "I hope to see you back in the free world someday." I said, thanks for everything sir and it was an honor to serve with you."

On June 23, 2003, at 0600 hours, the war in Iraq was over for me. I thought to myself only the dead have seen the end of the war, but, I bet they never served under two assholes like Sergeant Margie and Maj. Kate. I was now on my way to Camp Wolfe to depart for Ramstein Germany. Sergeant Margie along with Specialist Curry drove me to the flight line. Upon arriving Sergeant Margie tried not to give me my medical and dental records, but I made damn sure I had them in my hand. Then he threw my two duffel bags out in the sand and they drove away. I felt free and now it was time to go.

Within a few hours I was on a C130 airplane heading for Germany. Once there I was placed in a hold over and was given a cot in a gymnasium with other wounded soldiers. I called back to my soldiers. They told me Maj. Kate and Sergeant Margie were asking them to make statements about me, so they could try and get rid of me or give me a bad Non-Commissioned Officer Evaluation (NCOER). After talking to a few of them they said there was not one soldier who would make a bad statement about me. After reporting this too my doctor in Ramstein, Col. Hammond and telling him the situation, he got right on the phone and called down range to Camp Commando. He told Maj. Kate, "Major, this is Col. Hammond, Sergeant Dunn, is here to heal, he is not under your command anymore. He belongs to me; if he comes back I will make damn sure it is not to your unit. Now do you understand that Major. There was a silence and then Col. Hammond smiled after hanging up the phone. I am sorry you had to serve with that officer, thank you sergeant Dunn for your service." I said no, thank You Colonel." He smiled again.

I stayed at Ramstein for three days and got to eat in a real mess hall. The food was great and the people there took real good care of me. I then boarded a C141 airplane and headed for Andrews Air Force Base. I was now on my way to Walter Reed Hospital. When I got there I and other soldiers were met by a Colonel who welcomed us home. We then got on a bus and were taken over to be in processed as new patients. I spent two weeks at Walter Reed. They were really good to me at Walter Reed and they evaluated me and told me I would be going back to Fort Campbell for further evaluation and treatment.

FORT CAMPBELL
3397TH GARRISON SUPPORT UNIT
HOPKINSVILLE, KENTUCKY
JULY 2003-MARCH 2004

I arrived 1 July 2003 at Fort Campbell, Kentucky. It is on the border in Hopkinsville, Kentucky and Clarksville, Tennessee. I was checked in late at night and was put back in the same exact barracks I was in before I left with the 101st Airborne Division in March. It was déjà vu all over again. Except now I was assigned to the 3397TH Garrison Support Unit (GSU). I met my new first sergeant. Sergeant Demario. He told me the rules and when formation was and what was expected of me while I was here. Rule number one, make your doctor appointments and don't miss formations. He then introduced me to the commander, Capt. Fletcher who basically told me the same thing. There were about 200 soldiers in this company and we were all here for one reason to get better and go back to the war.

I was given a room and when I walked in there was Sgt. Cabot who had been with me in the 25th CASH in Baghdad. I looked at him and he said, "Funny seeing you here Sgt. Dunn I thought you were back in the war." I said, "I guess, they thought we would be better off if we were roommates back here at glorious Fort Campbell." He just laughed, then he told me how things were here and what to expect while I was waiting for doctor appointments.

It did not take me long to see what was going on here after being at Ramstein and Walter Reed. Appointments were spread out over a long period of time and soldiers were not being seen on a regular basis. There was a lot of malingering and some soldiers just took advantage of the situation. They had us on work details in between our doctor appointments, but there were still soldiers using the system for their advantage. Everyone was supposed to have a job. I worked at the fuel point and was in charge of three other soldiers who worked there with me.

A lot of young soldiers got medically boarded out of the Army. Most of them wanted this; it assured them of a life time disability rating and a monthly check. This made it easy for them to get out of the Army. I saw soldiers who had nothing wrong with them getting 30 to 60 percent disability. The process sometimes took up to two years to complete. While they were waiting to get medically boarded out of the Army, they got their full pay while staying at Fort Campbell as a medical holdover.

There were soldiers here that were never even deployed with their units. They would complain about an illness when they got here and while they were being looked at the unit was deployed. I saw soldiers who were still at Fort Campbell even after their units got back from a one year deployment. This made good employment for them till the doctors decided what to do with them.

It was not only here at Fort Campbell, but also at over 10 other mobilization sites across America. There were soldiers that had been to every doctor on post and had created illnesses just to stay at Fort Campbell and draw all they could out of the Army, and released with a disability percentage and check.

There were also female soldiers who got pregnant in Iraq, just so they would not have to go back to Iraq, we had two in my platoon. It took 6 months or more to get rid of them. There were soldiers who were hurt, but the majority just used this place as a hang out while they got paid and got disability.

If you had some kind of job, went to formations, and kept your doctor appointments no one ever kept up with you. There were soldiers who would also cover each other's backs on their jobs, while others just hung out on post and even went out to bars and drank their time away. There was drinking and gambling in the barracks every night. The first sergeant and commander did not even care.

After Sgt. Cabot left and went back to his unit. I had a Spec. Langston for a roommate. The bad part was this kid was a conscientious objector and never wanted to go to Iraq. He said he did not believe in the war. Well, his unit came back and a few of the soldiers wanted to beat this kid up for not going. There were some name callings and threats. I went to the commander and told him about the situation. I objected as an E-7 in a room with an E-4, but the commander would not move him. He was finally discharged out of the Army. The sad thing was the Army took over a year to do this; while he got to go to college and finish his degree.

There was one soldier who just went absent without leave (AWOL) for two weeks before they even knew he was missing. When they finally caught him all they did was bring him back and send him to the doctor. He never got charged for leave or disciplined for his actions.

My father was dying and getting worse with Alzheimer's. I had lost my wife's father a few years before. My mother was taking care of my father at the time and he was in the final stages of the disease.

My mother did not have nursing home insurance for him. He was really starting to get out of control. So every time I got the chance I went home to see him and help her. I was lucky; my mother lived 4 hours from Fort Campbell in Louisville, Ky. My wife and son lived in Dayton, Oh. At Wright Patterson Air Force Base, so at least once a month I was able to see them on a weekend here and there too.

I started working on a request for a Compassionate Reassignment to help my mother with my father. I went to the personnel warrant officer in the company and she helped me get a packet together to submit to the board.

She told me what I needed. If it had not been for CW3 Petry, I would not have ever got this packet together. She had also sat on reassignment boards and knew what they were looking for. It took me several months and a lot of doctor's statements on my father just to get this approved.

I was still recovering from severe anxiety, heat exhaustion and I had also had a colonoscopy. I was seeing three different doctors. I still did not feel right. I requested 30 days leave and had another colonoscopy at Wright Patterson Air Force Base so I could be with my family.

During this time Maj. Kate and Sergeant Margie called to see what was going on with me at Fort Campbell. When they told them I am on leave; they started their usual trouble with me. They called Col. Sullivan, the Battalion Commander and ask him why I was given leave. This did not satisfy Maj. Kate, he then calls my sergeant major, who I thought was my friend who years before had went to Advanced Non-Commissioned Officers Course ANCOC with when we were both staff sergeants back at Fort Benjamin Harrison. He sides with Maj. Kate and calls me while I am with my wife and son in Dayton, Oh. He orders me back to Fort Campbell. I had to travel back even before my leave was over. Sgt. Maj. Martin said, "I want to see your leave form, it better have a control number on it approved by that command."

I went back to Fort Campbell and saw Col. Sullivan. He told me he wanted to see my leave and my medical records. I showed him both of them. He looked at me and said, "Boy Sergeant Dunn, Maj. Kate, Sergeant Margie, and Sgt. Maj. Martin really hate you." I looked at him and said, "Sir, it seems to me that it is their problem."

He looked back at me and said, "You are right and I am going to make sure they are not to contact you or the command the rest of the time you are here." I said, "I would appreciate that sir." He asked me about my father and noticed I had a colonoscopy two days ago. He then turned to me and said, "Sergeant Dunn, you go back to the 3397th GSU Charlie Company. You have been a good soldier here and you have done what we asked of you." I will make damn sure Maj. Kate does not bother you again, just get well and move on." I said, "thank you sir that is just what I plan on doing."

A week later I had a doctor's appointment with Col. Christianson in Internal Medicine at the Hospital on Fort Campbell. He asked me about Maj. Kate and Sergeant Margie. He said, "They are real interested in your medical condition Sergeant Dunn, but I will decide if and when you go back to Iraq or duty." He also said, "I am the powers that be here." After this I never heard from Maj. Kate or Sergeant Margie. I did hear from my good friend Bob Williams in Little Rock, Ark, we always stay in touch. He told me he was at a Public Affairs Conference in Atlanta and Sgt. Maj. Martin was talking behind my back. Bob told me, that he said, I was absent without leave, AWOL. Bob said, "I know Sergeant Don Dunn and I think you are wrong, this does not sound like him." I called Sgt. Maj. Martin myself and ask him about this. He got on the phone at his office in Atlanta at Fort McPherson at the USARC and I asked him about what he told Bob. He was furious; because he knew I had talked to Bob who I know was my friend. He said, "Never call me again Sergeant Dunn unless it is business."I told him if you got something to say Sergeant Major, I am all ears." His last comment after that was and I quote, "I will see you in hell." He then hung up on me. I called Bob and told him what happened and he laughed. He said, "Don just watch out. I am out spoken and vocal and yes it has hurt my career over the years, but I will stand my ground.

Three soldiers in my Public Affairs Team in Iraq also came back to Fort Campbell. Staff Sgt. Sweet he had a liver problem. Sgt. Carter, he got real ill from a sand flea bite. Then there was my own team leader Capt. Finklestein, he had a separated shoulder. Of the six soldiers in my public affairs team in Iraq, there were now three of us who had returned. The only one to go back was Sgt. Carter. Well, they also tried to send me back with him, but Col. Christianson kept good on his word to keep me here.

After making sure Sgt. Carter got off and helping him and his family. My goal at this point was to get out of here and go back to the unit in Columbus Ohio. I got orders to go back to my unit on 1 March 2004. I finished up working at the fuel point; I also put two soldiers, Sgt. Hughes and Staff Sgt. Cranston in for Army Achievement Medals. When I left, Staff Sgt. Sweet and Capt. Finklestein were still there and were going to be there to meet the unit when it returned from the deployment in two weeks. Maj. Kate and Sergeant Margie's plan had failed to put me out of the unit. I also did not have to look at them when I got back to the unit, because they were at Fort Campbell after I left and they went back to their original units.

THE 88TH REGIONAL SUPPORT COMMAND 367TH MOBILE PUBLIC AFFAIRS DETACHMENT COLUMBUS/WHITEHALL, OHIO PART II 2003-2004

The unit came back in March 2004. Upon arriving, there were media to welcome them home along with all their families. I got my NCOER from Fort Campbell, Maj. Fletcher and 1st Sgt. Demario took care of me and gave me a good rating. They knew even though I was sick and injured, I helped them get vehicles fueled and ready to go everyday at Fort Campbell for other deployments. Then I got my NCOER from Capt. Finklestein, Sergeant Margie, and Maj. Kate. You see once again I thought Capt. Finklestein was not only my team leader, but my friend. I had done everything he asked of me up to the point where I was sent to Walter Reed. He even told me," don't worry Sergeant Dunn, I will take care of you on your evaluation no matter what Maj Kate and Sergeant Margie try to do to you." When I got my NCOER, he went along with them. I was told this by Capt. Wolfe who was there when it all went down.

Yes, my NCOER was very bad from them. I noticed the form was filled out wrong. They lied about the quarterly counseling form which never happened. I parted ways with Capt. Finklestein, and yes I told him what I thought of his involvement. I went to the Inspector General IG. I had a few cards up my sleeve and they were Aces. They did an investigation. They found out about the forgery signatures on my NCOER for the counseling and they asked to see the NCOER Checklist, which would have had my signature on it too. It was not there. Now we have an integrity problem with two officers and a senior NCO. They were caught lying. Oh, it gets better; the NCOER went to the Board of Correction of Military Records in St. Louis, Mo. They concurred with the IG's findings. My NCOER was revoked and was not put on my record and it was noted why.

I was just getting started, remember the Toga Party, Maj. Kate and Sergeant Margie had back at Fort Campbell before the deployment, well I turned in the video tape to the IG, it was noted and they kept it in house for fear that the Department of the Army would see it. I have showed it to a few of my friends and they said Sergeant Dunn, turn it over to DA and let them deal with these two dickheads. Also Maj. Kate had used government equipment and soldiers for his personal use. He had a video tape made of him and a few soldiers and submitted it to Texas A&M to win season football tickets. He won the season tickets, now the IG was looking into this. I do know that the IG decided not to peruse it. You see they also wanted to protect themselves and the command from the embarrassment of having a bad commander.

The 88th Regional Support Command knew who Sergeant Dunn was and then my compassionate reassignment went through. They could not wait to see me leave, because they knew I had things the Army did not want to talk about. I was isolated from them and even though I was right they were scared and on the run and I knew it. The IG told me not to discuss this. You have to protect yourself in the Army; there is more than one enemy. They could end my career till I turned the table.

I took care of the soldiers in the command before I left. I got 500 tickets from Shania Twain, the country music singer. I had written her and she had her promoter call me to tell me he had tickets for the soldiers. She had a concert in Cincinnati in May and I made sure soldiers and their families got tickets. I was put on funeral detail my last two weeks before leaving. I had to do two funerals before I left. I and Sgt. Howell a supply sergeant did this with me. It is the saddest thing to hand a family member the American Flag after they have lost a love one. Also to hear taps at a funeral is even harder. Just to take the flag off a coffin will bring tears to any soldier's eyes. I was glad to have the opportunity to do this, but I am glad I never had to do it again. Then, the two soldiers that took our place showed up in PT uniform at the next funeral, those two soldiers should have been kicked out of the Army for being so stupid and it was also a disgrace. Class A uniform or Dress Blues is the only appropriate uniform at a soldier's funeral.

I was on my way out, I was going home, but the bottom line is in the Army you got to watch what you wish for, because sometimes you just might get it. My last assignment was Fort Knox, Ky. I was being assigned to Army Accessions Command. Usually, a Compassionate Reassignment is good for one year, but it just so happened the slot I was going into was being vacated by a buddy of mine Sgt. 1st Class Brockberg and he was set for retirement. I asked him how long he had left. His answer was, "I am so short, I could suck an earth worm's dick." I laughed and said, "I guess that is shorter than sitting on a dime." I also knew Col. Phillips who I had served with when he was a Captain in the 77th Regional Support Command in New York City. He highly recommended me for the slot.

I talked with Sergeant Brockberg about the job and what was to be expected. He also mentioned a civilian

GS13 named Bill Larkin, the Outreach and Marketing Directorate for the Accessions Command who would be hard to deal with.

Just like at Fort Jackson, I got nothing from the 88th RSC, not even a farewell dinner. Besides fighting to get my NCOER rebutted, I did get an Army Achievement Medal; the citation did not even acknowledge I was ever in Iraq. I out processed, got my wife Telena and my son Donald III and we left out of Wright Patterson Air Force Base at the end of May 2004. This also gave me an opportunity to put my son in Waggener High School, the same high school I was in and graduated from. Also, most importantly, I got to help my mother with my father who was slowly drifting away with Alzheimer's. My wife's mother was close to Fort Knox too. I put my career on hold for my family, but I would not have it any other way. My parents raised me and now I owed it to my mother to help her with my father. This would be my last assignment and like the Army, it was not easy either.

CHAPTER 9

U.S. ARMY ACCESSIONS COMMAND
FORT KNOX, KENTUCKY
2004-2007

I went to basic training and Armor School at Fort Knox in 1981. Now this is where my final duty assignment was. It was full circle. I got my family settled in. This time I would build a house instead of living on post; this is where I would retire. I helped my mother every day before and after work with my father who was getting worse with Alzheimer's. It was a trying time. My son would be going to the same high school I went to, Waggener High School. He was glad to be near his grandparents and my wife was glad to be near her mother. I had just started the construction on my home next to my mother's house and we were living with her till it was complete.

I reported in to my new duty assignment on 28 June. I first met Maj. Paul Stamps who was my rater and new first line supervisor. He had also served in the 100th Division. We also had attended the same college Eastern Kentucky University. Then I met Lindsey Hershey, who I called "Hersh" for short. He was a recently retired Sergeant First Class and was now a Department of the Army DA Civilian. I was told by Maj. Stamps that I would be working with him and Hersh on outreach and marketing events.

Then I met Mr. Bill Larkin, who was the civilian directorate of the Army Marketing and Outreach Division. Right away I knew he would be hard to get along with. Sgt. 1st Class Brockberg had warned me about Mr. Larkin and told me to watch my back. He was right. He liked to be called just Bill. He was the bullying kind who liked to have things his way; He was a retired Master Sergeant in the Army. He was old school and liked to yell, use nicknames, and would be best described as a micro manager with little people skills. I did not like it how he bossed Maj. Stamps around. Bill also made sure he had the best office in the section and put Maj. Stamps in a lesser spaced office.

There were about 10 of us who worked in the office and he wanted everyone to make sure they knew he was the boss. His office meetings were long, sometimes three to four hours. Then he wondered why certain work was not getting done. I would sit there and listen to his bullshit while we all sat at our littler places at the table. It was like sitting at a home where he was the dad and we were all the children. One of my jobs was the Temporary Duty/TDY calendar. It did not matter if you were military, DA Civilian, or an agency contractor. He wanted to know where you were at all times and it was part of my job to keep up with this and report to him every morning. I had to know where the military personnel were, but civilian accountability and contractors was really not my job. If someone did not come to work it was my job to tell him and find out why. He was one of those DA civilians who thought being at Grade Level GS 13 made him a full bird colonel. He even had this little card he carried around in his wallet that said he was a colonel. Bill was intimidating to say the least. Everyone always knew when he was in the office and you could tell the difference when he was gone. He would always sneak up behind you to see if you were talking about him. I will say this Bill was better than Maj. Kate and Master Sgt. Margie who were just evil.

He also, use to call Maj. Stamps, "Pauly", instead of addressing him as an Army Officer. Even when Maj. Stamps got promoted to Lt. Col. Stamps he still treated him the same way. He also would blame him for things that were not his job and beyond his control. I really liked Lt. Col. Stamps and it made me mad when I would see Bill abuse him.

Hersh, was the program manager for the Cowboy Program. This was the Professional Bull riders and the Professional Rodeo. Lt. Col. Stamps handled the National Stock Car Association, better known as NASCAR. He also handled Air Shows and was the operations officer for the All American Bowl. Bill, besides overseeing things was involved with the National Hot Rod Association NHRA. He was also the program manager and producer as he like to be called for the Army All American Bowl. Also, Ms. Parsons was the Program Manager for the Army Convention Programs which included all the ethnic groups such as Black History Month, Essence, Farmers Conventions, and the wives and women's groups who attended the All American Bowl. There were other things they all did besides this, like Operation Orders, Pageantry, and of course pleasing Bill. He loved to delegate authority with no direction and blame you when it fell through. The best way to describe this was like being in the Wizard of Oz and Bill, thought he was the Wizard. You better have everything in order before an event or you were brought before Bill in his office with the door shut. I spent many a time in Bill's office with the door shut.

You see Bill would expect things, but he would never give you proper guidance and he was not a people person, it was always his way. Bill was also an information whore and by the time you found out what you did wrong it was too late. He never scared me; Hersh use to say," I wish I could get Bill out of my ass." He would give Hersh a harder time than me, because Hersh had also once been in this office as a soldier.

Lt. Col Stamps was his right arm and Hersh was Bill's left arm. Then Ms Parson's was his legs. Mr. Bagman handled all of the supplies needed for the events. I use to also help him too.

We also had contractors and agency people assigned to the Outreach and Marketing Division. They would get signage, tickets, and promotional items, among other things. I myself thought we could do this without their help. They knew nothing about the Army and when there was a mistake they would blame it on us. I did not trust them and they would undermine you to make themselves look good. My belief is this, if it is Army it should be run by the Army and its soldier's period.

They would show up at events and pass out lead cards to try and recruit future soldiers. They also claimed wages for work they never did. Then they would give you up in a heartbeat and throw you under the bus to Bill. The whole point of this Army Marketing Outreach Division is simple; it is Army Awareness for Recruiting. I want to break down each Army Accessions Command programs I was involved in to the best of my knowledge.

PROFESSIONAL BULL RIDERS (PBR)

The Army sponsored some bull riders from the Professional Bull Riders (PBR). I helped support the program. Hersh was the program manager. My job was to help with some of the assets and personnel for the pre pageantry at PBR events. The PBR is not a rodeo. They are Bull Riders period. They mostly ride for the love of it, not the money. They are sponsored and only get paid if they win.

Some of these bulls weigh in excess of 2500 lbs. I have seen Bull Riders ride the next day after concussions, broken legs, arms, broken backs and neck injuries. I have been back stage where the first question they will ask the doctor is "can I still ride." One bull rider was even paralyzed and his response was I wish I could ride again. They do not sit out to recover, they Cowboy Up. The meaner the bull the better they like it. Of all the sports I have covered in the Army, I admire these bull riders who give all.

Working with Hersh was great; he was one of the best program managers. He knew the program and was always prepared. He would tell me, "Don, we might drop a few balls, but not the big ones."

My first bull riding event was the biggest, it was the 2004 World Finals in Las Vegas NV. Hersh had to arrange a Color Guard, Repel Team, many soldiers, and vehicles for display. I was in charge of the Army Olympians. Maj. Anti had won a silver medal in the Army Rifle Competition in Greece. I was also one of the drivers and had to make sure Mike Lee one of our bull riders was at autograph sessions and a meet and greet at a National Hot Rod

Association NHRA Race which was also going on in Las Vegas at the same time. This was a two major event weekend. Bill was on site and nothing was fun with him there.

We got to Las Vegas a week before the event to recon and set up; I helped Hersh with everything he needed. We met with Randy Bernard, who is the Chief Executive Officer (CEO) of the PBR. He was a real professional person and gave us the support needed. Then there was Mr. Clayton, he acted like he supported us. He also tried to play us down, but Hersh just went around him.

Later that week right after final pageantry practice in the Thomas and Mack Center, I had mud all over me from walking around the bulls. I had to also take Mike Lee out to the NHRA Race at Las Vegas Motorspeedway for a meet and greet autograph session. I was driving the van with Mike and his wife. We arrived and I found a quick place to park and made sure Mike was not late. When I walked in the Army Hospitality Tent I had to set Mike up with Tony Schumacher. He was our sponsored NHRA Top Fuel Driver. Also, Angelle Sampey, and Antron Brown the Army sponsored NHRA Pro Stock Motorcycles drivers were there too.

There were these two Sergeant Majors looking down at me. I noticed them making their way toward me. I thought they were just coming over to see Mike and the NHRA drivers. I moved aside to let them through and they walked right up to me. The first one a Sgt. Maj Blunt, asked, "Who are you with Sergeant Dunn." I said, "I am with both of you." Then the next one a Sgt. Maj Roberts started a shark attack on me at the same time about my uniform, boots and haircut. My hair was not high and tight, but it met the Army standards. I just never liked shaving my head. I tried to explain to them about the pageantry at the PBR where I had been in the mud and had no time to do my boots or change, because Mike had to be out here on time.

Everyone there was looking at them and they kept getting louder and louder. I thought I was in basic training again. Talk about being unprofessional. They just walked off still yelling at me making a scene and left. Mr. Bagman who handled our supply came up to me and said, "Sergeant Dunn, don't worry about those two, you did the right thing not being late." The two sergeant majors were Sgt. Major Blunt, the USAREC Command Sergeant Major and Sgt. Major Roberts, the Army Accessions Command Sergeant Major. What a great first impression of two assholes trying to embarrass me for doing my job. The soldiers in the command stayed clear of them and always talked about them behind their backs.

Later, I ran into Bill, he was furious and told me that they came to see him about my boots and hair. He said you have one hour to go back to the hotel and change your uniform and get a haircut. So instead of arguing with him, I went and saw Hersh and told him where Hersh said he would cover for me so I went back to the hotel and got on another pair of boots and a haircut on the way back to the track.

Next, I had to get Mike back to the PBR event at the Thomas and Mack Arena. He did well that night and now had a chance to be world champion. The next day was the big event. This was the last day for the World Finals and Mike Lee was ready.

Sunday started with picking up Mike and his wife at Mandalay Bay. I remember watching Mike Lee eating a

Krispy Krème glazed donut and taking a big dip of Skoal Bandit Winter Green chewing tobacco at the same time. I looked at him and said, "Mike you should have been an infantry soldier, you have the perfect eating habits." He laughed and the donut fell out of his mouth on the floor of the van, he picked it up and ate the rest of it, and looked at me with a cowboy grin.

The World Finals were just starting to get under way and Hersh was making a last minute check and looking at the itinerary, all the sudden a bull blew snot on his paper and his shoulder. Hersh, at first looked disgusted then he saw one of the bull riders laughing and he just started laughing too.

Me and Hersh, stayed in the back by the bull riders and waited for the World Finals to start. First there were no lights and then a spot light hit the bull riders as they were all introduced. Then there was a song by the Blue Man Group. The National Anthem was next, then fireworks and explosions. This was followed by the Fort Campbell Repel Team coming out of the ceiling to the floor. Last a couple of Humvees came into the arena and picked up the soldiers and they drove to the back of the arena.

The PBR World Finals was ready to start. Mike Lee rode every bull and the last one sealed the deal. In the first year of Army sponsorship Mike Lee had won the 2004 PBR World Finals. He threw his cowboy hat into the crowd and reached his hand to the sky thanking God for his victory on his knees. Mike was a religious bull rider. I never saw him take a drink or curse. He always prayed before each event and when he signed autographs he would sign "God Loves You."

I remember driving him back to the hotel and asking him, "Well Mike now that you have won over a million dollars today, what are you going to do to celebrate."He looked at me and said, "I thought me and the wife would go bowling tonight." I looked at him and said; well you did not say you were going to Disney World." He just laughed and said, "they would throw me out of Disney Land for spitting tobacco."

Once back at Mandalay Bay there were reporters and journalist following him and asking him questions. He was very modest and all the hoopla did not really mean all that much to him. To Mike it was just another day riding bulls, the thing he loved.

I worked the PBR with Hersh for the next 2 years. I had the opportunity to meet Charlie Daniels, Kenny Wayne Shepherd, and Robert Earl Keen who each played the VIP Parties for the three PBR World Finals I worked. I also got to meet Ty Murray the only 5 time champion and Adrianno Moraes, who has won 3 PBR World Finals. The PBR was always fun and all the bull riders loved the Army.

BUCKMASTERS

This program was assigned to me by Bill and he set me up for failure from the beginning, with no guidance. Buckmasters was dead in the water in less than 3 months. It was an Idea of Mr. McGregor who was one of Bill's bosses at Fort Monroe. He was a big outdoorsman and hunter who created the program.

It was funny how these higher DA Civilians would piss money away. We referred to United States Army Recruiting Command (USAREC) as Useless Wreck.

As the program manager, I was left totally in the dark. There was no plan, Bill said, "You are going to make it happen. I received a pre-plan guidance. It was outrageous; the first thing I noticed was Buckmasters meetings were going to be held in some local bars. I went to Bill and asked about this and my concern for the Army being mixed up in a program that involved drinking alcohol.

His response was, "Get it done, Sergeant Dunn." I never thought USAREC would ever go along with a program filled with drunken hunters promoting the Army, but they did. The Army has strict policies about alcohol, but in this case no one cared.

The shit hit the fan when I was told to go with Lt. Col. Stamps to a NASCSR race that conflicted with me being at the Buckmasters Expo in Greenville, SC. When I came back, I was called into Bill's office. He went off and blamed me, because his boss and good buddy Mr. McGregor was furious at him. He told Lt. Col. Stamps to write me a counseling statement. After his temper tantrum ended I was thrown out of his office once again, with the words "just go back to your cubicle and get out of my sight." The thing was no one ever got recruited and the whole Return on Investment (ROI) was a waste.

With any program in the Army for recruiting there are lead cards. These are filled out by potential Army Recruits. The cards are given to the recruiters and turned into USAREC Cyber Cell for tracking future soldiers. This program had nothing to show. Speaking of lead cards, it is a fact that many are filled out, but few new soldiers are recruited. There was even little hand outs, like shirts, caps, key chains, and lanyards to lure in recruits, but there was rarely any follow-ups. This is what I saw, I never remember any soldier telling me he or she joined because they filled out a lead card and was given a t-shirt. I went to events where there was agency people running the whole Army Interactive Zone and passing out lead cards. How in the hell do you expect civilian kids working in the Army's Interactive Zones, to tell someone about the Army. I always said soldiers should run the Multi-Million dollar Army Interactive Zones. The soldiers know the Army and they should be the ones with lead cards and talking about it.

One of the stupidest things I saw was a young Army specialist dressed up in full desert gear. He looked like he had just returned from Iraq. I walked up to him and said, "Where were you at in Iraq?" He just looked puzzled at me and said, "Sergeant Dunn, I was never in Iraq." You never put a soldier out in front of everyone looking like he had been in combat in Iraq. Then finding out he had never been there.

NATIONAL HOT ROD ASSOCIATION (NHRA)

Once in 2000, I actually met Bill briefly at one of these events. I was stationed at Fort Jackson and covered the Bristol, Tenn., NHRA race for the newspaper "The Leader." I met Tony Schumacher, the Army Top Fuel Dragster Driver and I even took a picture of him with my son. Tony was really nice person even took time to talk to us and sign a few autographs. I then went into the Army Hospitality Tent and asked if I could get some water. Then this big fat guy came out of the hauler and looked at me and said who are you with? I told him, "my name is Sergeant Dunn and that I was doing a story." He did not even introduce himself to me and said," we are not suppose to give out water here, but I guess you and your son can get a coke." I said," thanks." I saw other soldiers in the tent drinking cokes and water. I thought to myself what a dickhead. I never knew four years later I would be working with him. The Army is funny, you might meet someone today and never see them again or you may work for them down the road.

Unlike Bill who only concerns himself with those above him, I remember people, especially those in the Army who are assholes. I went with Bill to Denver Colorado in early July 2004. The first thing I noticed when I got there was the Army Interactive Zone. It was set up by contractors from Relay a civilian agency. I watched as Bill went in and looked to make sure all the haulers and trailers were set up right. The Army signage was always something Bill always picked at along with the overall set up.

Bill would get on the Relay contractors, but he would really bitch at us if things were not right. Relay would get the tickets and held the parking passes and golf carts if we needed them. I hated asking them for something I should have already had. Also, they always thought they were in control and when something happened they would tell Bill behind your back. Bill thought he owned everything and every program in the Army was his. Unlike Bill, I realize everything belongs to the Army and the taxpayers.

Having met Tony Schumacher before, I liked him; he talked to everyone and was always nice to me. His father Don Schumacher was a great driver too in his day. The Pro Stock Motorcycle Drivers were Angelle Sampey and Antron Brown; they were nice and very appreciative of the Army's sponsorship.

Bill had all them fooled into believing he was the reason they were sponsored by the Army, the sad part was they believed it. Bill would come to a race and go in the haulers like he owned them. Bill used his power to intimidate. At first, I was intimidated, but later I knew he was a barker and not a bitter. He would yell and rave about something and even threaten you, but he was not really going to do anything, he just liked you to think he is in control.

One of my jobs was helping put soldiers at events. I would get at least four or five soldiers for every NHRA event. Bill would always come back from a race and complain about one of them. I was able to get soldiers from Army Reserve Units and Commands who would support from local areas where the races were. This also saved the Army a lot of money; it was all good Bill did not know this sergeant major was going to be at a NHRA race in Seattle. When he returned from the race he went to see Lt. Col. Stamps and then I was called into his office, again. He looked at me with fire in his eyes and said, "Sergeant Dunn, you think you can do whatever you want." Then, I looked over at Lt. Col Stamps and smiled, he hated that. Again he yelled and said, "Get out of my face and go back to your cubicle."

I heard him through the door telling Lt. Col Stamps to give me a counseling statement. About that time my phone rang and it was the sergeant major that I had put at the race. He asked me if I needed his help. I said; don't worry sergeant major I will take my lashes. He started laughing and said, "That Bill guy is intense and hard to deal with, but hey Sergeant Dunn you took it for the team."

Lt. Col. Stamps called me in and said, "This time Bill is not going to let this go. He wants me to give you a counseling statement. I said, "I know sir, I got you in trouble, so give me the counseling statement and I will sign it after all I don't have much time and I am going to retire anyway who cares."

Later in the week Bill came by where I was at in my cubicle and asked me "Did you get that counseling statement from Lt. Col. Stamps?" I said, "Yes I did." and Bill said, "I guess you know not what to do now."

Next we had a change of command ceremony for Maj. Gen Rochelle; he was the commander of USAREC. Tony Schumacher and Don Schumacher showed up. I was asked by Lt. Col. Stamps to go down and escort them into the building. I took them to Lt. Col Stamps. We all went over to Bill's office. He just looked at us like we were bothering him on the phone. He got up and shut the door in our faces.

I looked at Lt. Col. Stamps and we took Tony and Don over to our meeting room where we tried to entertain them by talking about the Army and racing, till Bill would see them. I thought to myself and even Lt. Col. Stamps mentioned it to me later how rude Bill was. I have to hand it to Don and Tony they realized this and I could tell Don was pissed. There are people who can walk in a room and you can feel there positive charisma. Then there are people like Bill who can walk in a room and you can feel like the way you feel before a doctor gives you a shot in the ass. One of my jobs was to keep up with the Personnel Calendar, so I could tell Bill where someone was and when they were coming back. Everyone use to ask me when Bill was leaving and when he was coming back. I could tell what kind of day it was going to be when Bill was there. If you came into work and everyone was talking to each other and smiling, you knew right away Bill was gone. When, you walked in the office and everyone looked busy on their laptops and never come out of there cubicle, except to go to the bath room, Bill was there. I actually spent more time telling co workers about Bill's coming and goings than I actually did working the calendar.

When Bill called you in the office, he would never come to get you. He would just yell one of his nicknames and you knew it was you. Example, when he would call for Lt. Col. Stamps, he would just yell, "Pauly get in here." He called me Dunny. It was bad, the fact that he did not recognize Lt. Col. Stamp as a officer. It was all lack of respect, if you were a Colonel or higher this is how he addressed you.

I had a lot of little jobs in the office besides getting soldiers for events. One of my jobs was feeding Bill. I had to go and get his lunch when he was in the office. One of the main reasons I put up with this was, it got me away from him for a while and he was usually quite when he was eating. Show me a fat body and I will show you someone who bitches and is miserable with themselves and others. I will not claim to be the fittest soldier, but I do try to take care of myself and treat others with respect they deserve.

THE U.S. ARMY ALL AMERICAN BOWL

The Army All American Bowl (AAB) is in San Antonio, TX, the full event last about two weeks. The game has 72 of the best high school football players from across the country with 36 players on an East Team and 36 on the West Team. It is played on a Saturday the first week of January.

There is a lot of pageantry. Also other events and the Army sets up a fan fair with interactive zones. These include Army show cars, Army haulers, and a variety of other Army exhibits.

My job in the 2005 game was to work with Master Sgt. Bradley and Lt. Col. Stamps in the AAB Operations Center. We had to make sure players and coaches had rooms, food, and meeting areas to before the game. There was a lot of driving back and forth to the Alamo Dome where the game was to be held. I had to pick up t-shits, supplies, and other promotional items.

I and Master Sgt. Bradley worked on rosters, schedules, and answered phones, along with other things. Lt. Col. Stamps had the hardest job. There were many moving parts and a lot of agency people to deal with from Relay to Sports Link. Lt. Col Stamps was juggling all these balls like a magician. He worked long hours and Bill constantly stayed on his back as more of a delegator than a worker helping him. I helped him as much as I could. Being this was my first time at this event it was a learning experience and we were short handed, which meant we got blamed for everything that went wrong whether it was our fault or not. Then there was a Lt. Col Bolton did some of the work, but Lt. Col. Stamps carried the load. Also Lt. Col. Bolton and his butt buddy Sgt. 1st Class Mackey, a recruiter and one of Bill's boys who he brought over to run the pageantry. I tried to get along with Sergeant Mackey, but he was an asshole like Bill and hard to deal with. Sergeant Mackey was one of those soldiers who thought he was hot shit and had power and Bill liked him. At our briefings every morning he would stand up and tell Bill the status of the pageantry like he was in control of the whole operations center.

Being a senior NCO with more time in grade and the same rank as Sergeant Mackey he thought he was my boss. One night I was out getting something to eat. My cell phone rang and I answered it and it was him. He needed a t-shirt for someone and he wanted me to come back from where I was and get it. I had one set of keys for supply and his boss Lt. Col Bolton had the other. Well, I asked him to get the keys from him and get a shirt. Sergeant Mackey, exploded and said, "Sergeant Dunn you need to get back here and do your God Damn job." I said, let me speak to Lt. Col. Stamps, and then he hung up on me. I decided right then I was not coming back to the hotel till, because he was an ass and not my boss. I got back and met with Lt. Col Stamps. I told him what happened and then Lt. Col Bolton came over to give me a hard time. I just let him rant and rave and walked away. Another one of my jobs at AAB was to take care of the Continental Color Guard. I also was put in charge of the Drill Sergeants. The Color Guard was no problem. I had a bad radio to communicate at the practice that Friday before the game. Also, Sergeant Mackey in his infinite wisdom did not give me any specifics on how the Drill Sergeants were suppose to come out on the field, even after I asked.

A clear set up for failure, the Drill Sergeants came out a few seconds late. I looked up and here comes fat ass Bill trying to run across the field after me and he was steaming mad. I had to laugh; His ass was dragging and wobbling. Lt. Col Stamps was standing right beside me and he just smiled. Bill was pissed, he started going off on how I made him do more Physical Training than he did when he was in the Army. Then he started bitching and threatening me and said. "If you screw this up tomorrow at the game, I will have you relieved for cause, and then he said I have the power to do it too." With his face red and his eyes about to pop out of his fat head, he said, "you have not done anything since you have been in this command and I have had it with you, Sergeant Dunn." Then he started yelling at Lt. Col. Stamps about something else. Everyone on the field was looking at me and Lt. Col. Stamps. It was embarrassing, but Bill showing his ass out there made him look like a fool and he did not even realize it.

I looked a Lt. Col. Stamps and said, "You know sir, with a laugh. Bill is a true asshole and Sergeant Mackey must be his son, he must think with his poor communication skills that I must be Marvin the Mind Reader." Lt. Col. Stamps kind of laughed and said, Sergeant Dunn, I am glad you did not say anything and took the high road." I looked at him and said, "Does this mean I will not be doing my part with the Drill Sergeants on the day of the game." Lt. Col. Stamps, said, I guess not." Then one of the Drill Sergeants walked over to me and said, "Who was that dickhead and why did you let him talk to you that way." I just looked at him and laughed and said, "That's Bill, he is the AAB producer. The Drill Sergeant said," I don't care who he is; I would not take any shit off that fat body civilian."

Back at the Operations Center, I was tasked to help Hersh with some things. I always liked working with Hersh, he was a hoot. I remember one time after dinner Hersh cut a nasty fart. I said damn Hersh you should put a warning sign on your ass. He laughed and said, "How do like that aroma therapy." I looked at Hersh and said, "I like you Hersh you just don't give a damn," he just gave me a shit eating grin and said, "Don, you just got to relax and don't worry so much."

I was watching over the Operations Center while everyone went to dinner. There was some bowl game on TV and I was just watching it to past the time. Then, I looked behind me and there was Coach Herman Boone and his assistant Coach Bill Yost, they were the coaches for the 1971 high school, T.C. Williams Virginia State Champions AAA Division. They were the coaches whose story was told in the movie "Remembering the Titans." They looked at me and said, "Where is everybody," I told them they were at dinner. Then they sat down right beside me and watched the game. They were guest speakers and VIP's for the All American Bowl.

I asked them if they had everything they needed and they said yes. It was interesting to watch them and their analysis of the game. They signed a couple of index cards for me before they left. It was one of those moments. I knew they were coming to the game, but I did not expect to be watching a game with them. I told Lt. Col Stamps that they had arrived. Bill also did not give me an access pass to the game, but Lt. Col Stamps gave me one and told me Bill did not want me to have one. I said, "Well sir if that is the case I will go home now. If I can't do my job, I would much rather spend New Year's with my real family at home." Then Lt. Col. Stamps said, "that is not going to happen, because I need you."

The game was at noon and was nationally televised. I was in the operations center at 0630 that morning to help Lt. Col Stamps and Master Sgt. Bradley with any last second things that might come up. Bill came in thanking everyone for their part in the game. He looked at Lt. Col. Stamps and called him an all star, he looked at Master Sgt. Bradley and called him a great NCO, He never mentioned or even looked at me. I don't care much for being patronized and I could care less what he thought of me.

Later me and Sgt. Bradley loaded up some soldiers in the van for the Pageantry and headed over to the game. Bradley said jokingly, "I can tell Bill does not think much of you." I said with a laugh, I will be here for two more years, so he has to deal with it." Also Bill told Lt. Col. Stamps that I would never work in his directorate after I retired. I got a news flash for his fat lard ass. I don't have too. I saved my money and I was really retiring. I had no plans to leave as a retired NCO and come back as a DOD mister. I had to get the Continental Color Guard ready to go out on the field before the National Anthem. Everything went well and they made it out and presented the colors. After the game we had another dinner and some award ceremony. Everyone received an AAB Army coin, but me. Once again Lt. Col Stamps made sure I got one. This was my first AAB and truly I hated it and Bill's fat ass was the reason.

The football game is a good thing for Army awareness, but there is a lot of waste. First, there are at least eight weeks planning for a three hour football game. Every month or two most of the office excluding me were gone to San Antonio planning for it. In one of the last meetings I was at, I thought I would have a little fun. I was asked if I had completed a task assigned by Bill and I said "no." He looked at me and said, 'why not Dunny." So I handed him a memo my father's doctor had written while he had Alzheimer's. Being we have the same name except I was Donald Dunn II. I handed it to Bill and it said, "I am doctor Sheffield, Donald Dunn, is incompetent and will remain that way for the rest of his life, therefore he can't complete instructions given him." Lt. Col Stamps thought it was hilarious and so did everyone else at the table except Bill. He just looked at me and said, "I already knew that." This one game a year took preference over everything that went on in the Army Marketing and Outreach Program. We did a lot of other things in this office to include NASCAR, NHRA, PBR, Conventions, and etc. Well, nothing was more important than the All American Bowl. I never saw more than 25,000 people at the AAB game and most of them were soldiers who were placed in the stands to make the Alamo Dome look full. The return on investment for all this was a joke. Lt. Col Stamps, alone with sometimes my help would go to NASCAR events and see higher numbers and there would be over 200,000 fans in the stands, besides the soldiers we would bring and Bill hated NASCAR. The waste was here and he could not see it.

The 2006 All American Bowl, my second year here. There was a little surprise this year. Col. Neal was training his predecessor, Col. Stark for his job as the new Colonel for the Army Outreach and Marketing Division Chief. It was Bill's turn to feel the heat. You see along with Col. Neal, Bill was supposed to train Col. Stark. He flat out told Bill he was in charge and Bill did not like it at all. Bill started scheming against Col. Stark. Bill, being the information whore he is tried to keep Col. Stark in the dark and still run it his way. Then right in the middle of AAB Col. Stark let Bill have it right in front of Lt. Col. Stamps. He told Bill, if he did not like it his way, he could get rid of him and he looked at Lt. Col Stamps and said, "Do you understand me." Lt. Col Stamps said, "yes I do sir." You see he knew Lt. Col Stamps would obey him and he wanted Bill to see that and do the same.

At the beginning of the first week Col. Stark came to me and said, "Sergeant Dunn, do you have a copy of the AAB Operations Plan and Annexes." I said, 'yes sir," he said, "would you email me everything you have." I said, "right away sir." So I emailed him everything on AAB and the things he did not ask for. He emailed me later thanking me; Col. Stark also wanted me to make some copies for his afternoon briefing. You should have seen Bill's face when I walked in the afternoon Operations Meeting. He looked at me when I came in and said, "What are you doing here Sergeant Dunn?" I did not have to say a word; Col. Stark got up and said, "I told him to come in here and thanks again for the AAB Info, Sergeant Dunn it was a big help."

Later that evening, Lt. Col. Stamps told me Bill wanted to see me. So I went to Bill's room in the Westin Hotel in San Antonio. He said, "who gave you the permission to email Col. Stark." I said, "He did." He replied, "You are not to email any Colonels without my permission first."

Supply was handed over to Hersh with me as his helper. Some of the officers and sergeant majors thought they could just come in and get free t-shirts, sweaters, footballs, tennis shoes, coins, or anything else we had. The worst two soldiers for trying to do this were Lt. Col. Richards and Sgt. Maj. Blunt. Well not only did I not Blunt, I was not going to give anything out unless I was told to do so by Hersh. I told them flat out no, and Sgt. Maj. Blunt tried to bully me, but sergeant major or not he was not getting anything, especially if he was not on the list we had. The list was mostly the units and soldiers who were supporting AAB. I would give a private something before I would give it to a Colonel or useless Sergeant Major, like Blunt, who probably had a whole closet of

Army stuff at home. To me the lower enlisted always came first. Sgt. Maj. Blunt, after the way he treated me at the NHRA, he was definitely on my shit list and he would not get anything. He wanted something from me and now it was payback time.

Then another thing happened while I was in the supply room out of nowhere came Maj. Kate the asshole commander I had in Iraq. He wanted a pair of football shoes and Hersh told him no way. Then he left, Hersh looked at me and said, where do you know that idiot mooch from?" I said, he was my commander in Iraq." Then Hersh rolled his eyes and said, "God help us." I laughed and said, he got a Bronze Star and how would you like him to be in charge of you for a deployment? "Hersh said no thanks."

Maj. Kate then went back and started bad mouthing me in front of Maj. Axelrod who I had helped with some things he needed. It was funny because. Maj. Axelrod told Maj. Kate that I was one of the best NCO's he had ever seen and Lt. Col. Stamps backed his play. I knew a week earlier that Maj. Kate was coming, so I was not surprised to see his sorry ass. Now not only did I have to deal with Bill, I had to look at Maj. Kate in the Operations Center, this time he was not my boss and he knew it. Maj. Kate thought he was special and would only work about half a day, and then he would take off to who knows where after lunch and never come back. The other officers in the Operations Center noticed this. He always talked about Iraq and bragged about how he got a Bronze Star. He never mentioned the fact that he never saw combat. Ms Parsons, who I worked with and helped with supplies for her functions, said it best, "Maj. Kate is an oxygen thief." The last straw was when

Maj. Kate walked out on the football field with the lower enlisted soldiers to stand next to the football players before the game. It was a sight, he was the only officer out there and Bill said who is that major out there where he doesn't belong? This was the last time I ever saw Maj. Kate. He was not invited back to AAB.

Then there DJ, he was a real arrogant little shit who thought he was over everything too. Like AAB did not have enough chiefs. The bad part about DJ as he was called was he would give you up in a heartbeat and he was one of the Relay agency contractors. He had been with Bill awhile and got where he did because Bill liked him. He was also the typical kiss ass and he liked to give me a hard time. He also thought he was my boss too. He was like an overgrown college kid. He had gone to college at the University Of Southern California (USC) and thought he was a know it all on college football. It was funny when USC got beat by Texas for the national championship that year. He threw a fit like a baby in the Operations Center. The funniest part was we were in Texas and everybody was celebrating, but him.

We also had a new comer in our office his name was Mr. Harris. It was funny, all he wanted to do was hang out and look for women; he thought he was a playboy. He would get on the computer and act like he was working. I would see him on the singles web sites looking for women in San Antonio. He could make you think he knew what he was doing and he had Bill buffaloed. He hated Bill too and when this was over he went back to Florida where he was from and found another job.

The day of the game was just like the year before. The players would announce which colleges they were going too. I liked the game itself, what I got to see when

I was not running back and forth out of the Alamo Dome working. I was one of the gofers. This is how I was treated as a Sergeant First Class. I would have been better off as a towel boy for one of the teams. After the game and all my humiliation leading to it, there was the awards dinner. I got a coin again, yes from Lt. Col. Stamps. The worst day came on December 2nd 2006 a month before AAB. My father succumbed to Alzheimer's and died. It was a Saturday morning and I had checked in with my mother and saw him late Friday night after I got back from TDY at a PBR event. I knew it was just a matter of time. He had the disease for almost 10 years. I told my mother two weeks before I knew he did not have long, because he was bed ridden and sleeping with his eyes open. I had seen people die and most died with their eyes open, but this time it was my father.

I got a frantic call from my mother. When I got there he was turning blue and gray. I called 911 and they came about 5 minutes later. The paramedics ran to the side bed room in our house. They asked me and my mother what hospital they wanted us to take him too. Then a few minutes later they pronounced him dead. I was there with my mother when he died. We were the two that cared for him the most, especially my mother no one did more for my father than her. She stood by my father through all this. My dad was a Christian and a God fearing man. I do know this, if there is anyone in heaven it is him. He loved God. It was sad, but I know where he is. Alzheimer's is a terrible disease and it takes a person's whole identity. One day they know you and the next thing is a blank stare. The best way I can describe this disease is you are dead before your dead. We could have put my father in a nursing home. My mother wanted him home and that is where he died. Now with all this said, I served in the Army during all this, but my family always came first. At the funeral home the day we were to bury my dad, my mother saw Bill and my Army staff. She told Bill how I cared for my father and how I helped her. He then realized when I left work where I was going all the time. Now with my father gone and my wife's father gone too. I helped both of our mothers. The way I see it, it is God, family, and then country in that order. I miss my father, but I did what I could to help him. Family members would charge my mother money to watch my father, but I would have none of this. Like I said, he was a Christian and I owed it to him as my father.

I on the other hand help my mother and I ask nothing in return. Others in the family still take advantage of my mother's good graces. I have never asked my family or my wife's family for financial help, because they owe me nothing. My mother and father raised me and I could not take anything from them. I even put my career on hold and I retired two months later. I wanted to stay in the Army, but I did not have the desire for it after 26 years service. My family to this day is my most important thing to me.

My last AAB was in January 2007. Once again I worked with Hersh and Lt. Col Stamps. A soldier got hurt and fell off one of the display vehicles, a Stryker and I was tasked with taking him to Brooks Army Medical Center in San Antonio. He had to have surgery for a few broken bones in his face along with some stitches. I took him to his doctor appointments and made sure he was taken care of. I also, helped him with getting his orders amended so he could return to his unit. All this took about a week. I enjoy taking care of lower enlisted soldiers and this soldier was my first mission. Once he was able to travel, he went back to his unit and his first sergeant thanked me and they left together. Then I went back to the operations center. Upon entering to the operations center I was met by Sgt. Maj. Roberts, you might remember him from the tag team him and Sgt. Maj. Blunt gave me at the NHRA race in Las Vegas, a real asshole. He looked at me and said, "Sergeant Dunn come over here I want to see you for a minute. I walked over and said, "what is it Sgt. Maj. Roberts. He looked at me and said, "I have been here for three days and I have not seen you doing anything where have you been."

I told him about the injured soldier and what had happened; he did not care and started giving me a hard time about being accountable while I was here. He did not even ask how or who the soldier was. He just wanted to be a dickhead to me again. I did not care what he thought anyway, I was going to be retired in another month. I was accountable and I was taking care of a soldier this what an NCO does.

I was then put over at the AAB Interactive Zone to work with Mr. Anders. He was a newly assigned DA civilian in our office and he needed some help with all the Army equipment.

I also got to work with helping set up an autograph session for the Army's new NASCAR Driver Mark Martin, also NHRA Drivers, Tony Schumacher, Antron Brown, and Angelle Sampey were on hand to sign autographs for the fans and soldiers. I also got to meet Anthony Munoz, Tim Tebow, and a lot of other Medal of Honor recipients. I kidded with Joe Nemecheck about how I was driving him around in San Antonio, he just laughed. This was my last AAB and I was glad it was over.

Even after I was retired, I tried to get Lt. Col. Stamps to bring Cpl. Frank Buckles the last American survivor from WWI to the next AAB. At age 109 Mr. Buckles would have done it, but Bill killed it because it was my idea. When Lt. Col. Stamps showed Bill a picture of me and my son with Mr. Buckles at his farm house in Charles Town, WV, he just looked at Stamps and smirked. Then he told Stamps, "He would probably be dead before the game." If it was not Bill's idea it was not going to happen. I was just glad to know next year my Christmas holiday would be with my family and not at AAB getting bitched at or humiliated by Bill, his cronies and contractors.

NATIONAL STOCK CAR ASSOCIATION (NASCAR)

This was my favorite of all the events and programs I covered as a Public Affairs NCO in the Army. I love this sport more than any other and the drivers are great to the military and fans. I volunteered for any race that Lt. Col. Stamps needed support. He was the program manager for Army NASCAR. This was the sport that put soldiers in front of the crowds. I would have stayed in the Army if this was what I could exclusively do. Lt. Col. Stamps said, "Sergeant Dunn, "you are the most enthusiastic fan I have ever met and you truly like this." Yes, and I liked to support the Army doing this.

To me racing was more American than baseball. There is nothing like going to the track. It was a lot of work, but I enjoyed it. The bonus was Bill hated NASCAR. He said the Army spent too much on it and it did not pay off. We never had to worry very much about Bill coming to the track. He would usually show up at the Daytona 500 to see some of the new Army Interactive Zone displays, also he would show up maybe in Charlotte around Memorial Day, or Homestead in Miami for the last race of the season, but other than those three races he was never around much. He was too much into the NHRA.

My job was to put soldiers at races and I made the most of it. One time I and Lt. Col Stamps, with the help of Maj. Griffin put over 3,000 soldiers at a Memorial Day Race in Charlotte, NC. I put over 100 soldiers at the Daytona 500 to unfurl a massive American Flag. It made me proud to watch the pre race ceremony and see that flag with the soldiers holding it in front of over 300,000 NASCAR fans. Bringing some of the heroes from the war in Iraq and Afghanistan was what it was all about too. Lt. Col. Stamps would bring in Drill Teams, 82nd Airborne Chorus, and Color Guards etc. There was an Army Interactive Zone for the fans. In my opinion this was the best program the Army had. Unlike the other Army events we did not have to try and fill the stands, because they were already filled. NASCAR is one of the biggest fan base sports in America and they love the military.

Once I did a story on the Army Interactive Zone at NASCAR for the Recruiter Journal, which was a USAREC publication. Everyone I talked to liked the article, but Bill. I remember being called into his office shortly after getting back from the Texas Motor Speedway in Fort Worth. Bill took a deep breath and went off, he started ranting and raving about how I did not have his blessing to do this and that I did it on my own. He even threatened to make me a Staff Sergeant if I ever did this again. Lt. Col. Stamps just sat there, we looked at each other, I almost started laughing in his face. He had no authority to do this. Bill, said, "I wonder if you think it will be funny when you are sitting in front of the Col. Neal." Lt. Col. Stamps looked at me and Bill said, "You are his supervisor did you know about this, and he said, "Yes. Bill went off again. He said, "You all just get out of my office." The funny thing was when I walked out of his office; there were some of the Relay Agency people out there waiting to see Bill about AAB planning. They looked at me and Lt. Col. Stamps. I turned to them and said, "He was just apologizing to us about something that happened at the track." They all busted out laughing and Bill did not even know what it was about. All I know was I set the tone for their meeting and I think Bill needed a valium. I was never allowed to cover any more stories. Lt. Col. Stamps did not like the way Bill was, but he put up with it and I admire him for it. He was a better man than me, because Bill was always ragging him about something. I know this, the next Lieutenant Colonel who comes in this office after Lt. Col. Stamps won't take it off him.

Mr. Thiesman was the NASCAR program manager for the Relay agency, so he worked with Lt. Col. Stamps. My first dealings with him were over golf carts. He thought he owned them at races. Also he was a rat and he told on us constantly. I could not talk to anyone with him around and if I ask for a drivers autograph, he would give me up in a heartbeat. Lt. Col Stamps told me to beware of him. Lt. Col Stamps would carry the load while he was putting in hours at the golf course. I told Mr. Thiesman, I knew about the hours he kept. The funny thing was Bill found out from other sources and his days were numbered. After the 2006 NASCAR season he was gone.

Once in the Marriot Hotel in Miami before the last race of the season, DJ was bitching at the desk clerk about his room. I looked at him and said, "what's wrong Daniel?' He exploded; he told me if I ever called him by his first name again he was going to whip my ass.

I said, "well Daniel if you feel like a frog leap.' He just kept popping off his mouth and I laughed at him. He just walked away in a rage. Then the desk clerk looked at me and said do you want me to call security on him. I said, "That won't be necessary, he is just mouthing off." Then she said, "He is an asshole and told me about the fit he threw over his room. I told Lt. Col. Stamps about DJ and he laughed.

Then there was this Mr. Sewerd everywhere I turned he was tattling. I used to call him the stalker. What an ass and he would email Bill at the track and talk shit behind my back on his blackberry.

He was also a do nothing. One time he brought his son to the track at Pocono with one of his son's friends. They both had Hot Passes. The Army also paid for those passes and he used them like they were his. I was working the race and I only had a workers credential. Talk about fraud, waste, and abuse.

I felt like the luckiest soldier in the Army going to NASCAR Races. I told Lt. Col. Stamps many a time, "Sir, this is the best job in the Army. I would go to about 10 out of 36 races a year. If I could I would have done them all for free.

One agency person I worked with in NASCAR was a great guy. His name was Brian Gaines; he worked with me and Lt. Col Stamps. Gaines was a Football player from the University of Louisville before he got this job. I am also a Louisville fan in both basketball and football and we got along great. I had seen him play football and he was a savage. If you got hit by him you knew it. He never got his chance to go to the National Football League (NFL), but he was that good. He loved all sports and he was good at what he did. He even helped me get into a few races and also made sure I had the right credentials. I have been a NASCAR fan for decades and I am a member of Richard Petty's fan club and I would go to Randleman, NC every year to see him at his reunions. He was my favorite driver until his retirement in 1992 at Atlanta Motor Speedway and yes, I was there. This was Jeff Gordon's first race. After that I was a Gordon fan. There has never been a greater ambassador of a sport, than Richard "The King" Petty. He always talks to fans and signs anything they give him. His Victory Junction Gang for disabled kids. He established this after losing his grandson Adam Petty to a car accident at Loudon, NH. He also loves the soldiers. He asked me once, where I was stationed and I told him Fort Knox. He said, "Sergeant Dunn, are you taking good care of my money." I told him, "I wish I had your money." He laughed and said, you're a soldier and that is something money can't buy."

I started covering racing when I was at Fort Jackson in South Carolina in 1997. I went to Darlington and Charlotte religiously every year. I would sneak into garages, meet drivers take pictures, and hang out and listen to everything about the sport and yes I talked to them about the Army. I started covering a young driver a few years back named Brian Vickers, who ran a car under partial Army sponsorship. He was still in high school and racing in the Busch Series before he even graduated. His father and mother invested all they had in him. He was the youngest driver to win the Busch Series at age 20. I first met him at Charlotte and I took pictures for his website. Now he is with Red Bull Racing.

Once I was at Charlotte and Bobby Allison was walking and needed a ride. I gave him one in my golf cart and when we got to the gate, security did not want to let him in. So I looked at them and said, do you know who this is and they did not have a clue. It is amazing how everyone knows the new drivers, but has no idea of the history makers behind the sport and who they are. One time at Miami Motor speedway Jeff Bodine was walking and three golf carts passed him by and never offered him a ride. So I picked him up and drove him to his Brother Todd Bodine's hauler who was racing in the Truck Series.

Another driver the Army sponsored was Bill Lester; he raced in the Truck Series too. He had a job as an engineer and gave it all up to follow his dream as a NASCAR driver. He was part of the Army's diversified driving program.

One of the biggest thrills I got was when I was working with Lt. Col. Stamps at a race in Kansas in 2004. The Army 01 car driven by GI Joe Nenecheck took the checked flag. I had the opportunity to stand in the Winners Circle and be with the crew and other soldiers. It was a dream comes true for me. I had been too many races, but this one was special. I stood right next to Lt. Col Stamps and Joe Nemechek. It was one great day for the Army. I was proud just to be a small part of it. The week after the race however when Bill saw me and Lt. Col. Stamps on the front page with Joe in the NASCAR Scene Magazine, all he could say to me and Lt. Col Stamps was "why are you two in the picture, the winners circle is for winners." One thing really cool did happen; Lt. Col. Stamps said they were going to put all of us in the winner's circle on a Crock Pot. I said to Lt. Col. Stamps, "We are immortalized forever now." He just laughed.

Joe Nemechek, he was a great person besides being a great driver. His mother was at all of our races and she use to dress up like a drill sergeant. Martha Nemechek was just a fun lady to be around. She would get patches for her uniform from other soldiers and wear them. She was a great ambassador for the Army and the soldiers loved her and she loved the soldiers. She would stand right at the pit box at every race in a Drill sergeant hat and uniform and cheer the Army on. She use to even wash and wax Joe's car before every race and she made the best chocolate chip cookies. I looked forward to seeing her more than I did Joe, a driver could not have a better mother than Martha Nemechek. Even now without the Army sponsorship, I still look for Martha when I go into the garage. It is a shame Joe is no longer the Army driver. He is the only Driver in the Army Car to win with full U.S. Army sponsorship.

Lt. Col. Stamps gave Martha a Liberty Bell trophy and I was there with him. We hated to see her and Joe go without giving them something to show we cared. I remember her crying that day in Miami Homestead before the last race of the season, but she knew Lt. Col Stamps and Sergeant Dunn cared. Lt. Col. Stamps has a big heart and I admired him for making sure Martha knew we cared and she and Joe would be missed as part of the Army family. I still see Joe at the track and his career is winding down and his sponsorship is not what it used to be, but I made sure he would be remembered. I personally bought a brick to put in front of the new NASCAR Hall of Fame and it has his name on it and when he won that race in 2004 at Kansas Motor speedway for the Army.

I was in the winner's circle two other times once with the National Guard, in Michigan with Greg Biffle and Jack

Roush his owner. Lt. Col. Stamps was there too. Also I was at Charlotte when Casey Mears won. But those two were nothing like that win in 2004 with Joe Nemechek, that one was special. A funny thing happened at Pocono a guy in a golf cart rode up to me and Lt. Col. Stamps and asked us if we would watch the race trophy till he got back. So Lt. Col. Stamps took a picture of me holding the Pocono Trophy, then the guy realized we were not the right people to give the trophy to.

The next Driver to take the wheel behind the Army car was Mark Martin, Mark was different than Joe. He had more wins and had been driving longer than Joe. His merchandise sold better, but he never won in the Army Car which had went from the number 01 to the number 08. He was probably the only driver who deserved a championship, but never got one yet. At 50 years old Mark could still drive with the best of them. My last race with the Army Team was Mark Martin's first, in February 2007 and it was three days before I retired. Bill tried his best not to let me go to the track, he just wanted me gone. He really got pissed when Maj. Moore asked me if I wanted to go. Of course, I said, "yes sir." I thought he was kidding, but he went to Col. Neal and he called me and told me I was going. Oh, now this really pissed Bill off. You see Lt. Col Stamps told me Bill said, I had no more events to go to after AAB that year. He specifically told Lt. Col Stamps to leave me off the roster for The Daytona 500. Col. Neal told Bill I was going and that he wanted me there. There was nothing Bill could do. In his anger, he called Lt. Col. Stamps into the office and they were in there for over 30 minutes. Bill kept ranting and raving over all the reasons I should not be there. Then he found out Maj. Moore went to Col. Neal and asked if I could be there for my last event. Bill did not say anything to Maj. Moore, because he was Col. Neal's officer in his office.

Well, I went to The Daytona 500 and Bill tried everything he could to keep me out of the track. He even tried to leave me at the hotel the day of the race, because of a rain delay, but I always went to the track with Lt. Col. Stamps. Bill also only gave me a workers credential to keep me out of the garage, but that did not work, because I always went to the garage with Lt. Col. Stamps who had a hard card, which is a season unlimited garage pass. The sad thing was the year after I left Lt. Col. Stamps never got another hard card, not because of me. Bill turned the NASCAR program over to someone else, because Lt. Col Stamps was being assigned to OCAR.

My last event with the Army turned out to be one of the closest Daytona 500 races ever run. With two laps to go, I was watching the monitor on the Army pit box and Mark was leading under a caution flag. The restart was about to begin. I was hoping Mark would win and this would be the greatest retirement present I could ask for. It was not to be unfortunately while coming out of turn four in the final lap, without a drafting partner Mark was on his own. Out of nowhere came, Kevin Harvick in the number 29 Richard Childress Shell Car. It was a drag race to the finish. Even though Mark got a little loose he was leading, then a bunch of cars behind Mark and Kevin started wrecking. With Mark still ahead, the caution flag never came out, which would have locked the field and Mark would have won. Mark looked for the caution flag, but it never came, Then Kevin Harvick won the Daytona 500 by a half of a front fender. You could have heard a pin drop in the Army pit area. It was like someone let the air out of his tires. Now the only thing I had left to do was to head back to Fort Knox and retire.

MY RETIREMENT

I came into work on Monday and finished my processing. I turned in my cell phone and laptop computer. I was glad most of all to turn in my government credit card and it was paid up. Other soldiers ask me, what are you going to do now sergeant Dunn? My reply was I am going to retire and they would say then what? I told them I was leaving as a sergeant and not returning as a mister DA civilian. I also told them, jokingly, "I am going to grow my hair long and eat out of garbage cans. I would talk shit to everyone working. I have plans now to do what I want to do and that is enjoying me, family, and travel."

I saved my money all these years and I had everything paid for. I will go on Military Aircrafts with space available (MAC) Flights and do the things I want to do. I don't need someone to tell me how to spend my time or my money, because now I have both. It was Wednesday February 23rd 2007 and my day of reckoning. My retirement was set for 1300. I retired with 25 years, 8 months, and 2 days service. I was now just waiting for my mother and my wife's mother and some of my relatives to come. It was a warm day for late February. I was ready to retire at Fort Knox. It seemed like yesterday back in September of 1981 when I first came here for basic training and Armor School. It was full circle. I started on this post and now I was finishing my career on this post. It felt like any other day in the Army, the difference was today was my last day to wear the uniform.

Col. Neal was in charge of my retirement ceremony, he was also supported by Lt. Col. Stamps, and Maj. Moore. Even Bill, along with Hersh, Dottie, and a few agency contractors from our office were all there. I will say this Lt. Col. Stamps and Maj. Moore cared about me as a soldier and even Bill did not treat me bad that day. Like some of my previous assignments where I received nothing. I was treated great on my way out.

Col. Neal was the speaker for my retirement, he talked about me and my career and then I received my second Meritorious Service Medal. I received a full length American Flag for my service to this great country. I also received a few personal awards. The best award however was a letter of appreciation for my service signed by President George Bush Jr. There was also another letter by the Chief of Staff of The Army, Gen. Peter Schoomaker attached to it.

After all this my family joined me for pictures and my wife Telena was given a certificate for her support over the years and a bouquet of flowers. My mother Peggy Dunn and my wife's mother Mable Shimfessel got hugs and flowers from me and Col. Neal. I was just glad I could share this with my family. I just wish my father and my wife's father were there. To me this was just another day in the Army. It did not dawn on me till much later that my career was over. To this day I still miss being in the Army and taking care of soldiers. I truly loved being a soldier and it was all I ever knew and was good at. It was also the best decision I ever made for me and my family, and now it was over.

My cousin was there, Joe Biller, remember he was the one who talked me into joining the Army with him in 1981. He was now a lawyer and was a former Lt.

Commander in the U.S. Navy. After meeting with all the family and friends we all went to lunch on Fort Knox at the Leaders Club. There we ate and I was given a few more command awards. Bill spoke and thanked me for my service. He also said he admired me for watching my father with my mother all those years with his illness. My mother knew I had put my career on hold when my father was ill. He died two months prior to me retiring, I felt like this was for my dad.

It is stressful to say the least serving many years in the Army, now it was time for me to go. The Army will always be in me and I still talk about it. You can never understand a soldier unless you have been a soldier. It will be with me till the day I die and I still love being around soldiers and going to where soldiers are at. After being a soldier you can never go back to being a civilian. I had done and seen too many things and I survived. I went through the gamut. I was threatened in my career by everything imaginable. I was told I would never retire by two different commanders. One said he was going to bar me from reenlistment, another told me I was a disgrace to the uniform. I also was told I would retire only as a Staff Sergeant if I was lucky. I also had a few NCO's and Officers tell me they were going to call my Branch and get me relieved. This ever happened. It is what it is. You see, I took care of soldiers and I was not always right in the way I handled some things, but to those individuals who thought they could end my career; this is all I have to say. I made it and no one can take that away from me. My soldiers know who I am and what I did for them and their families. Most people never see things through to the finish. I had stayed the course. I think I made a difference and I liked being in Public Affairs. I already saw the jealousy in some of my friends, who laughed at me when I joined the Army, because they never thought I would make it. Say what you want, like me or not, I did it and I also sleep well at night. The teachers, friends, relatives, and many others can call me a loser and keep laughing, because I am the one who is laughing now. I did not win all the battles, but I won the war.

My son has now stepped up and he is in the Army now. Sgt. 1st Class Donald Ray Dunn II is retired, but Sgt. Donald Ray Dunn III carries the torch. He is only 21 years old and he is an Information Technology Specialist. I never talked him into joining the Army; it was something he wanted to do. He has been in now 3 years. I only wish we both could have been in at the same time, but I did get a chance to wear my Class A uniform at his AIT graduation at Fort Gordon in Georgia.

I am real proud of him and he has done more than I even thought he was capable of doing. I have to say I think he is a better soldier than me. Why, because he listens more than me and I was always a rebel with authority. I believed in taking care of soldiers and I would do anything for my soldiers. I am vocal, if I think something is wrong I express it. My son on the other hand handles things just the opposite and I give him good advice when he asked for it. He calls me almost every day and we have always been close. Now he is not just my son, he is my brother too. He told me "dad it is because of you and the example you set for me, that I wanted to be a soldier in the Army too." If there is nothing else I ever did, I am proud that I have a son who is a good person and has never caused me any problems. Also without the help of my wife Telena this would have never been possible too.

She raised him when I was gone and he listened and obeyed her. I and my wife survived together, I have seen a lot of broken marriages in the Army, it is beyond hard on a family in the Army, we all stuck together like a unit and a team and made it. My stripes are my wife's too.

One of the things I remember most was the saying, everyone wants freedom, but few are willing to fight for it and freedom is not free. I had seen the Army go from manual gray typewriters to cell phones and computers. I had also seen uniforms change from fatigues to ACU's and jeeps to humvees, and old school ways to new school ways. My next assignment will be traveling to Fort Living Room, cruising on the USS Recliner. It is now my time to wake up each morning to Capt. Crunch and enjoy Col. Sanders for supper. The hardest thing I ever did in the Army was that afternoon after my retirement, I went home and took off my boots, hung up my uniform, and put my black beret on the closet shelf for the last time. Then I looked in the mirror and smiled. I will always remember this, once a soldier always a soldier!

Would you like to see your manuscript become a book?

If you are interested in becoming a PublishAmerica author, please submit your manuscript for possible publication to us at:

acquisitions@publishamerica.com

You may also mail in your manuscript to:

**PublishAmerica
PO Box 151
Frederick, MD 21705**

We also offer free graphics for Children's Picture Books!

www.publishamerica.com

PUBLISHAMERICA